A LIFE

IN THE STRUGGLE

Critical Perspectives on the Past

A SERIES EDITED BY

Susan Porter Benson, Stephen Brier, and Roy Rosenzweig

A LIFE
IN THE STRUGGLE

Ivory Perry

and the Culture of Opposition

BY GEORGE LIPSITZ

Temple University Press

PHILADELPHIA

Temple University Press, Philadelphia 19122
Copyright © 1988 by Temple University.
All rights reserved
Published 1988
Printed in the United States of America

The paper used in this publication meets the minimum
requirements of American National Standard for
Information Sciences—Permanence of Paper for Printed
Library Materials, ANSI z39.48-1984

Library of Congress Cataloging-in-Publication Data

Lipsitz, George.
A life in the struggle.

(Critical perspectives on the past)
Bibliography: p.
Includes index.
1. Perry, Ivory. 2. Afro-Americans—Biography. 3. Civil
rights workers—United States—Biography. 4. Civil
rights movements—United States—History—20th
century. 5. Afro-Americans—Civil rights. 6. Afro-
Americans—Civil rights—Missouri—Saint Louis.
7. Saint Louis (Mo.)—Race relations. I. Title. II. Series.
E185.97.P49L5 1988 973'.0496073024 [B] 87-33618
ISBN 0-87722-550-8 (alk. paper)

Contents

Acknowledgments

Scholars often work in solitude but never in isolation. While working on this book, I have been nurtured and sustained by the kindness and caring of many good friends and colleagues. I am grateful to all those who helped shape the design and execution of this inquiry, but I want to single out a few individuals for special recognition.

Ivory Perry allowed me to examine every aspect of his life and never once ducked the hard questions I posed to him. Perry read the entire manuscript and offered many valuable comments and criticisms. Many of his friends, relatives, acquaintances, and even a few enemies generously gave their time to me, and they carefully directed me toward a full understanding of the significance of his beliefs and actions.

In the early stages of research I received important advice and encouragement from Paulette Lipsitz, Kathy Corbett, Alex Yard, Dick Miller, Marline Pearson, and Ed Robbins. Mel King and the members of the Urban Fellows Program at MIT allowed me to present some of my research to them, and their comments helped me a great deal. Later on in the project, Jeff Prager, Daniel Czitrom, Elias Vlanton, and Michael Fischer provided much-needed advice and assistance.

When the manuscript was completed, I received the benefits of exceptionally fine criticism from Lawrence Levine, Michael Schwartz, Gerald Gill, Stan Weir, William McFeely, Clayborne Carson, and John Dittmer. Mitchell Aboulafia, Elizabeth Long, Don and Jean Quataert, Bruce Palmer, and Ed Hugetz also provided indispensable dialogue and commentary.

Throughout my research, Melvin Oliver served as a source of inspiration and enlightenment; his many interventions on behalf of this book are deeply appreciated. Ramon Gutierrez helped me discover what I wanted to say about this topic; his scholarship and friendship add an important dimension to my life. As always, the towering intellect and political acumen of George Rawick inform all of my academic and cultural understandings; his influence is on every page of this book.

Roy Rosenzweig offered me the benefit of his fine skills as a scholar and editor in revising the manuscript, and Janet Francendese of Temple University Press provided me with all the help an editor can extend to an author. I am deeply grateful to both of them. Barbara Tomlinson contributed her skills as an editor and critic, and the final manuscript was immeasurably improved as a result of her efforts.

Finally, between 1980 and 1985 part of my teaching responsibilities at the University of Houston–Clear Lake involved courses at the Texas Detention Center at Ramsey. At that prison, I encountered some of the best students, and some of the best people, I have ever met. They challenged me to develop a deeper understanding of power relations in American society—to confront the consequences of the history and culture that I tried to teach them. They understand what is at stake in a book like this, and it is to all of them that the book is dedicated.

A LIFE

IN THE STRUGGLE

Introduction: Peace in the Struggle

I first became aware of Ivory Perry's importance as a historical figure in 1982, when I assembled a photographic exhibit and organized a series of panel discussions about the history of social protest in St. Louis.[1] In the photographs, citizens linked arms during marches and demonstrations. They sat down in front of cars and buses to stop traffic. They chained themselves to the doors of businesses charged with discriminatory hiring practices. Taunting crowds and armed police officers menaced the demonstrators; angry protesters clenched their fists and shouted defiantly at law enforcement officers and onlookers. Men and women stood shoulder to shoulder in an effort to change society and their place in it. Their faces reflected a range of emotions—rage and pride, bravado and fear. I wondered who these people were. How did they reach the point where they decided to run the risks of direct-action confrontation? What had motivated them at those crucial historical moments and what had happened to them since?

In the discussions, recognized leaders of civil rights groups spoke about the organizational imperatives of mass mobilization—about raising money, maximizing political influence, and securing long-range objectives. While their remarks addressed relevant historical issues and concerns, there seemed to be a wide gulf between the carefully planned and disciplined struggles they remembered and the disorderly contestation evident in the news photographs depicting decades of dramatic demonstrations and direct-action confrontations in that city. The panel discussions presented a "people's history," but the people who waged the disorderly, chaotic, and emotional mass struggle portrayed in the news photographs had not been represented on the panels.

My perception of a disparity between the content of the discussions and the nature of the photographs grew stronger during an open forum on the night before the close of the exhibit. I had placed advertisements in local newspapers inviting interested citizens to discuss the words and images that had been presented in the panel discussions and pictures.

About forty people attended, and I offered the microphone to anyone wishing to speak. For the most part, those who addressed the group came from college campuses or from community groups involved in actions related to social change. They spoke with sophistication, passion, and erudition about the history of social protest in St. Louis. But toward the end of the evening, a powerfully built black man stood up in the back of the room and directed attention toward the photographic exhibit in the next room. "I'm in half of those pictures out there," he proclaimed, "and I want to talk about the things that I did."

His name was Ivory Perry, he said. He had been active in social protest movements for years, and there were parts of the struggle that the general public knew nothing about. Unlike most of the previous speakers, Perry focused his remarks on actions in the streets, on confrontations between protesters and their opponents. He contended that real social change came from the bottom up, insisting that the civil rights movement had involved mobilization of an entire community, not just a few leaders and organizations. Emphasizing social protest as the main resource for oppressed groups, Perry concluded with an appeal to "any historians here" to "write this up because a lot of young kids and a lot of the older people out in the community don't know nothing about all that's gone on." I was one of the historians there: I decided that I should respond to this invitation.

Historians routinely travel halfway across the country to visit archives that yield no more than a footnote; rarely do we find historical sources demanding our attention by calling out to us across a room. I invited Perry to show me the pictures that included him, and as we walked through the exhibit together, I discovered that indeed more than half of the photos that I had selected solely for their dramatic properties included incidents involving Ivory Perry. In one picture, he lay sprawled under the wheels of a car, blocking traffic to call attention to complaints against police brutality. In another, he chained shut the doors of an office building to dramatize charges that the company headquartered there discriminated against black job applicants. A third photograph presented Perry outside the editorial offices of a daily newspaper, protesting the paper's treatment of racial issues by holding a match to a copy of that morning's edition and setting it on fire.

Many of the images of social protest that caught my attention when I assembled the exhibit had been composed in advance in Ivory Perry's imagination and brought to fruition by his direct actions. Assorted news photographers had snapped the pictures and I had collected them and displayed them on the wall, but the true author of the text represented in them was Ivory Perry. I did not know at that time if he actually had an important story to tell, but I was sufficiently intrigued to arrange for an interview.

Arranging an interview with Ivory Perry turned out to be far easier than actually conducting one. Every time we planned to talk, some crisis intervened. One time his car broke down. Another time a meeting ran late. To make matters more difficult, at the time he had no permanent address and no telephone. He lived with various friends and relatives, and any attempt to contact him meant leaving messages all over town. But eventually, after almost four months of missed connections, we sat down to tape an interview. Except for a few flecks of gray in his hair, Perry looked much as he had in photographs taken twenty years earlier. The callouses on his hands and the muscles on his arms and shoulders told me something about the hard physical labor he had done in his life even before he spoke. In a deep, rough, and resonant voice, he began to tell me his life story.

It was a story of struggle and commitment. Raised in a sharecropper family in rural Arkansas in the 1930s, Perry became accustomed to hard work in the fields at an early age. He served in the last all-black unit in the army during the Korean War, and in 1954 he moved to St. Louis, where he began work at a series of unskilled and semiskilled jobs. During the 1950s and 1960s he marched and picketed for school desegregation, fair employment legislation, and equal access to movie theaters and restaurants. He participated in St. Louis's most important civil rights campaign: the effort to win jobs for blacks at the Jefferson Bank in 1963. He also went off to join in some of the most significant civil rights confrontations of the 1960s in places like Selma, Bogalusa, and Cicero. He endured assaults and imprisonment for demonstrations in both the North and South, and he learned about tactics and strategy in direct-action campaigns led by many of the civil rights movement's most famous spokesmen, including Martin Luther King, James Farmer, Stokely Carmichael, and Jesse Jackson.

But Ivory Perry participated in the civil rights movement and subsequent efforts at social change as a rank and file activist, not as a celebrated leader. As he answered my questions, Perry touched on all the important historical themes that I associated with the movement of the 1960s—public protests, energetic organizations, and prominent people.

But his words contained another narrative as well, a story of continuous commitment at the grass-roots level. Perry led no important organizations, delivered no memorable speeches, and received no significant recognition or reward for his social activism. But for more than thirty years he had been distributing the leaflets, carrying the picket signs, and planning the flamboyant confrontations essential to the success of protest movements in St. Louis and elsewhere. Brought into the streets in the late 1950s by the ferment of civil rights protest, Perry had never ceased his activism. Civil rights protests in the 1950s and 1960s led him into community organizing around issues of housing, employment, and health care in the 1970s and 1980s. His unflagging commitment at the local level prodded others into action, kept alive hopes of eventual victory in the face of short-term defeats, and helped provide a seemingly powerless community with effective levers for social change. I soon realized that I had access to a very important story.

From the start, Perry and I agreed that we should tell the whole truth: we should talk about defeats as well as victories, reveal his faults as well as his strengths, acknowledge the bitter frustrations of his life as well as its triumphant satisfactions. Perry spoke about his life in a direct and factual manner, treating me with neither deference nor condescension. In thirteen separate interviews conducted over a five-year period, we engaged in more than twenty hours of dialogue about his memory of events and his evaluation of their meaning in his life. These interviews were an introduction to his life as an activist, a means of surveying its chronology and eliciting his comments about his own experiences. I used his remarks as a guide to further interviews and archival research. Except for purely subjective reflections, I used no piece of evidence on Perry's word alone, choosing instead to check his information against archival records and the memories of others. Only if I could find independent verification of facts he presented did I use them in this narrative. But his memory proved remarkably accurate, and I drew freely on his comments for illustrative anecdotes and subjective responses. In addition, Perry's subjective responses constituted "facts" in themselves, primary evidence about the mindset and internal resources of a grass-roots activist.

Like all oral history interviews, my talks with Ivory Perry relied on the subject's memory, perspective, and credibility. I could verify his factual statements through outside research, but I also had to develop the capacity to analyze critically his opinions and to find ways of encouraging the most productive dialogue with him. During our first interviews, Perry's political priorities made it difficult for me to learn much about his personal life. He tended to speak in political epigrams and aphorisms, answering questions about his private life with statements presenting political conclusions. For example, he first described sharecropping exclusively as a set of experiences that motivated him to fight against exploitation and racism. He remembered the church services that his mother compelled him to attend in his youth solely as a lesson about the hyprocrisy of white people who claimed to be Christians but still practiced racism. He recalled military service in Korea as an experience that taught him the injustice of risking his life in war for freedoms that he could not enjoy in peacetime. All these recollections accurately reflected Perry's memories and sentiments, but they were incomplete, focusing on political conclusions while ignoring the conflicts and contradictions, the emotions and experiences that led to those conclusions.

Perry's long history as a community organizer had made him a master at creating stories that encapsulated complex social issues into readily understood political lessons, but that skill also led him to obscure some of the personal and social dimensions of his life, dimensions that I wanted to explore. The powerful political messages encoded in the photographs of his activism—the very thing that had drawn me to him in the first place—now worked against me, for I found it difficult to get beyond discussion of his political views. But as I reconstructed his life history from legal documents, personal records, published sources, and interviews with others, I found that I could frequently come back to him with questions that led to full and rich descriptions of both his private and public experiences.

With Ivory Perry's help, I secured his military, medical, employment, and police records. During visits to archives and research collections in Arkansas, California, Illinois, Louisiana, Maryland, Missouri, Pennsylvania, Texas, Virginia, Wisconsin, and the District of Columbia, I documented the historical transformations that shaped Ivory Perry's life: the demise of sharecropping in the 1930s and 1940s, black participation in the Korean War, migrations to industrial cities in the 1950s, the origins of the modern civil rights movement, the federal antipoverty program, and the contradictions of inner-city life in industrial and postindustrial America.

In addition, I conducted more than fifty hours of interviews with more than thirty of Ivory Perry's relatives, teachers, employers, friends, and enemies. I conducted interviews in the back room of a ghetto bar and in the reception area of a Baptist church, in the plush offices of successful corporate lawyers and in the modest kitchens of families on welfare. I learned about Ivory Perry from federal judges and from career criminals, from black nationalist revolutionaries and from police officers assigned to monitor and contain social protest. The people I spoke with had plenty of criticisms of Ivory Perry. Some felt that he had neglected his family responsibilities in favor of political activism. Others saw him as impatient and undisciplined, too eager to provoke confrontations and too reluctant to engage in negotiations. Some perceived him to be living in the past, foolishly pursuing opportunities for social change that had long since passed. Yet even his harshest critics praised Perry's sincerity, courage, and perseverance.

Each of my research trips and interviews provided me with new information about Perry and new questions to pose to him. By conducting followup interviews, examining archival sources, and obtaining independent confirmation of first-person testimony, I provided the context, commentary, and corroboration necessary for placing oral history interviews in useful social and historical perspective. As Perry and I retraced familiar topics on the basis of new information, we invariably fleshed out previously skeletal accounts. Interview information provided important illustrations, anecdotes, and guides to further research. When used in conjunction with archival research and evaluated by strict standards of proof, it provided me with useful links between public events and personal perceptions. It demonstrated the existence of common memories, traditions, and attitudes that underscored the shared values and community networks behind Perry's social vision. Had I been content to use oral interviews as uncorroborated primary sources or had I limited my dialogue with Perry to only a few interviews, the results would have been far less useful and credible.

My research also compelled me to evaluate Ivory Perry's reliability as an interpreter of personal and historical experiences. In some respects his recall of specific facts was amazing: he described accurately the color of a rental truck that he drove to a demonstration in 1965, the exact words that he exchanged with a police officer in 1960, and specific dates and incidents of his Korean War service in 1950. In each case, I subsequently discovered documents that verified his recollection of these specific details. More significant, he had an extraordinary memory of the issues, events, and personalities that he encountered as a social activist.

His reflections proved extremely valuable in guiding later research because they displayed such a thorough understanding of the individuals and institutions that had shaped his values, beliefs, and actions.

In our interviews, recollections about intimate personal experiences and feelings came less easily to Perry. He could not remember all of his seven children's birthdays, his cousin's married name, or his parents' birthplaces. Other personal information emerged slowly. During our third interview, I learned that Perry had been hospitalized for a nervous breakdown caused by depression. In our sixth conversation, he revealed that he had been arrested (although never convicted) for crimes unrelated to civil rights protest. Only after eleven interviews did I discover that he had received a dishonorable discharge from the military. Each of these revelations made me wonder whether I was getting the whole story about the complexities of his personal life. Through research and interviews with others I discovered that the nervous breakdown included an incident where Perry threatened to take his children away from their mother because she was a "false prophet," that his dishonorable discharge from the army stemmed from prosecution for insubordination and possession of heroin, and that his arrest record included charges of assault and stealing.

My research established Perry as an honest and straightforward respondent. When I asked him for details about the things that I had discovered, he always answered fully and frankly. He did not remember all the details about the threat to take his children away from their mother during his nervous breakdown, but he conceded that it had happened. He related in detail the story of his army court-martial, claiming that he had never been insubordinate or used drugs but had been the victim of a racially motivated frameup. He insisted that the criminal charges of assault and stealing stemmed from police harassment and never resulted in convictions.

I would have had no hesitation about contradicting Perry if his accounts had turned out to be untrue; my intention was to be as accurate as possible about the story of his life, with all its complexities and contradictions, not to present him as an untarnished hero. It would neither have surprised nor upset me to discover unflattering information about him on these matters. But my subsequent research showed Perry was telling the truth about each of these episodes. His memory of his actions during his nervous breakdown corresponded directly to what other eyewitnesses told me. Police reports showed his arrests for assault and stealing were based on unsubstantiated charges that collapsed under scrutiny, resulting in acquittals or charges being dropped. The verbatim transcript of his army court-martial made his case seem even stronger than he had reported it, and left me convinced that he had indeed been unjustly convicted in a hearing marred by racial prejudice. These discoveries did not smooth off all the rough edges of Perry's life history and leave him an uncomplicated symbol of virtue. In my eyes, Perry remains a complex and contradictory figure who has hurt himself and others even while pursuing noble goals.

My inquiry into Ivory Perry's life history brought forth a unique body of evidence about black history, social protest, the civil rights movement, urban history, and American political culture. As a scholar specializing in twentieth-century U.S. history, I was already familiar with many of the things that Perry related to me. I knew about the mechanization of agriculture in the 1930s and 1940s that drove sharecroppers off their land and into the big cities, about the bitter and costly fighting waged by American troops during the Korean War, about the emergence of the modern civil rights movement. But Perry had lived through those changes; the entire course of his life had been shaped by them, and his memories illumined the personal consequences and effects of historical change. In some cases, Perry's recollections educated me about subjects that I wrongly thought I already knew well. He told me about a degree of active black resistance to white racism in the small southern community in which he was raised that I would not have thought possible in the 1930s and 1940s. He described segregation and discriminatory practices against black soldiers in Korea in 1950 and 1951 that I thought had been eradicated by President Truman's 1948 edict desegregating the armed forces. He revealed a long history of planning and preparation behind civil rights demonstrations often portrayed as spontaneous reactions to immediate grievances. But beyond any specific bits of factual information, the most important thing Ivory Perry had to offer me was himself, or more specifically the story of his continuous commitment to social change at the grass-roots level.

In addition to participating in the historically significant civil rights demonstrations and campaigns of the 1960s, Ivory Perry has also thrown himself into hundreds of less publicized local struggles over the years to secure jobs, housing, and medical care for people in need. He orchestrated dramatic demonstrations against police brutality, discriminatory hiring practices, and slum housing, but he also worked quietly to aid individuals lacking the basic necessities for survival. His efforts to obtain screening and treatment programs for children susceptible to lead poisoning saved thousands of young people from permanent brain damage. His leadership during rent strikes and other tenants' struggles won better housing at affordable rents for hundreds of families.

Social activism enabled Perry to make exceptional contributions to society, but it also subjected him to extreme dangers and strains. It left him with economic and psychological difficulties that took a cumulative toll on his happiness. Publicity about his activism led him to be dismissed from jobs, and his many acts of civil disobedience brought him repeated terms in the city jail. Preoccupation with politics drew him away from family life and contributed to the dissolution of his two major relationships and to some alienation from his seven children. The relentless physical dangers and emotional pressures of activism strained his nerves and contributed to disorders that required periods of hospitalization and extended psychiatric treatment. Yet Perry expresses pride and satisfaction in what he has accomplished, and views his life as a success.

PEOPLE LIKE Ivory Perry rarely appear in history books, but they often make history. Without them, leaders have no followers and ordinary citizens have no means of translating their wishes and desires into coherent political contestation. The story Ivory Perry told me about his life had its unique elements, but he personifies a broader social type. Everywhere social conflict takes place, people like Ivory Perry emerge. The Italian Marxist theorist Antonio Gramsci called such people "organic intellectuals," and his term helps to identify what is representative and significant in the life of Ivory Perry.

In Gramsci's view, organic intellectuals direct the ideas and aspirations of their class even though they hold no formal status or employment as "intellectuals." Social action constitutes the indispensable core of their activity. Organic intellectuals not only analyze and interpret the world, they originate and circulate their ideas through social contestation. As Gramsci explains, "The mode of being of the new intellectual can no longer consist in eloquence, which is an exterior and momentary mover of feelings and passions, but in active participation in practical life, as constructor, organiser, 'permanent persuader' not just simple orator."[2] Unlike traditional intellectuals, whose support from patrons, universities, and cultural institutions allows detachment from practical life, organic intellectuals learn about the world by trying to change it, and they change the world by learning about it from the perspective of the needs and aspirations of their social group.

As Gramsci defines them, organic intellectuals use their knowledge and imagination in the way that intellectuals do, although they lack formal recognition from society that they are engaged in intellectual activity. All people think and therefore all people engage in some sort of intellectual work. Organic intellectuals resemble traditional intellectuals in that both manipulate signs and symbols to make the interests of their social group appear synonymous with the interests of all of society. But organic intellectuals not only represent a different set of interests from the traditional intellectuals: in Gramsci's view they also engage in a different kind of cultural practice. Traditional intellectuals can distinguish themselves purely through the originality of their ideas or the eloquence of their expression, but organic intellectuals must initiate a process that involves people in social contestation.

As the exercise of power in the modern world increasingly comes to depend on communication and culture, the exercise of critical, creative, and contemplative faculties becomes a matter of self-interest and survival for dominated groups. Organic intellectuals try to understand and change society at the same time. They conduct their intellectual inquiries through the practical activities of social contestation; they measure their own efforts more by their effect on changing society than by their correspondence to preestablished standards of eloquence and originality. Organic intellectuals generate and circulate oppositional ideas through social action. They create symbols and slogans that disclose the commonalities among seemingly atomized experiences, and they establish principles that unite disparate groups into effective coalitions. Most significantly, they challenge dominant interests through education and agitation that expose the gap between the surface harmonies that seem to unite society and the real conflicts and antagonisms that divide it.

Through social action, Ivory Perry has articulated and circulated ideas of singular importance to the black community of St. Louis. He has organized protests that legitimized the perceptions and aspirations of the powerless by propelling them to the forefront of public consciousness in such a way as to provoke responses from those in power. Perry has presented the interests of his constituents as synonymous with the interests of all of society—by stressing the negative consequences of injustice and the positive potential of social change. His appeals have brought people of diverse backgrounds into coalitions that worked effectively for common goals, and his manipulation of words, signs, and symbols brought to the surface hidden areas of theoretical agreement that facilitated group action.[3]

As a strategist and organizer, he has had to discover which issues troubled people and which strategies might transform their ideas and inclinations into action. Activism has required Ivory Perry to understand existing conditions, to generate new ways of thinking about them, and to circulate his ideas so that others would help put them into practice. Organic intellectuals cannot be merely troublemakers or loudmouths; they succeed only when their organizing efforts articulate and activate ideas already present in the community, and when they tap existing networks of communication and action. Perry's demonstrations and direct-action protests have served as part of a larger "war of position," transforming the needs and aspirations of his community into symbolic and real acts of contestation. On picket lines and marches, at mass meetings and rallies, in the streets and in jail, Perry has functioned as the quintessential organic intellectual.[4]

Ivory Perry has drawn others into his activities through the use of participatory democracy, both as a goal and a tactic, as a vision of an ideal society and as a way to involve people in solving the problems of the one we now have. But Perry realizes that political activism can bring only token changes as long as dominant American values privilege individualism, materialism, and privatism at the expense of collective, moral, and public concerns. In the course of challenging the exclusion of poor and black people from the American dream, Perry has gone on to question the validity of the dream itself. He has tried to change immediate power realities, but also to educate people about the need for a revolution in values—the need to replace competition and exploitation with cooperation and fellowship.

As an organic intellectual mobilizing his community for remedial social action, Ivory Perry has embraced not only the unconventional behavior of direct-action protest, but unconventional values as well. In a society that places so much emphasis on the accumulation of riches as the road to happiness, Perry has directed his energies toward receiving spiritual and emotional rewards. In a culture rife with images of the "rugged individual" and the "self-made man," he has devoted his time to serving the needs of others. In an environment that most commonly connects love to the pleasures and comforts of home and family, he has insisted on trying to demonstrate his love for strangers by ministering to their basic needs for food, shelter, clothing, and health care.

Yet even a rebel against dominant values has been shaped by them, and Perry has engaged in a continuing dialogue with materialism, individualism, and privatism as a matter of necessity. He has not so much ignored the American dream as he has reinterpreted it. He has chosen not to seek personal wealth, but he has battled long and hard to win material gains for poor and working-class people. He has shunned the kind of individualism that makes one person's self-worth dependent upon the degradation of others, but he craves recognition for his exploits as a freedom fighter and a humanitarian. He has sacrificed many of the comforts and satisfactions of family life in order to look after the needs of strangers in the larger human family, but at the same time he longs for closer ties to his own biological family. Much of what makes Ivory Perry interesting as a person makes him significant as a historical actor. His many contradictions and conflicts are not his alone, but rather they illumine important aspects of what both social adjustment and social contestation mean in this society.

The value conflicts central to Ivory Perry's life hold particular meaning for me because of my previous scholarly research. In my first book, *Class and Culture in Cold War America: A Rainbow at Midnight,* I explored the ways mass strikes and demonstrations by American workers after World War II helped win enormous material gains for the working class while they also stimulated democratic sentiments throughout society.[5] Even though workers failed to secure many of their articulated demands in those years, they changed society in significant and lasting ways. Because rank and file aspirations in that period found only partial expression in organizations and institutions, workers engaged in what seemed to be spontaneous and leaderless mass actions. These direct-action protests expanded the boundaries of social conflict, raising demands and reaching constituencies that would not normally have been included within the parameters of labor-management struggles. The pervasiveness and power of grass-roots activism during the postwar years led me to rethink my understanding of oppositional movements and their relationship to dominant power groups and prevailing ideologies.

I concluded that societies are shaped through contestation and conflict, that even the most static, placid, and hierarchical social structures draw determinate shape from past and present antagonisms. In my view, power is wielded within limited confines formed by the interplay of conflicting forces at any given time and place.[6] The relative power of dominant and oppositional groups determines the ideological and practical contours of elite domination through concessions granted to dominated groups in order to make the rule of those in power seem legitimate. Thus even when aggrieved populations fail to seize power or to fashion autonomous spheres of opposition, they still influence the exercise of power in their society. In addition, when existing institutions and organizations prove inadequate for the expression of rank and file aspirations, grass-roots activists devise alternative vehicles of contestation to articulate and implement goals that remain unrecognized by those working within conventional channels.

My previous explorations of collective mass action have examined largely neglected aspects of activism and social change, but they have emphasized group activity more than the actions of individuals. To investigate social protest at the stage of mass insurgency, I had to slight the historical currents and oppositional consciousness predisposing individuals toward direct action; I implicitly accepted a definition of social protest as an unexpected rupture with an otherwise acceptable status quo.[7] In Ivory Perry's social activism, I encountered another example of seemingly spontaneous social protest, of dramatic moments when human will pushed objective social constraints to their limits. In newspaper photographs, Perry appeared again and again engaged in some flamboyant act of passive resistance, disrupting business-as-usual to call attention to unresolved grievances. His repeated resort to direct-action protest suggested an extraordinary continuity beneath the appearance of rupture. The fire in the heart propelling Ivory Perry back to the picket line time after time is too powerful a force to attribute to momentary frustrations and resentments; it reflects moral and intellectual resources honed through a lifetime of personal and collective experiences with long-term social contestation.

The combination of personal pain and public accomplishment that characterizes Ivory Perry's life illumines an important contradiction common to many social activists, but one that is poorly understood by scholars more disposed to consider the cohesion of public political action than the chaos of an ordinary person's life. Scholars tend to portray activists as either exemplars of bourgeois morality, striving to make the public realm conform to the standards of their private lives, or else as deviants driven to political action by the distortions imposed on their psyches by historical and social forces beyond their control.[8] Either way they assume that discomforted individuals become the nucleus of movements for social change.

But this analysis overlooks the ways in which social contestation can become a means of comfort and contentment for strong individuals from discomforted populations. Ivory Perry's experiences demonstrate this dialogic relationship between political and personal identity, illustrating how a cohesive public identity can emerge as a logical response to personal frustrations and form a unified totality.[9] He is proud of what he has accomplished, and secure enough with his chosen role that he concludes his letters by writing "Peace in the Struggle." Coherent political activism was neither the cause of Perry's chaotic personal life nor simple compensation for it. Rather, it functioned as a means for fusing his personal and his political beliefs into an organic whole, reflecting his critique of society, while at the same time expressing his desired relationship to it.

To summarize, my interviews with Ivory Perry led me to certain propositions that form the core argument of this book. Perry's story demonstrates the existence and importance of organic intellectuals in movements for social change. It illustrates the important role that Perry and other activists have played in resisting and altering dominant values in American society, while initiating and circulating oppositional beliefs. It reveals the ways in which oppositional movements, even when they fail to attain their stated goals, change power realities in the present and hold open the possibility for even more radical change in the future. It shows that while activism involves pain and stress, it is not primarily an expression of personal discomfort but an outgrowth of an individual's analysis and understanding of collective discomfort. It expresses a logical and collectively sanctioned response to hierarchy and exploitation on the part of strong-willed individuals with clear and comforting connections to networks of opposition.[10]

Finally, Ivory Perry's life story offers a unique window into recent U.S. history. All the significant social changes of the recent past, which we generally read about from the perspective of decision makers at the top, had an impact on Ivory Perry. In some cases, he had to deal with the negative consequences of social change when no one else would. But he has never been a passive victim. His struggle to influence and change American society illumines some of this nation's darkest tragedies, but it also testifies to the endurance of its best hopes.

CHAPTER 1

Pine Bluff: The Moral Resources of a Southern Black Community

Ivory Perry's story begins in the fertile farm country along the banks of the rivers flowing through central and southern Arkansas—the Ouachita, the Saline, the Arkansas, and the Mississippi. Born on May 5, 1930, in a sharecropper cabin in Desha County near Dumas, Perry got his first lessons about life from labor in the cotton fields during the hard Depression years of the 1930s in rural Arkansas. As soon as he learned to walk, he learned to work. Perry was just two years old when his mother tied an empty twenty-five-pound flour sack for holding cotton around his neck and brought him to work alongside her in the fields. With his sisters Kathen and Earline, he picked and chopped cotton all day long; the entire family earned perhaps $1 per day. Pearl Barnes Perry supplemented what little money she and her children earned in the fields by cooking and cleaning in white people's homes at the end of her long days picking cotton.[1]

Pearl Barnes had known little but hard work her entire life. She grew up on a farm near Bastrop, Louisiana, where she cut sugarcane, raised chickens, chopped wood, and picked cotton. Her father died in a sawmill accident when she was young, and her stepfather treated Pearl and her sisters cruelly. He would feed his own children first, giving the stepchildren only leftovers. He made them work in the fields all day and forbade them to attend school. He subjected all the children and his wife to frequent beatings. When her family moved to Arkansas in the 1920s, Pearl Barnes met and married a young sawmill worker, Ivory Perry, Sr., known to his friends as "Son" Perry. Together Pearl and Son worked as field hands and sharecroppers, but he often went off to jobs in the lumber camps and sawmills, leaving his family behind. Pearl never knew when her husband would be home, and she gradually took on more and more of the task of raising and supporting their three children.

In 1933, Son Perry left for good, and started living with another woman. Kathen, Ivory, and Earline still saw their father from time to time, but their upbringing and their survival depended solely upon their mother.[2]

Ivory and his sister Kathen remember their mother as a woman whose only activity outside of work was church services. Kathen Perry Wright explains, "I never knew her to do nothing else, really I didn't. Like a ballgame or a dance—she didn't care for that. She didn't even wear makeup or nothing like that. I don't know nothing she liked to do. Nothing. She didn't like to listen to the radio; I never knew her to go to a movie." Ivory remembers his mother wrapping her legs in burlap so she could walk through the snow to her job as a cook for a local judge, and he recalls her enjoyment at spending all day Sunday in church—at least on those Sundays when she could get the day off from work. "She was just a hard working lady," says Maggie Lewis, Pearl's sister. "She'd chop cotton, cut wood, and take care of her kids." A neighbor, Katherine Jiner, tells how Pearl Perry would work all week long in white people's kitchens to bring home $2.50. "His mother worked *all* the time," emphasizes Ivory's cousin Doris Caldwell; "sunup to sundown, she had to work all day."[3]

The peculiar injustices of sharecropping and day labor made Pearl Perry's unremitting work necessary. Landowners allowed families like the Perrys to live and work on their land in return for half the crop outright and the rest at a stipulated price. When political and technological changes in the 1930s undermined the sharecropping system, many workers found themselves even worse off than before—reduced to working as day laborers, paid only for the crop they picked each day. Most owners required tenants to do all their shopping at plantation commissaries, which inevitably offered inferior goods at inflated prices. The commissary system also enabled the owners to exert paternalistic control over their tenants by instructing storekeepers to refuse selected tenants the opportunity to buy candy, alcohol, or other "unnecessary" items.[4]

Ivory Perry remembers that sometimes his family had to pick hundreds of pounds of cotton a day just to break even and pay for the food, clothes, and tools they had purchased on credit during the previous winter. Even when they picked enough cotton to come out ahead, Pearl Perry and her children had to contend with the discretionary power wielded by the people who employed them. Plantation owners prevented sharecroppers from looking at the scales that weighed how much they picked and from seeing the ledger books that recorded how much money they owed. No matter how many bales of cotton her family managed to pick, every year Pearl Perry heard the same story: "You almost got out of the hole this time; try again next year."[5]

The Perry family "worked the shares" and performed day labor on plantations near Dumas and Grady, seldom staying on any one farm for more than two years. From six in the morning until six at night they chopped and picked cotton. Pearl worked one row by herself; the three children took the next one together. At night, Kathen cooked dinner for her brother and sister while their mother went off to cook and clean house for other people's families. On days when they were not needed in the fields, the children went to school, sometimes walking as much as eight miles in each direction. Ivory liked going to school, he enjoyed fishing and hunting expeditions with other boys, and he even derived a certain satisfaction from work in the fields. "I'm a Taurus, an earth sign," he explains, "and I like farming and working with my hands in the soil—if I could own my own farm." But working for others meant having to labor at their pace and for their benefit, and it meant having to endure their manipulations of the ledger books and scales. "Sharecropping would have been ideal for some people with large families," he observes, "but you always get tricked in the end."[6]

The "trickery" of sharecropping meant poverty and dependency for Pearl Perry and her children. Throughout his youth, Ivory suffered from severe and recurrent earaches caused by an infection. Kathen remembers their mother's concern over his condition and her efforts to get some treatment for her son. She took him to a doctor, but the physician wanted $25 in advance, which she did not have. She prayed instead, asking God to take the infection away. Fortunately, the infection got no worse and eventually did go away, but other problems emanating from the poverty and dependency of sharecropping remained.[7]

One plantation owner used to come to their cabin to get Ivory to help him with his illegal bootlegging excursions. The child had no choice but to help. "My mother really didn't like it," he recalls, "but what could she do?" One time they drove off during a thunderstorm to deliver some homemade whiskey to a new customer. The plantation owner kept sampling his own product as they rode, and every time it thundered he would shout out curses against God. "I was afraid of what would happen with him yelling like that," Perry remembers. "With all that thunder and lightning going on, I expected that lightning to strike him, because, man, he was hard on God!"[8]

The plantation owners also worked to keep black and white sharecroppers hostile to each other. They told the white tenants that black workers held everyone else back, reducing income for all sharecroppers. Ivory recalls the situation confronting the white sharecroppers:

> They were treated worse than we were, but there was a lot of racial problems there because the plantation owners didn't want them to socialize with us. But there wasn't nowhere else for them to go. They couldn't socialize with them [the owners]. I made some very good friends with some of the white sharecroppers, young boys my age. We used to go hunting and fishing together and we had a lot of fun.[9]

Racism discouraged black and white sharecroppers from uniting to press for solutions to their common problems, and racial discrimination left black sharecroppers with few alternatives to farm labor. On a personal level, black and white tenants might get along and be friends, but the owners had a stake in perpetuating a social structure that kept the races divided.[10]

In their lives as sharecroppers, the Perry family inherited the burdens of hundreds of years of racism and exploitation. "History is what hurts," claims Fredric Jameson, referring to the ways past events and their consequences impose inexorable limits on each of us: certainly Pearl Perry and her children knew something about that kind of hurt.[11] The experiences of their ancestors as slaves and the traditions and hierarchies that arose after slavery ended had a lot to do with the hardships they faced every day.

But history can also be what helps, a resource from the past that addresses present hurts and eases current pains. The collective memory of communities contains historical information that expands the present by infusing it with the experiences and accumulated wisdom of past generations. Ivory Perry's personal experiences as a child had a collective historical dimension; they had been shaped by events and attitudes that originated before he was born. But just as his history contained legacies of oppression, so did it involve traditions of resistance. The experiences of slaves, sharecroppers, and social activists in his community's past permeated collective memory and legitimated demands for decency and justice in the present.

All Afro-American history begins with slavery, but we sometimes forget that contemporary individuals have direct as well as indirect connections to that institution. When Ivory Perry was growing up in Arkansas in the 1930s and 1940s, some of the old people that he saw on the street had been born slaves. In 1938, interviewers from the Federal Writers' Project of the Works Progress Administration contacted some of these people and recorded their memories of slavery and its aftermath. Their recollections display the values and traditions shaping the community that nurtured Ivory Perry and they shed important light on the sense of legitimacy that guided Perry's subsequent social activism. For example, James Davis, a ninety-six-year-old cotton farmer, remembered with pride his efforts to harass the Ku Klux Klan during their first reign of terror after the Civil War. He told the WPA interviewer:

I've seen them Ku Klux in slavery time and I've cut many a grapevine. We'd be in the place dancin' and playin' the banjo and the grapevine strung across the road and the Ku Klux come ridin' along the run right into it and throw the horses down.[12]

Attitudes about the 1930s revealed in these interviews proved no less combative. "The way things is goin'," said eighty-year-old George Benson, "I don't think the white man wants the colored man to have as much as the white man." J. N. Brown, seventy-nine, voiced a similar sentiment:

We colored people are livin' under the law, but we don't make no laws. You take a one-armed man and he can't do what a two-armed man can. The colored man in the south is a one-armed man, but of course the colored man can't get along without the white folks. But I've lived in this world long enough to know what the cause is—I know why the colored man is a one-armed man.

And in words that would prove somewhat prophetic, seventy-eight-year-old Tanner Thomas argued:

God intended for every man in the world to have a living and to live for each other but too many of 'em living for themselves. But everything's goin' to work out right after a while. God's goin' to change this thing after a while. You can't rush him. He can handle these people. After he gets through with this generation, I think he's goin' to make a generation that will serve him.[13]

These men, and their contemporaries, had witnessed enormous changes in a lifetime. Born as slaves, they remembered the promises of emancipation and the achievements of Reconstruction. They participated in the economic and social system that replaced slavery, a system built around the imperatives of tenant farming. Faced with an uncertain labor supply after the Civil War ended slavery, southern planters devised a means of tying their work force to the land and of paying less for labor—the sharecropping system. In Arkansas, sharecropping expanded dramatically after 1900 when lumber companies had finished clearing much of the land in the eastern part of the state, and when floods, the boll weevil, and soil exhaustion undermined the cotton economy in other parts of the South.[14]

Everywhere the system existed, sharecroppers faced the same abuses that confronted the Perry family—instability, low wages, and fraudulent bookkeeping. A 1935 study found that 57.1 percent of Arkansas Delta sharecroppers had lived on their current farms less than two years. The average annual net income for sharecroppers in 1934 totaled $284; wage laborers averaged only $203.[15] Historian Lawrence Levine's studies of black folklore identify numerous tales based on the propensity of plantation owners to cheat their tenants. In one version

> a black sharecropper, tired of doing nothing better than breaking even year after year, decides to report only ten of twelve bales of cotton he raises one exceptionally good year. After elaborate figuring, his white landlord informs him, "Well, well, you done putty good dis year too, Fred. You broke dead even." "Well, dat's good," the sharecropper replies, "but dere's two mo' bales I didn't tell you 'bout." "The hell you did," the white man screams as he tears up the paper on which he had been figuring. "Don't you never do nothin' like dat again, nigger. Have me refigurin' yo' crop all over so you can come out dead even."[16]

Sharecropping enabled plantation owners to share the risks of farming with their tenants while keeping a disproportionate share of the benefits. The system secured a steady and inexpensive work force for wealthy landowners, but it also provoked resistance and rebellion among the workers. In 1919, Robert Lee Hill, a black sharecropper from Phillips County, organized the Progressive Farmers and Household Union, a self-help group based on the principles of Booker T. Washington's Negro Business League. Their main aim was to get fair reward for their labor by obtaining accurate information from plantation owners on how much money they owed and how much cotton they had picked. When police officers stumbled upon a union meeting in October 1919, an exchange of gunfire touched off a complicated series of events known as the Elaine Riot.

Rumors spread that blacks planned a general uprising and that they intended to kill all whites; the white population formed vigilante posses to round up the "troublemakers." Within five days, five whites and anywhere from twenty to two hundred blacks, depending on which estimate one uses, had been killed in the fighting. A self-appointed committee of plantation owners and storekeepers interrogated the more than one thousand blacks taken captive by law enforcement officers and federal troops, and they held seventy-nine of them for trial on charges of insurrection and murder. In five days, they convicted sixty-seven defendants and sentenced them to jail terms ranging from twenty years to life in prison. Twelve of the accused were convicted of murder and sentenced to death.[17]

Investigators for the NAACP contended that the police started the violence by opening fire on a peaceful meeting, and that the trials violated American standards of due process. They noted that not a single white person faced any legal action as a result of the violence that left many blacks dead, and that intimidation and torture had been used to secure confessions. Charging that the real crime of the Elaine Riot victims had been their decision to form a union, the NAACP appealed the convictions to the federal courts and eventually the jail sentences were overturned. However, union organization among the sharecroppers died out until the formation of the Southern Tenant Farmers Union fifteen years later.[18]

The problems of sharecropping facing the Perry family were hardly unique, but they entered the world of tenant farming at a particularly crisis-ridden time. By the time Ivory Perry was born in 1930, 78 percent of the nation's 2,803,756 black families lived in the South, 44 percent in rural areas. Of those in the countryside, 80 percent worked as tenant farmers or day laborers. In Jefferson County, where the Perrys did much of their sharecropping, more than half of the entire population lived in the country, with blacks constituting 83 percent of the rural population. Cotton covered three-quarters of Jefferson County's cropland and accounted for 90 percent of the land worked by sharecroppers. The largest plantation in the county had 1,560 acres devoted to cotton, with 1,014 of those acres worked by 107 sharecropping families and the rest tended by hired day laborers.[19]

During the Depression, cotton prices fell from seventeen cents per

pound in 1929 to seven cents per pound in 1932. President Roosevelt's
Agricultural Adjustment Act (AAA) sought to alleviate the farm crisis by
raising crop prices and reducing acreage through subsidies for fallow
land. As a result, Arkansas plantation owners received $72 million from
the federal government by 1938 to take land out of production—which
the owners accomplished largely by evicting sharecroppers. From 43
million acres under cotton cultivation in 1929, southern farms fell to 23
million acres by 1939. Displacement of sharecroppers provoked two responses: collective resistance and individual migration.[20]

Collective resistance coalesced around the Southern Tenant Farmers
Union (STFU). In 1934, seven black and eleven white men formed the
STFU near Tyronza, Arkansas (about 150 miles from Pine Bluff). By 1935,
the organization's membership soared to 15,000 tenants from the Mississippi Delta cotton fields, and it waged a fierce strike that year, seeking
better pay and improved living conditions. In Arkansas alone, 22,000
workers joined the STFU between 1934 and 1938, and total STFU membership throughout the South in 1938 exceeded 38,000.[21]

The rapid growth in STFU membership stood in marked contrast to
previous attempts at organizing Arkansas sharecroppers. Violence and
intimidation still characterized relations between plantation owners and
sharecroppers in the 1930s, but historical changes created a new determination to resist on the part of the workers. Declining cotton prices,
AAA subsidies, and increased agricultural mechanization all undermined the stability of the sharecropper system. STFU members had
even less economic power than their predecessors in the Progressive
Farmers and Household Union, whose labor had provided an indispensable resource for the owners. In addition to the traditional problems of
low wages and poor working conditions, sharecroppers in the 1930s also
faced eviction from the land and an end to their way of life. By the early
1940s, federal policies, mechanization, and repression combined to defeat the STFU and to force sharecroppers off the land in large numbers.[22]

Pearl Perry and her children participated in the exodus of sharecroppers from the countryside when they moved to Pine Bluff in 1943. In that
city they encountered a different kind of historical legacy, one composed
of decades of Afro-American struggle and accomplishment. In the nineteenth century, a former slave named Wiley Jones had amassed a fortune
in Pine Bluff by investing the money he earned as a barber and shop-
keeper in local real estate and transportation ventures. Jones built the
city's first streetcar line, and he owned the local fairgrounds, park, and

racetrack. He served as treasurer of the Annual Colored Industrial Fair held each October to display the accomplishments of local blacks.[23]

During the Reconstruction era, a series of compromises between whites and blacks in the Pine Bluff Republican party organization divided local elective offices between the two races. Ferd Havis, a black man, was elected alderman in 1871, state legislator in 1872, and Jefferson County assessor in 1873. Havis and Wiley Jones attended the 1880 Republican National Convention as delegates from Arkansas, and for ten years Havis served as Jefferson County circuit clerk. Another black officeholder, John Gray Lucas, served as state representative and commissioner of the U.S. Circuit Court, while other blacks routinely won election as county coroner and common council representative.[24]

Business and political achievement led to opportunities for black education in Pine Bluff. J. C. Corbin had come to Arkansas from his native Ohio in the 1870s, and he quickly became one of the most influential black leaders in the state. A graduate of Ohio University who spoke nine languages and published scholarly articles on mathematics, Corbin served as chief clerk in the Little Rock branch of the U.S. post office and filled the office of state superintendent of public education for one term. At the behest of Governor Augustus H. Garland, Corbin moved to Pine Bluff and established Branch Normal College for Negroes in 1875, an institution that later became Arkansas AM&N and then the University of Arkansas at Pine Bluff.[25] The existence of that institution helped secure an important role for Pine Bluff as a center of black education, culture, and business in the state of Arkansas.

Thus Ivory Perry grew up in a region characterized by a rich history of Afro-American struggle and accomplishment. Born in a rural area known for militant activism by sharecroppers, he moved to a city with rich traditions of self-help and political mobilization. But neither the urban nor the rural strains of activism had much of a direct effect on him personally. In the mid-1930s the STFU had eighteen locals in Jefferson County and enjoyed a following among both black and white sharecroppers. When county officials denied welfare relief to destitute black sharecroppers under the pretense of having run out of application forms, the STFU staged successful protest demonstrations. Yet Ivory Perry never heard of the organization when he was growing up, and to this day his relatives cannot recall any contact with it. The STFU had its greatest strength in Jefferson County north of the Arkansas River, while the Perrys did most of their farming south of it. But even if they had known of the union's existence they would not necessarily have joined it. They certainly resented the terms and conditions of sharecropping, but like most people they tried to survive as best they could under the system that existed, giving little thought to prospects for systemic change.[26]

In Pine Bluff, the Perry family lived with relatives on Mississippi Street as they made the transition from rural to urban life. Even though his father had long since abandoned the family and even though his mother spent much of her time away from home at work, Ivory grew up in a warm supportive atmosphere, surrounded by aunts, uncles, cousins, and neighbors who treated him like a family member. That experience conformed to a larger pattern among southern black families in which kinship clusters, flexible extended families, and neighborhood support networks provided a stable source of affection and identity even when economic pressures disrupted the nuclear family.[27] To a youth raised in the country, the city had a lot to offer, and Ivory especially enjoyed going to school right down the street without having to miss class regularly for work in the fields. After school, he explored the shop windows and motion picture theaters downtown, both of which helped stimulate his curiosity about the rest of the world.[28] Yet even after moving to Pine Bluff, Ivory continued to work in the fields. He often got up at four in the morning to catch the truck that stopped at the corner of Ohio Street and Twenty-ninth Avenue to take day laborers out to the plantations. He also took jobs in the city—delivering packages for a grocer, caddying at a golf course, and shining shoes.

While Perry encountered new surroundings in the city, poverty and racism continued to shape the contours of his experience. Sometimes the labor contractors who took him out to pick cotton in Grady or to shuck rice in Stuttgart would just pocket the money Ivory had earned, knowing full well that the youth could not afford to complain and risk not being hired again. In addition, Pine Bluff made the nature of white racism more evident to him than ever before; signs everywhere designated public facilities for "whites only" or "colored only." At the Strand Theater, blacks had to sit in the "colored balcony," and Perry remembers being careful not to laugh at the funny parts of the films until the white people had laughed first. Even white children could pose a threat, as Ivory discovered one day when he told a white boy that he had seen another white boy break the first's bicycle. Pearl Perry, overhearing the exchange, beat Ivory. She knew that he had told the truth, just as she had always instructed him to do, but she felt she had to impress upon her son the dangers of antagonizing white people—even those who were only nine years old.[29]

His family taught Ivory Perry more affirmative lessons as well. Through family stories he received instruction in what made for a good life. His relatives cultivated moral and psychic resources in the children by celebrating family members whose exemplary conduct provided useful lessons. Ivory's cousin, the Reverend Robert Pierce, remembers one hero venerated in those stories:

> We had an uncle in those days, who was real old, that we considered to be a success. He had migrated out of the state of Louisiana and came to south Arkansas where he was a little teacher and a little preacher. And he could read and write, which was rare for people his age. And to us, we considered Uncle Willis a very successful man. And our parents kind of disciplined us into his tracks—to stay in school and learn how to get along with people, and help people, for you can't make it by yourself.[30]

Robert Pierce took those lessons to heart and became an example himself to Ivory and his sisters. When Pierce was in the ninth grade he did yard work for a white family and became friendly with their son, who was in the seventh grade. He noticed that his new friend's seventh-grade books were the same ones that he got in the black school in the ninth grade. In addition, the boy had supplies at home, like long pieces of chalk, that Pierce had never seen in his school. The black schools got only little end pieces of chalk once they had been discarded by the white schools, just as they received only hand-me-down books and science equipment. Wanting to win the approval of his teachers, Pierce borrowed a long piece of chalk from his playmate and brought it to school. But when he showed it to the teachers, they assumed he had stolen it. Pierce escaped punishment when the white youth verified that he had given him the chalk, but the experience left Pierce with a lingering resentment against the constraints imposed on him by racism, and with a determination to fight against them.[31]

When Pierce returned to Pine Bluff from military service in World War II, racism bothered him more than ever before. He remembers boarding the Main Street bus and observing that the sign ordering black people to sit in the back read "COLORED SIT FROM THE REAR OF THE BUS." Seeing no whites on board, he sat down on the seat directly behind the driver. The driver ordered Pierce to move back, but Pierce retorted that he was in full compliance with the sign, and that if the bus company wished to convey some other message by that sign, then they should change its wording. "We had gone to war and given our guts for our country," he says, "and we felt like we deserved the same privileges as anybody else." With that principle in mind, Pierce quietly tested the limits of segregation whenever possible. He took a drink from the "whites only" water fountain in a downtown store, refused to move when a white man sat down beside him on the bus and then insisted Pierce should move farther back, and suggested to white store owners that hiring black employees would increase their sales to black customers. In one hardware store, a black employee routinely helped customers with all their selections but was not allowed to work the cash register. Pierce told the owner that he faced a mass exodus of black customers unless he changed that policy. Soon the black employee began to work the register.[32]

Robert Pierce followed his conscience in defiance of those who considered him to be a troublemaker.

> Here's what the white man calls a troublemaker. If you were black and a white man walked up and started talking to you, if you found a way of not saying "yes sir" to him, then you were a "smart nigger." I could find a hundred ways never to say "yes sir." I could talk all day and don't have to say "yes sir."[33]

Another of Ivory Perry's cousins, Doris Caldwell, echoes Rev. Robert Pierce's sentiment. "I ain't never said 'yes, sir' or 'no, sir,'" she insists. "I just couldn't use the words. I didn't. Why should I?" Like Pierce she waged her own battle with segregation. She remembers having to confront whites on the street when she was a teenager, whites who expected her to step off the sidewalk to let them pass. "I fought many a day with kids my own age when they tried to push us off Main Street," she recalls. "They tried, but they didn't get nowhere because we fought back." Shortly after Caldwell married she went to Newberry's department store to buy handkerchiefs for her husband. The clerk refused to let her touch the ones she wanted, insisting instead that she tell him her preference so that he could pick them up from the display case. Incensed by his refusal to let her touch the handkerchiefs, Caldwell waited until he had wrapped the box and then told him, "OK, now you pay for them and take them. You picked them out, they must be yours." Caldwell stormed out of the store, never to shop there again.[34]

Attitudes of self-respect and antagonism toward racism permeated

Ivory Perry's family and childhood community. What he learned at home found powerful reinforcement at school, especially in the classes of Miss Myrtle Jones, his tenth-grade teacher at Pine Bluff's Merrill High School. By the time Ivory entered her class, Miss Jones had already established her identity as an indispensable resource and role model for black children in the area. Being her student entailed special responsibilities and offered special rewards, according to the things Ivory had heard people say, and once he became a student in her class she did not disappoint him.

Before students could enter her classroom, Miss Jones held inspection to make sure that they had combed their hair, cleaned their fingernails, and shined their shoes. "They had to prepare themselves to go into manhood and womanhood," she explains, adding that she wanted them armed with respect for themselves and respect for others. "We were striving for the virtues, honesty and truth," she recalls, never acknowledging the vices—"we didn't even call their names"—because she wanted her pupils to be guided by positive aspirations. "Above all, tell the truth," she told them. When students asked what they should do if someone threatened to cut off one of their arms unless they lied, she told them, "Lose the arm, but tell the truth."[35]

Black educators like Miss Jones had the difficult task of encouraging their students to work for success in a society that had stacked the deck against them. Too much emphasis on racism and the limitations it imposed on black people might lead to despair and resignation, yet insufficient attention to the obstacles ahead might give students a dangerously unrealistic notion about life in a segregated and racist society. Like other teachers in that situation, Miss Jones asked her students to dig deeply inside themselves for internal resources to transcend unfair, unjust, and immoral circumstances.

Self-discipline constituted the core of Miss Jones's philosophy. She took an active role policing the extracurricular lives of her pupils, driving up and down Pine Bluff's notorious Third Avenue in her big white Chevrolet looking for young people about to enter taverns or juke joints. All she had to do was honk her horn at her students, and they would dutifully turn around, go home, tell their parents that Miss Jones had seen them on Third Avenue, and accept their punishment. On occasion, Miss Jones would walk right into the Strand or Vester theaters to search for students skipping school, and she would drag them out on the spot. After she retired from teaching, Miss Jones continued youth work for twenty years as an officer of the juvenile court. Even after retiring from that job, she continued to do the same work on her own, without pay.[36]

Miss Jones worked tirelessly to help her students avoid the temptations of drinking, dancing, and motion pictures, but she wanted to do much more. It was important to her that young people do something for others and that they recognize their responsibilities to society. She organized "tag day" sales every year to raise money for needy families. She encouraged her pupils to share with one another and to take an interest in one another's well-being. She never directly addressed racism, but she told her classes as emphatically as she could that they should "treat everybody like you've been raised to be—polite, honest, and truthful." She reminded them, "Have respect for yourself and then respect for others."[37]

Ivory Perry learned those lessons well; the things Miss Jones taught stayed with him his whole life. "If it weren't for Miss Jones, I'd probably be dead now," he says. "She taught me respect for people and a respect for truth—that your word is supposed to be your bond." Her emphasis on caring for others became second nature to him and helped prepare the groundwork for his later social activism. Robert Pierce observes, "He walked to school through the mud in the rain and carried his little lunch in a brown sack. And he learned to share what he had with others, because somebody always shared with him." Yet Perry also learned at school about the divisions in the black community, about the status rivalries and petty jealousies that divided him from his classmates. "If one little kid got a new shirt and I couldn't afford one, he called himself better than me," Perry recalls. "And they had little societies and cliques based on what church you went to or how much money you had."[38]

The moral lessons that Ivory Perry learned at home and in school were supplemented, at least in part, by his experiences in church. Whenever she could get away from work, Pearl Perry went to church and always took her children with her. Most of the time in Pine Bluff they attended Rev. Albert King's St. Hurricane Baptist Church at Thirty-fourth Avenue and Ohio Street. Church activities included Sunday services, choir practice, weeknight prayer meetings, Bible study groups, Baptist Training Union, and home mission visits.[39]

Ivory believed in the existence of a Supreme Being and accepted the moral imperatives taught in church, but he had his doubts about organized religion, especially as it related to racism. "These whites doing lynchings, they was Baptists too," Perry remembers thinking, "and I couldn't figure out, if they was such good Christians, why were they killing innocent people?" In addition, the preaching in church about humility and meekness in this world in return for eternal reward in heaven made no sense to him. "I want to get my reward in this world," he insists, "because I never been to the other world and I don't know how it's going to be; but you know the whites running this world, so you know they gonna be trying to run the next world—so I want to get mine while I'm here."[40]

Questions of race occupied his mind on subjects other than religion. Merrill High School had no black history courses, and Ivory's textbooks never touched on the specific experiences of black people, but one of his teachers used to talk to him privately about the civil rights activist and scholar W. E. B. Du Bois and about the black nationalist leader Marcus Garvey. "At the time I heard about Garvey and how he wanted to go back to Africa, I was hoping it would become a reality, because I knew I just had to get away from all this racism," Perry remembers.[41] But like many others attracted by Garvey's message, he had to postpone thoughts of exodus to Africa while he grappled with the problems and concerns of his immediate surroundings.

Ivory tried to learn about racism from every available source. When he worked in white people's houses, he surreptitiously read the books and magazines he found there in the hope that they would have answers to his questions about racism. He listened to the radio at home, and drew particular satisfaction from the triumphs of the black boxing champion Joe Louis. Conversely, the demeaning stereotypes of black people in radio programs like "Amos 'n Andy" made him feel both embarrassed and angry. He found no humor in that program's presentation of blacks as lazy, shiftless, and amoral. He felt that southern blacks like himself suffered directly from the racial stereotypes perpetuated by "Amos 'n Andy," as typified by an incident that happened to him in Warren, Arkansas when he was seventeen years old.[42]

Working as a bellhop in the Southern Land Hotel in Warren, Perry began to shine the shoes of a white salesman from Shreveport, Louisiana. Without warning, the man began to slap Ivory's face and punch him, screaming, "You're the blackest nigger I've ever seen." The hotel manager, an elderly white woman, made the salesman stop and ordered him to apologize. Contritely the salesman explained that he had been drinking, and he gave Perry a $20 tip. But the irrational rage behind the attack underscored the menacing presence of racism in his life, and Perry felt suffocated by the obsession with skin color that seemed to dominate the thinking of white people. Everywhere he looked he saw evidence of it—on the signs that differentiated white water fountains and restrooms from those designated "for colored only," in the words of white people who assumed that they could address any black man as "boy," and in the obvious discrimination that relegated black workers to menial and low-paying jobs.[43]

One respite from the indignities of racism and the alienations of labor came from leisuretime activities with his friends. Perry liked to ride horses through the open fields around Pine Bluff with his best friend, Jewel Gonder, whom everybody called Sam. They pretended to be the cowboys they saw in the movies, with Ivory imagining himself as Don "Red" Barry and Sam pretending to be Lash Larue. Sam and Ivory stayed overnight at each other's houses and played until dark in their back yards. They filled up their weekends with marble games, fishing trips, and hunting expeditions.[44]

When they became teenagers, Gonder and Perry sneaked into places like Eddie's Pool Room, the Swingland Grill, and other juke joints along Third Avenue. Neither of them drank alcoholic beverages, but they liked to dance and to listen to the music of blues singers like Muddy Waters and Louis Jordan. They had to conceal these excursions from their strict parents and from the eagle eye of Miss Jones as she cruised up and down in her big car. Miss Jones did pull them out of the Strand Theater once, but she never caught them in the juke joints. Perry and Gonder reflect upon their youth in Pine Bluff with happy memories. They recall a closeness with each other, as if they had been brothers. They remember how you could trust people and never have to lock your door or worry about someone stealing from you. They cherish the atmosphere of mutual respect that characterized their community as well. "It wasn't a whole lot of jonin' [aggressive teasing] like a lot of these kids do today," observes Jewel Gonder.[45]

At the same time that life in Pine Bluff increased Ivory Perry's exposure to white racism, it also enabled him to learn about methods of resistance and contestation. In Pine Bluff, the Perrys came into contact with civil rights activism, although more as spectators than as participants. An active NAACP chapter dominated by small-business owners and civil service professionals made its presence felt in the city, but within the limits mandated by the realities of southern racism. When the local chapter participated in the national NAACP campaign for federal legislation against lynching in 1937, they had to return 150 campaign buttons to the national office because they could not be displayed safely in Pine Bluff. As postal worker and chapter chairman W. B. Cloman wrote to the national office, "It was found in some cases to be dangerous to display them in some parts and places of our city and county. The wrist bands and large placards we could not handle at all on account of prejudice here among the whites."[46]

If that atmosphere of intimidation constrained the actions of business owners and professionals whose livelihood did not depend upon white approval, it virtually precluded social protest by sharecroppers and day laborers. Yet one incident played an important part in the Perry family's understanding of racism and their desire to struggle against it. It took place before Pearl Perry and her children actually moved to Pine Bluff, but their relatives talked about it often as a lesson that proved they need not submit passively to racist provocations. The incident involved two brothers from one of Pine Bluff's most distinguished black families—Leo and Wiley Branton.

On an early September day in 1940, eighteen-year-old Leo Branton and his younger brother Wiley walked into the Henry Marx department store in Pine Bluff to buy clothes for the impending school term. A salesman showed Wiley Branton a gray "by-swing," a jacket with pleats and a belt across the back. He was anticipating a nice commission on the sale—until the young man asked his brother's advice. Leo pointed out that Wiley already had a gray suit and that the by-swing was out of style. Angered by the prospect of losing his sale, the store employee whirled around and asked Leo, "What the hell have you got to do with it, nigger?" Leo replied that he had a right to advise his brother, but that response only made the salesman more irate. "If you don't shut up, nigger," he warned, "I'm going to hit you in the mouth." The youth vowed that he would do no such thing, and with that, the salesman struck him.[47]

Leo Branton put his hand to his mouth. When he saw blood, the 135-pound teenager hit back, knocking the 200-pound salesman against the wall. In his fury, Leo knocked the bigger man to the floor, jumped on his stomach, and began to pound the man's face with both fists. Store personnel finally intervened, enabling Leo Branton to stand up and step back. As they dragged the salesman to the back of the store, the owner asked what had happened, and Leo Branton explained, "He struck me and I hit him back." The owner told the Branton brothers that they should leave before there was any more trouble. As they turned to walk out of the store, Leo Branton heard someone shouting, "No, Carl! No, Carl! For Christ's sake, don't do that!" When he turned around, Branton saw the salesman coming toward him from the back of the store, brandishing a handgun. He chased the teenager behind a rack of clothes; in self-defense Branton pushed the rack over on top of his pursuer. Leo and Wiley Branton ran from the store to their father's taxi company office four blocks away. They told Leo Branton, Sr., what had happened in the store. Believing his sons and supporting their actions, Branton nonetheless sent Leo off to stay with his grandfather for safety's sake.[48]

A fight between a black teenager and a white man violated the southern code of racial deference, but Leo Branton had no thought of that at the time. Looking back on that day, he reflects:

> I never thought about it. I'm just not a person who allows people to run over them. The thought never occurred to me that this is a white man I'm fighting with and the consequences are going to be great. I mean, the man struck me and I did the natural thing. I struck back.

Yet the salesman hardly thought of Branton's response as a "natural thing," and he demanded prosecution. The Pine Bluff chief of police refused to act because he considered Branton had acted in self-defense, but the county sheriff agreed to arrest the youth.[49]

Leo Branton went to court thinking he would face a minor charge of disturbing the peace, but the racial implications of the case soon produced a bizarre turn of events. Pine Bluff had only two black attorneys at that time; one did not handle criminal cases, and the other had spoken out so frankly against discrimination and segregation that the Brantons feared that his involvement in the case would surely lead to conviction. The family hired a white attorney, but he withdrew from the case on the morning of the trial, leaving Leo Branton to face the charges without benefit of legal counsel. To his shock, the youth discovered that in addition to a charge of disturbing the peace, he faced prosecution for assault with a deadly weapon. The salesman needed sixteen stitches and alleged that Leo Branton had used the butt end of a knife in the attack. Wiley and Leo Branton told the court their version of what had happened in the store—that Leo had acted in self-defense and had used only his fists. But the judge found him guilty on all counts. "He sounded like a tobacco auctioneer," Leo Branton recalls, remembering how the judge called out "thirty days on the county farm for this and thirty days on the county farm for that." Before the sheriff could take Leo off to jail, his father arrived with an attorney who informed the judge of his intention to appeal the case, which under the system then in effect meant an automatic retrial in front of a jury.[50]

Within the Pine Bluff black community, the Branton case became an important symbol. The president of Arkansas AM&N, Dr. John Brown Watson, discussed the issues raised by the trial in a speech that helped mobilize the entire black community. As Wiley Branton remembers it, "Dr. Watson did not exactly call for a boycott of the Henry Marx department store. But he did say that if he saw any faculty members coming out of that place of business, they should tell him where to send their final check, and if he saw any students coming out of that store they should tell him where to send their final transcript." The response to Dr. Watson's appeal was immediate and emphatic. With no central organization or public meetings, all the important black groups in Pine Bluff, including the NAACP and the Prince Hall Masons, spread word of the boycott. The removal of black business cost the Henry Marx store thousands of dollars, and when Leo Branton's case finally came to trial before the jury, black people filled up their designated area of the courtroom to demonstrate support.[51]

Yet that very solidarity made prosecutors determined to secure a conviction. Leo Branton remembers that when he testified in his own behalf, the prosecutor asked him nothing about the events in the store, but instead posed a series of questions designed to establish that Branton attended college at Tennessee State University. Branton discovered the reason for that line of questioning during the prosecutor's final speech to the jury. Branton remembers him saying:

> If this was an ordinary cornfield nigra, I would tell you to fine him and let him go, because fining him would be punishment for him. But here's a nigra that's got money, got enough money to go away to college, and in another state! So fining this nigger wouldn't be no punishment for him. The only thing that would be punishment would be to spend some time on the county farm, and I want him to spend some time on the county farm.[52]

The jury returned a guilty verdict and the judge sentenced Leo Branton to a term on the county farm.

The Branton family vowed that they would never let Leo serve a day in jail, and they had their lawyer file another appeal. As he went back to school while awaiting the outcome of his appeal, Leo Branton decided that he would never return to Pine Bluff if it meant going to prison. "I never would have gotten out of the jail alive," he contends. "They would have gotten me down on that county farm and they would have killed me." Anger over the verdict within the black community and embarassment over it among whites led to a compromise solution, however, that kept Leo Branton out of jail. The judge who presided over the case told Leo Branton, Sr., that he felt the verdict was unfortunate, and that he would welcome information about any extenuating circumstances that could be used to suspend the sentence. They worked out an agreement to have a physician certify that confinement would damage Leo Branton's health so that the judge could commute the sentence. That outcome satisfied the prosecutor, who still had his conviction, and it delighted the black community, which from that point on looked at Leo Branton not only as one who stood up and fought back but as one who "got away with it."[53]

The Branton case illustrates the important role played by independent black businesspeople in building community resources for social contestation in southern cities. Leo and Wiley Branton's grandfather on their father's side owned the taxi company; their grandfather on their mother's side drove a parcel post truck for the post office. Along with other black families whose incomes came from insurance, undertaking, and other businesses serving a primarily black clientele, they provided an economic basis for civil rights activity in Pine Bluff. Of course, the community was not monolithic and not every black business owner could or would support civil rights activity, but they did serve as a potential and sometimes an actual base of support.

Even in the course of their everyday functions, black businesses sometimes provided vital services to the community. For example, the Branton taxicabs transported sick people to hospitals when the public ambulances would not serve blacks, and they picked up children from school on inclement days. The cabs connected people on the outskirts of town with friends and relatives in the city at a time when few black people in Pine Bluff owned automobiles. On more than one occasion they provided a radio-dispatched fleet of cars descending on the scene of potential racial violence to remove black people from possible physical danger. But their most important contribution was providing a base of support for civil rights activism. Wiley and Leo Branton's grandmother waged a fight to get black people to vote against funds for a new library because city officials announced that only whites would be able to use it. They didn't always win, but as Wiley Branton says of his parents' and grandparents' generations, "Even though they knew that white folks were in control, they would by and large give them a run for their money."[54]

The presence of Arkansas AM&N also made a difference in black activism in Pine Bluff, as evidenced by President Watson's stand on the Leo Branton case. Black educators worked quietly to lobby for funds for black schools and they insisted on high standards of educational quality at Merrill High School and at Arkansas AM&N. They also engaged in delicate negotiations with the white community over scarce resources. One folk tale collected in Pine Bluff by folklorist Richard Dorson underscores the diplomacy demanded of these educators. "The appropriation for the negro school was used for the white school. The superintendent explained this to the negro principal who of course couldn't make a direct protest. So he said, "The one thing we need most of all is educated white folk."[55]

The community resources of Pine Bluff and its environs established a firm foundation for social contestation within the black people raised there. Leo Branton went on to become an internationally renowned attorney who successfully represented black activist Angela Davis in the early 1970s. Wiley Branton became the first black graduate of the University of Arkansas law school and a leader of legal efforts to secure voting rights for blacks in the 1960s. But for Ivory Perry, raised in the same community, the translation of childhood memories and resources into social activism took a more roundabout path. It is perhaps significant that much of his later activism mirrored the pattern established in the Branton case—resistance to racism by individuals provoked official reaction and overreaction, which in turn mobilized collective support from the aggrieved community. Many of the coalitions that he formed later in life resembled the alliance among educators, business owners, fraternal organizations, and individuals that rallied in support of the Brantons in Pine Bluff in 1940.

Yet while Ivory Perry and his family took pride in the civil rights activism in Pine Bluff, they did not participate in it directly. They had no independent income and could not afford to alienate white employers. The matters decided in voting booths and courtrooms seemed very distant from the daily struggle for survival that occupied most of their time. Although the Branton case and its aftermath inspired and encouraged the Perry family, the economic and social circumstances of their every-day life demanded a more personal struggle. In subsequent years, when he became a community organizer and social activist, Perry realized his childhood experiences gave him some important insights into the obsta-cles that keep poor people from joining movements for social change.

It seems understandable that the child raised in an extended family and community kinship network would develop a philosophy as an adult that called for helping everyone in need, not just blood relatives. Similarly, one can see why a child stung by playmates' scorn of his old clothes and his membership in the "wrong" church might come to dis-trust materialism and status hierarchies later in life. But Perry also learned from his youth that people do not become involved in activism simply because they are unhappy. Poor people fight a battle every day to put food on their tables and to keep a roof over their heads, and they cannot afford to waste any energy on behalf of abstract principles. Politi-cal action requires risk and presumes that short-term sacrifices will yield long-term benefits. But most poor people have no assurance that there will be a long run for them, and regardless of their sympathies, they often cannot afford to think about political change. Ivory Perry came to feel that social change had to touch the lives of people on the bottom of society to really make a difference, and that in order to reach these peo-ple it had to begin with their everyday needs and concerns.

But those perceptions fell into place only after adult experiences made Perry reflect back on his youth. At the time, he had his hands full just trying to understand the personal and historical circumstances facing him and other blacks all across the country. Mechanization of agriculture drove his family to the city and disrupted the rural life they had always known. World War II cushioned part of the impact of that displacement by providing job opportunities in the cities, but war mobilization also disrupted the fabric of urban life. Defense spending in the 1940s ended more than a decade of economic depression, and in a relatively short period of time a chronic labor surplus became a labor shortage. Fourteen million Americans entered the armed forces and millions of others crossed city, county, and state lines looking for work in defense produc-tion centers.

These migrations disrupted old networks, strained the resources of the cities, and created unprecedented transformations in race, class, and gender identities. Black people responded to war mobilization with de-mands for "double victory"—victory over fascism abroad and over racism at home. A. Philip Randolph organized the March on Washington Movement, which secured an executive order from President Roosevelt mandating fair hiring in defense industries, and a new militancy invigorated civil rights protests nationwide.[56] War mobilization also accelerated changes in family structure that had been underway since the start of the Depression. With large numbers of men in the military, greater numbers of women entered the work force and became the major source of support for their families.

In Pine Bluff, the Committee on Negro Organizations (CNO), under the leadership of black attorney Harold Flowers, engaged in highly publicized battles to desegregate bus station waiting rooms and city parks.[57] Juvenile court records showed a tremendous rise in delinquency cases during the war years and a gradual lowering of the average age of delinquents.[58] Ivory Perry moved from a rural society in transition to an urban community undergoing profound changes itself. As a result he spent his entire youth in unsettled and unsettling circumstances. Old patterns of social relations rooted in sharecropping had broken down, and new patterns remained fluid and transitory. Economic changes undermined traditional avenues for employment, and families faced extraordinary changes that left them uncertain about the future. Social strain displaced and disoriented individuals and it disrupted the patterns of the past for communities and institutions.

But for Ivory Perry, important continuities endured and offset the effects of rapid social change. Within his family, at school, and out in the community at large, he absorbed lessons in self-reliance, mutuality, and struggle. His family respected hard work and education, provided examples of sharing and compassion, and offered role models who did what they could to resist racism and exploitation. His favorite teacher demanded punctuality, cleanliness, and moral excellence. She instructed him to care for others and to share with them, and she insisted that he speak the truth no matter what the consequences. His community honored the memory of achievers in business, education, and government; it established networks of support to help those in need; and it mounted a sustained effort on behalf of the Brantons and others in pursuit of racial justice. In collective memory about the past, in the institutions indigenous to the black community, and in the practices and traditions of family, Ivory Perry learned standards of behavior that would anchor all his moral and political commitments in the years ahead.

Yet as Ivory grew older, a series of economic and personal hardships hit his family. Pearl Perry contracted bronchial pneumonia and the doctor ordered her not to leave the house. But the children had no food, so she walked in the rain to her two jobs that day. Shortly after, she suffered a stroke, and on November 20, 1946, she died at the age of forty-two.[59]

Ivory tried to stay in school after his mother died, but he had to put in ever-increasing hours at work just to earn enough money to survive. Kathen had gotten married by this time, so Ivory and Earline moved in with their older sister and her husband. But money was scarce in the household, and Ivory had trouble finding a job that paid enough to support himself, much less contribute to the rest of the family. He set out to find his father in hopes that Son Perry might be able to lend him some money. He searched on foot, walking the back roads of rural Arkansas, asking sharecroppers and timber workers if they knew Son Perry. When he finally found him, his father wanted to help but had very little money himself, and his new wife frowned on lending any of it to Ivory.

Ivory returned to Pine Bluff empty-handed and dropped out of school to find a full-time job. For more than a year, Perry worked wherever and whenever he could, but he never made more than $18 a week. Frustrated by low-paying menial jobs and unhappy about not being able to contribute more to support his sisters, he decided to leave Pine Bluff and join the army. That meant leaving home and leaving his family. But his room and board would be provided in the military, and he might even have enough money to send some back home. On November 2, 1948, Perry enlisted in the U.S. Army.[60]

CHAPTER 2

Korea: The Lessons of War

The night before his induction physical, Ivory Perry worked behind the desk at the Southern Land Hotel in Warren, Arkansas. Alone for most of the night, distracted only by the few guests who checked in, he reflected on his past and his future. Nervously he drank an entire case of Coca-Colas to keep awake. In the morning he reported to the recruiting station at Pine Bluff; they sent him on to Little Rock. Because of the Cokes he had too much acid in his system to pass the physical, and so he had to spend the next night in a boardinghouse in Little Rock. It gave him another lonely night to reflect on his decision to join the service. Eighteen years in Arkansas had provided him with a strong desire to see more of the rest of the world and less of his home state. He thought of the salesman who had slapped him at the hotel in Warren. He pictured his mother in failing health, walking off across town to her jobs in white people's kitchens, remembering how she used to sing "Meet me on the other side of the River Jordan." He thought about segregation—of the places that he could not go and the jobs that he could not get. He decided that he had to get out, that the army would enable him to leave his problems behind.[1]

Perry passed his physical exam and found himself on board a train taking him to basic training at Fort Knox, Kentucky. As he looked around the railroad car, he saw young black men like himself leaving Arkansas in hopes of a better life. At the swearing-in ceremony he had noticed many enlistees who had already served in the army during World War II, and he concluded that they must have felt that the military offered them more opportunities than civilian life. If they saw no future for themselves as black men in Arkansas, why should he? When the train arrived at Fort Knox, recruits scrambled off in a dozen directions, confused by the sergeants shouting instructions and screaming at them to move quickly. During eight weeks of basic training they kept moving, following orders, and learning about military discipline. They did fifty push-ups and ran five miles a day. Commands from tough officers rang in their ears, and any breach of military discipline could lead to tedious punishments like KP—kitchen patrol, where they had to peel potatoes and wash pots and pans. But to Ivory, the officers seemed no more ferocious than the tough black supervisors he had known on the plantations, and KP did not bother someone accustomed to kitchen work. "I'd been doing service work in kitchens practically my whole life," he remembers, "so that didn't bother me at all."[2]

After basic training and a short stint in California, Perry was assigned to service in Japan with the all-black Twenty-fourth Infantry Regiment (Twenty-fifth Division, Eighth Army). Although President Truman had ordered the desegregation of the armed forces in 1948 (in response to threats by A. Philip Randolph to launch a massive campaign of black draft resistance), the Twenty-fourth Regiment remained all black until 1951. Wherever segregation went, injustices followed.[3] Black soldiers found that they could not become high ranking officers, even in all-black units. Each military post had separate service clubs for blacks and whites. White soldiers could bring Japanese women on post with them, but black soldiers could not. Even off the base, white soldiers frequently refused to patronize Japanese businesses that served black customers. These practices did not surprise Ivory Perry, but they did disappoint him. He had hoped to leave racism behind when he joined the army, but it looked as though the same old things that had troubled him in Arkansas existed in the military too.[4]

In contrast, Perry felt that the Japanese people treated black soldiers very nicely. He met students and professors from Japanese universities who could speak English and who knew as much, or more, about the racial situation in the United States as he did. From them, he learned that differences in skin color did not automatically have to mean prejudice and hatred. As he learned more about Japanese customs and beliefs, he came to feel that all human beings had the same basic desires. Army life had its problems, but Perry felt that as a soldier, he got to see other places and share other cultures, and that he could develop skills and abilities that would have remained dormant at home.[5]

On June 25, 1950, his unit had just completed maneuvers on Mount Fuji and returned back to their base at Gifu, Japan. That same day, North Korean forces crossed the thirty-eighth parallel as part of a full-scale assault on South Korea. Two weeks later, Ivory Perry found himself in combat on the front lines in the Korean War. The Eighth Army rushed the Twenty-fourth Infantry Regiment from their base in Japan early in July in an attempt to slow the North Korean advance on South Korea. Undertrained and underequipped, the regiment suffered serious casualties but helped hold the line against disciplined North Korean troops. That resistance enabled General Douglas MacArthur to make his successful landing at Inchon in September, and to launch the invasion of North Korea. But when MacArthur moved his forces toward the Chinese border, China entered the war and its troops confronted the Twenty-fourth Regiment and other American units with some of the most ferocious fighting of the entire conflict.[6]

Combat service in Korea meant battling the enemy and the brutal Korean climate, but Ivory Perry and other black soldiers also had to contend with white racism within their own army. Segregated into all-black units under the supervision of white officers, they accumulated a list of grievances about their treatment. Perry saw the words "nigger go home" scrawled on walls wherever white GIs had been, and he resented publicity given to white units when victories by black troops went unreported. Black soldiers felt that white officers with inferior qualifications received promotions ahead of qualified black officers, and that some white officers in command of black units considered their assignment demeaning. Their condescending attitudes toward their troops ruined morale. On a personal level, Ivory Perry lost promotions due him to white soldiers, some of whom he had trained. He suffered when white officers eager for promotion took unnecessary risks in combat, sacrificing the lives of black soldiers to their own ambitions. "I saw a lot of black soldiers get killed over there because they had a racist company commander," he declares.[7]

Ivory Perry's cousin Harold Terrell served with him in the army in Korea. Terrell left Pine Bluff in 1949 to join the service because his parents could not afford to send him to college, and he could find no employment at home other than picking cotton for poverty wages. Like his cousin, Terrell did basic training at Fort Knox, and served in Japan and then Korea. Terrell's unit, the Seventy-seventh Combat Engineers, built bridges and roads for the Twenty-fourth Infantry Regiment among their other duties, so the two cousins got to see each other in Korea regularly. They compared impressions about race relations in the army and found that their views coincided, especially in regard to one important incident—the court-martial of Lieutenant Leon Gilbert.[8]

According to army prosecutors, Lieutenant Gilbert quit an outpost line in the face of an enemy attack on July 31, 1950. They charged that he refused a direct order to take his company back into combat because he was afraid to fight. His regimental commander arrested him on the spot, and on September 6, 1950, a court-martial board convicted Lieutenant Gilbert of cowardice in the face of enemy fire and sentenced him to death.[9]

The lieutenant told a different story. "I thought I was doing the right thing—I still do," he claimed after his trial. Gilbert explained that his company covered a retreat by the entire regiment by holding on to an important bridge, even though his men had no machine guns or automatic weapons. When driven back from that position, they encountered a colonel with no knowledge of their stand at the bridge. The colonel ordered them up the hill as if they had never been there in the first place. Lieutenant Gilbert later told reporters, "I did not refuse to obey the order. I was trying to explain why it couldn't be carried out. There were twelve men in my command. I considered it my duty as an officer to show why the order meant certain death."[10]

Ivory Perry and Harold Terrell knew Lieutenant Gilbert from their days together at Camp Gifu in Japan, and they were involved in the regimental retreat that included the incident for which he was sentenced to death. "Lieutenant Gilbert was a very good officer who was only trying to save his men," Perry claims, remembering storming up the hill that night himself. Outnumbered by the enemy and fighting on a steep hill that afforded little cover, the Twenty-fourth Regiment secured its objective three times, only to be knocked down the hill each time. After Lieutenant Gilbert's arrest, the regiment lost whole companies in the fighting, and the army reported 323 battlefield casualties that night.[11]

Although not eyewitnesses to the exchange between Lieutenant Gilbert and the colonel, Terrell and Perry believed the lieutenant's version of the incident. Furthermore, they felt that Gilbert's court-martial typified the predicament of black soldiers in Korea. "The colonel wouldn't go up the hill himself," says Perry, "but he'd send the men." Terrell adds, "It was just a colonel trying to make a name for himself without resources to do it." Terrell remembers relating the incident to other grievances felt by black soldiers, especially the press praising white troops but reporting on black units only when they suffered defeats. "They had the best equipment and the best officers," Terrell says of the white soldiers, yet they performed no better than the underequipped and poorly led black soldiers who won no praise from most of the media. Terrell notes that black heroes—like Lieutenant Harry E. Sutton from F Company of the Twenty-fourth Regiment, who made possible an evacuation of white troops by single-handedly holding a hill under enemy fire, or Medal of Honor winner Cornelius Charlton—never became known to the American public.[12]

Lieutenant Gilbert assumed command of the Twenty-fourth Infantry Regiment's A Company on the front lines of the Pusan Perimeter fighting during the afternoon of July 31, 1950. A veteran of more than ten years of military service, Gilbert had worked briefly as a machinist and supply clerk in Mechanicsburg, Pennsylvania, immediately after World War II, but he reenlisted in the army in 1948. Efficiency ratings showed Gilbert to be an excellent soldier, and he wore several medals awarded to him for his World War II service including the Combat Infantry Badge, the American Campaign medal, the European–Africa–Middle East Theater medal with two stars, and the World War II Victory medal.[13]

When Gilbert took command of A Company, the regiment had faced eleven consecutive days of heavy combat in the steep hills near Sangju. and Lieutenant Gilbert himself had been on the front lines for four days. On the afternoon that he took command of the company, he attempted to organize a roadblock, but enemy fire dispersed his men. According to the charges brought against him, Gilbert refused to take them back into combat even when ordered to do so a second time by Colonel Horton V. White. White testified at Gilbert's court-martial that he had asked the lieutenant why he left the outpost line with his men. Colonel White claimed that Gilbert told him that they feared getting cut off from the rest of the battalion and that he then ordered Gilbert to take his men back to their post, and that Gilbert agreed to comply with the order. Twenty minutes later, Gilbert allegedly returned to the colonel and informed him that he would not obey the previous order because "he was scared." Lieutenant Gilbert elected not to testify in his own behalf, but cross-examination of Colonel White revealed that the company commander had not known about the roadblock or about the battle situation on the outpost line. Other officers testified that Lieutenant Gilbert could not have reassembled his men because of enemy fire, and that Colonel White had misunderstood what Gilbert told him about not wanting to go back up the hill. Yet the hearing board found Lieutenant Gilbert guilty of violating Article 75 of the Uniform Code of Military Justice (cowardice in the face of the enemy) and sentenced him to death.[14]

Protests against the verdict poured in immediately, and they focused on two main issues: the quality of Lieutenant Gilbert's defense counsel, and the state of his mind on July 31, 1950. Critics charged that the defense attorney erred by not putting Gilbert on the stand, that he failed to secure testimony from key witnesses, and that he allowed the trial to take place in an emotional atmosphere within two-hundred yards of the battlefront.[15] A psychiatric report, completed after the trial but before sentencing, judged Lieutenant Gilbert had been suffering from an acute and severe anxiety reaction, "which would prevent him from carrying out his duties as ordered."[16]

Gilbert's defense attorney initially raised the issue about his state of mind. In an emotional atmosphere, with little time to prepare an adequate case and insufficient opportunity to subpoena friendly witnesses, the defense counsel raised what he considered to be his strongest argument. Rather than have to question the testimony of top-ranking officers, the attorney chose to use mental impairment as his defense, but he was not happy about the circumstances that forced him to do that. After the trial he wrote to Gilbert's wife, "The sentence of death was a direct result of the hysteria of the crisis in Korea, where the individual is sacrificed for what is deemed the good of the whole. The military authorities wanted to make an example of someone and through circumstances your husband was selected."[17]

The counsel's efforts did not fail completely. On appeal, President Truman took account of Lieutenant Gilbert's mental health in commuting his sentence to twenty years in prison.[18] But a subsequent investigation into the Gilbert case and into similar trials of black soldiers in Korea uncovered a pattern of behavior that called into question the legitimacy of Gilbert's trial and conviction.

Distressed by reports about the Gilbert case, NAACP Chief Counsel Thurgood Marshall went to Korea and conducted a detailed inquiry into disciplinary prosecution there, particularly with respect to black soldiers accused of cowardice in the face of the enemy. One out of every 3.6 men on the front lines in Korea during those first tough months of fighting was black, but almost 90 percent of those charged with violating Article 75 were black soldiers. Sixty blacks and only eight whites faced charges of misconduct in the face of the enemy between August and October 1950. Military tribunals convicted only two of the white soldiers, sentencing one to three years and one to five years in jail. The thirty-two black soldiers found guilty faced sentences of death (one), life in prison (fifteen), fifty years in prison (one), twenty-five years in prison (two), twenty years in prison (three), fifteen years in prison (one), ten years in prison (seven), and five years in prison (two).[19]

Marshall discovered that there were absolutely no acquittals for any soldiers tried between August 25 and October 2 (before and after the Gilbert trial), and he identified serious shortcomings in the processes by which those convictions had been obtained. Defendants told Marshall that after the Gilbert case they gave up any hope for acquittal, feeling that they would not get a fair trial. Few reported making deliberate choices about their defense attorneys; most accepted counsel chosen for them by the army. Many first met their attorneys on the day of the trial; others complained about too little time to discuss their case with counsel and too little opportunity to summon necessary witnesses. Harried defense lawyers faced multiple trials, and the time spent trying individual cases appeared excessively brief. Four soldiers charged with offenses that could bring death sentences had trials lasting less than fifty minutes—and that included reading of the charges, presentation of evidence, rebuttal, cross-examination, defense, summations, deliberations, and verdict.[20]

Marshall complained to a reporter from the *Pittsburgh Courier*, "I've never seen such ramrod justice handed out in all my experience. The life of a Negro meant nothing to those courts. Some soldiers were convicted for misconduct under fire when they were not even near enemy lines." In other cases, Marshall found a pattern in the filing of charges that revealed more attention to race than to behavior. Black soldiers who fell asleep on sentry duty were charged with "misconduct in the face of the enemy"; white soldiers faced a lesser charge of "sleeping on duty."[21]

To the NAACP and other black organizations, Marshall's investigation demonstrated the pervasive nature of white racism in the army and called into question the validity of court-martial convictions against black soldiers. But many officers and civilians believed that the figures uncovered by Marshall merely confirmed a dismal conduct record on the part of black soldiers. They argued that black troops faced a higher incidence of disciplinary actions than whites because they made poorer soldiers, and they contended that the combat record of units like the Twenty-fourth Infantry Regiment substantiated the claim. Colonel Horton White, the company commander who brought charges against Lieutenant Gilbert, voiced especially vehement criticisms of the regiment. "The tendency to panic continued in nearly all the Twenty-fourth Infantry operations west of Sangju," he told an army historian, noting that "men left their positions and straggled to the rear. They abandoned weapons and positions."[22]

In a highly publicized report, Brigadier General J. H. Michaelis claimed that his observations between July 1950 and May 1951 showed that "Negro units of the 24th Infantry Regiment repeatedly demonstrated their inability to either secure an objective against determined resistance or to defend particularly at night against enemy attacks of any size."[23] He noted that the division commander, Major General W. B. Kean, began placing groups of Negro enlisted men with white units because of the Twenty-fourth Infantry's repeated failures in combat. General Kean himself wrote to his superiors, "It is my considered opinion that the Twenty-fourth Infantry has demonstrated in combat that it is incapable of carrying out missions expected of an infantry regiment."[24]

Popular newspapers and magazines played up stories of cowardice among black soldiers during the Korean conflict. In 1951, the *Saturday Evening Post* "reported" alleged shortcomings of the Twenty-fourth Infantry Regiment in a series of articles, even offering a vehement, if self-contradictory, defense of the sentence meted out to Lieutenant Gilbert. In the process of ridiculing Thurgood Marshall's charges that racism caused the prosecutions of black soldiers for violations of Article 75, the magazine quoted an unnamed army officer who blamed Gilbert for leaving the prosecution with no choice: "In the tactical situation that prevailed at the time, he could have saluted, said 'Yes, sir,' taken his men out of sight around a bend in the road, and sat there. Nobody would have known the difference. You never knew whether your orders were going to be carried out or not."[25]

Tensions between blacks and whites in the military during the Korean War reflected a much larger social crisis in the making. Mechanization of agriculture in the South encouraged black migration to industrial cities, but automation, discriminatory hiring practices, and increases in overseas capital investment hit hardest at the industries most likely to employ blacks and contributed to deprive blacks of a proportionate share in the prosperity of the postwar era. Public and private home loan policies denied blacks access to expanding suburbs, while urban renewal programs built up central business districts at the expense of black home-owners and renters. At a time when white unemployment hovered between 3 and 6 percent, black unemployment stayed above 10 percent. At the start of the Korean War, the economic picture facing young black men was so bleak that they accounted for 25 percent of enlistments in the military, more than double their proportion of the population as a whole.[26]

The social crisis at home and the infusion of black soldiers into the army made the military a locus of racial tension during the Korean War. In addition, the nature of the conflict as a part of the Cold War struggle between capitalism and communism made issues of equality and fairness of paramount concern. The rhetoric of the Cold War made both sides attentive to practices that revealed a disparity between ideals and performance, and repeated invocation of terms like *freedom* and *self-determination* encouraged critical evaluation of conditions previously taken for granted. These crosscurrents converged in the U.S. Army in the summer of 1950, but never more so than in the Gilbert court-martial. The controversy emanating from that trial focused worldwide attention on American race relations, eventually involved the energies of historical actors as diverse as future Supreme Court Justice Thurgood Marshall, General Douglas MacArthur, and President Harry Truman, and in addition, may well have contributed strongly to the civil rights insurgency of the 1950s.

Sociologist Leo Bogart conducted two studies of racial attitudes among troops in Korea in 1951 that further document the controversy. White officers in command of the Twenty-fourth Infantry Regiment echoed the criticisms raised by Michaelis and Kean. "I don't believe that anyone could ever make a fighting outfit of them that would be reliable and could be counted on at any time," explained one officer. "Of course, they think they're hot stuff," complained another about the black soldiers under his command; "they think they're a lot better than they are."[27]

Black soldiers and black reporters covering the war told another story. They talked about poor command decisions by white officers, inadequate equipment, insufficient rest periods, unfair and dishonest publicity, and high casualty rates in battle. They pointed out that wounded white soldiers could expect evacuation by helicopters, but black GIs had to carry their wounded away from battle on stretchers. They noted that white units pulled back from battle enjoyed long rest periods, but that black outfits had to drill and stand inspection during their brief rest periods before rushing back into combat. They stressed their resentments over the disproportionate share of publicity and medals that went to white soldiers.[28] Many of the black soldiers participating in Bogart's survey were convinced that white officers considered them expendable.

One related a pattern of carelessness that exposed the Twenty-fourth Regiment to fire from U.S. planes and artillery: "They order artillery on a hill and then send us up the hill before the artillery aid came. We take the hill and no sooner than we get on top and our own artillery open up and kill most of the boys. Then our own planes kill a lot of the boys."[29] Other sources confirmed that soldier's perceptions. The *Pittsburgh Courier* correspondent covering the Twenty-fourth Infantry Regiment reported numerous incidents of that character. In one dispatch he told of U.S. Navy planes bombing the regiment by accident. In another, he reported the case of a white officer who ordered his black troops to take a hill, then left them in combat while he reported back to company headquarters with a foot wound that his soldiers claimed had to have been self-inflicted.[30] Perry remembers that incident. He recalls that although the officer displayed a bullet wound to the foot, his boot was not damaged.

Surveys, interviews, and reports from the black press all detailed the same complaints about the army that Ivory Perry remembers from his experiences in Korea. Corroborating data on Harold Terrell's Seventy-seventh Combat Engineers underscore the veracity of his reminiscences as well. David Carlisle, a black West Point graduate researching the history of the Seventy-seventh Combat Engineers, uncovered the case of Lieutenant Charlie Bussey. Bussey directed fire at the enemy from two machine guns, killing 258 North Koreans near Yechon in July 1950. His sergeant recommended Bussey for the Congressional Medal of Honor, but Bussey claims that company commander John T. Corley told him that he would not pass along the request because it would challenge the racial status quo. Bussey told the *Los Angeles Times* in 1984 that Corley confided to him, "If it had been a posthumous thing or if I were an inarticulate black private, it would have been O.K. 'But you' he said, 'would use it for integration.' And he was right. I wanted integration of the service and he knew it."[31]

Black and white observers agreed on one fact about the Twenty-fourth Infantry Regiment—its white officers suffered a far greater casualty rate than officers in other regiments. To critics of the Twenty-fourth, that statistic offered one more confirmation of the unit's incompetence and unsuitability for combat. To its defenders, the statistic emphasized the poor leadership and low morale facing a regiment with little rapport between its white officers and black troops. A middle position contended that "misunderstandings" between officers and the ranks led to increased casualties for both.[32]

Subsequent historians writing about the Korean War have tended to accept the negative judgment about the performance of black troops presented at the time by army officers and the mass media. In his recent book on the Pusan Perimeter fighting, Edwin P. Hoyt claims that "throughout the fighting the U.S. Twenty-fourth Infantry Regiment which was composed of black soldiers proved to be almost totally useless." Hoyt dismisses complaints by NAACP officials Thurgood Marshall and Walter White as unfounded accusations that did more harm than good to blacks because they tried to evade responsibility for demonstrably inferior performance by black soldiers. Drawing on the official army history of the war as his major source, Hoyt argues that the abundance of prosecutions for violations of Article 75 and the paucity of medals given to black soldiers reveals no pattern of discrimination, but rather a pattern of undistinguished conduct by black troops. Yet Hoyt's own evidence indicates more substance to charges of discrimination than he acknowledges. Many of the instances he cites to demonstrate unwillingness to fight on the part of black soldiers also reveal terrible confusion and incompetence among top-ranking officers.[33]

Despite his dismissal of the Twenty-fourth Infantry Regiment as "almost totally useless," Hoyt presents several cases where ferocious fighting by the Twenty-fourth contributed significantly to American victories. In addition, Hoyt offers no primary source material to back up his contention that the army was more than ready to reward black soldiers for superior performance, nor does he document his charges against Thurgood Marshall or Walter White, whose career records and demonstrated credibility certainly demand more respectful treatment. Most important, Hoyt fails to confront the historical antipathy to black soldiers in the military as well as the social circumstances during the Korean War that aggravated racial tensions among American soldiers.[34]

Black writers and historians have tended to interpret black soldiers' performance in Korea very differently from Hoyt and others. L. Albert Scipio's history of the Twenty-fourth Infantry Regiment emphasizes the unit's successes in Korea, especially at Yechon and Battle Mountain. David Carlisle has done extensive research on heroism by individual black soldiers in Korea and has campaigned for the army to award them the medals now that were denied them at the time.[35]

Writing more than twenty years after the end of the Korean conflict, Samuel L. Banks contributed a personal memoir to the *Negro History Bulletin*.

> Blacks made up a disproportionate number of workers who were engaged in the hardest and most arduous assignments in my unit (i.e. 840th Engineer Aviation Battalion). As a medic and chief administrative clerk of the dispensary, I saw the emotional and physical toll reflected in the daily "Sick Call" and the monthly "Morbidity Report."[36]

Banks's connection between the assignments and treatment meted out to black soldiers and their incidence of casualties certainly seems plausible. Psychologists examining combat stress during the Korean conflict found that it took soldiers defending positions under seige an average of thirteen days to recover physiological normality after an attack. Yet black soldiers in Korea during the summer of 1950 found themselves engaged in front-line combat for weeks at a time with inadequate opportunities for rest and recuperation.[37]

Controversy over the performance of black troops in the field masked an extremely complex situation. The Twenty-fourth Infantry Regiment won the first U.S. victory of the conflict near Yechon in July, but it came in for criticism once the fighting began to go badly for the American side. By making scapegoats out of black soldiers, the military hierarchy and American public could explain away defeats that stemmed from complex causes. "Every unit there gave ground," remembers Harold Terrell; "every unit there got kicked in the butt—but the white generals didn't get blamed for the defeats at all." When the war started, U.S. fighting forces were unprepared for sustained combat but they nonetheless expected to coast to an easy victory over the North Koreans. Hoyt presents as typical an opinion voiced by one soldier: "As soon as those North Koreans see an American uniform over here, they'll run like hell."[38] Instead, Americans faced relentless advances by disciplined troops that proved difficult to stop. In the first months of war, the ineffectiveness of South Korean troops placed heavy burdens on American forces, and the ambiguous aims of this U.N. police action made soldiers less motivated to fight than they had been in World War II. Under those circumstances, blaming the black soldier for problems in the field could avoid critical reassessments of basic assumptions while tapping a familiar strain of racism to provide a further argument against racial justice.

To an America consumed with fear of worldwide communism, failure to secure quick victory in Korea raised the specter of impotence in the face of the enemy. Ever since the declaration of the Truman Doctrine in 1947, U.S. policy makers asserted the right to help allies faced with outside invasion or internal revolution, and Korea provided an important test of that policy. Early in the fighting it appeared to be a test that the United States would not pass. Operating on the assumption that all Communists all over the world followed direct orders from Moscow as part of a unified plan for world conquest, Americans viewed defeat in Korea as a threat to their own peace and security. In theory, they might have interpreted the frightening news from Korea as evidence of policy makers' poor judgment or military leaders' tactical errors. But in an atmosphere of uncritical nationalism and anti-Communist hysteria, no such reevaluation could take place. Instead a reactionary search for scapegoats dominated public discourse, ranging from accusations of treason directed against State Department officials to repressive assaults on civil liberties through prosecutions of dissidents sanctioned by the Smith Act, which was later declared unconstitutional by the Supreme Court. Part of that reactionary scapegoating manifested itself in the attack against black soldiers, which presented the modest desegregation steps of the preceding years as the cause of the nation's woes. Thus desegregation could be presented as the cause for the demise of "quality" troops in the field, legitimizing a broader reactionary position in other areas of social life, leaving undisturbed some misplaced assumptions about the strength of Korean nationalism or the limits of American power.[39]

But contestation by black soldiers and their supporters prevented that scapegoating from succeeding, at least completely. Recognizing the threat posed by distortions of the battlefield situation, black soldiers fought a dual battle—to perform well in the field and to demand recognition for that performance behind the lines. The many acts of valor that disproved white supremacist assumptions and the quiet courage of ordinary soldiers following orders neutralized important parts of the reactionary attack. Informal networks among soldiers communicated expected standards of behavior and circulated the truth about both the failures and successes of black troops in the field. In the United States, black reporters and editors challenged the biased picture presented of black troops, and community organizations like the NAACP intervened with the military to expose the double standard applied to black soldiers. These actions had their limits, but the fact that the black community at all levels responded so vehemently to the racism in the military testifies to a common storehouse of values and a broad community consensus supporting acts of contestation. From Lieutenant Gilbert to Walter White, from Thurgood Marshall to Ivory Perry, blacks drew upon a common political stance to oppose a trend that threatened to turn back the clock on justice.

As early as 1963, Amiri Baraka called attention to the fundamental connection between the Korean War and the emergence of the modern civil rights movement. Baraka detailed the impact of the war on his own consciousness, and suggested that the conflict marked a distinctive ideological turning point for many of his generation.[40] Despite the significant chronological sequence it illumines, and despite the prominence of Korean War–era veterans like James Foreman, Bobby Seale, and James Meredith in civil rights activism, historians and social scientists have generally ignored Baraka's suggestion.[41] Ivory Perry's wartime experiences offer an opportunity to further explore the relationship between the Korean conflict and the civil rights movement. They reveal the emergence of a broad community consensus among blacks that historical and social changes in the early 1950s reversed rather than advanced progress toward social justice, and that prevailing conditions required coordinated resistance. Most important, in their protests against racism in Korea, black communities displayed and developed their capacity for independent responses to the political and ideological needs of those in power. Military officers and mass media figures might insist that black troops in Korea caused their own problems, but an independent network of communication and organization challenged those views on a wide variety of fronts. The very same network would be in the vanguard of the civil rights movement in the decades that followed.

Black organizations took advantage of the complicated realities of domestic and world politics in order to wage their struggle against racism in the military in Korea. Army traditionalists might have preferred a segregated army that kept black troops out of combat whenever possible, but political and logistical realities undermined that possibility. Racial tension in the armed forces damaged morale at home and in Korea, and it undercut America's image in the world. In addition, the dislocations in the U.S. economy led to a shortage of combat-ready white soldiers and a surplus of black ones. When combat losses mandated massive replacements, desegregation of the army became the only way to keep all units at appropriate strength.[42] Desegregation provided a partial answer for both sides in the controversy over the conduct of black troops in Korea. Those who had derided their performance could argue that they would improve when exposed to the good example of whites. Defenders of the black units could take satisfaction from their access to better equipment and leadership and from the erosion of prejudice that would inevitably occur in a desegregated environment.

Yet the underlying racism that caused problems between blacks and whites in Korea persisted. White soldiers still harbored contempt for veterans of the Twenty-fourth Infantry Regiment and other black units that they believed had fought poorly, and they retained stereotypes about black cowardice and inefficiency. Conversely, black soldiers retained expectations of unequal treatment and remained suspicious of soldiers and officers in their new units. It fell to soldiers like Ivory Perry to make their own responses to institutionalized racism in the military, even as they carried on the already difficult work of waging war.

The first time he killed an enemy soldier, Ivory Perry could hardly believe what he had done.

I had to check it out two or three times. I used to shoot, but a lot of times you see people fall but when you get over there, they're not there. I just couldn't believe it. I got the jitters. I said here I just killed somebody I don't know nothing about, never had any conflict toward each other. They were shooting at me too. I know they probably had the same feeling.[43]

In Korea, starting in the summer of 1950, Perry found many opportunities to shoot and to be shot at. He saw action at the front lines as a combat infantry rifleman, fighting the Korean weather and shortages of supplies as much as he battled the enemy. For six months he had no combat boots because the army could not find a pair the correct size, so he marched in weather thirty degrees below zero (with a wind chill of minus sixty) wearing only tennis shoes and borrowed jump boots. Hospitalized twice for frostbite, he nonetheless fared better than some of the soldiers in his regiment. He remembers one particularly extreme case.

Like my platoon sergeant, he was standing in line one morning, sun shining, but it was cold—forty-five below zero. He was waiting to get the food, but they had to bring it up from the rear. It was piping hot when they put it in the jeep, but by the time it got to us, it just turned to ice. And I asked him, "Sergeant Jackson, what's wrong with your hand?" And he said, "Where?" I looked and he had his glove on. It had just swollen up. It had split the glove open and his hand split open. There wasn't a drop of blood coming out of it.[44]

Early in December 1950 near Sinanju, Perry and his battalion ran into heavy fire from Chinese troops using mortars and automatic weapons. Cut off from the rest of the battalion, Perry's company had to fight their way back. During the combat he felt a stinging sensation in his leg while running from one position to another. He guessed that a rock had hit him, but when his leg began to feel cold and numb he looked down to see blood on his leg. He realized that he had been shot. Pulling the bullet out by himself, Perry continued fighting, but his next injury proved more serious.[45]

Engaged in an exchange of weapons fire with the enemy near Chongaree on December 18, Perry jumped out of the way of a hand grenade, only to propel himself into the path of a mortar shell explosion that knocked him down a rocky hillside. The fall fractured his hand. Medics moved Perry to a MASH unit where doctors ordered him evacuated to the 395th Station Hospital in Nagoya, Japan. After nearly two months in the hospital he returned to combat in Korea, but exposure to the cold there made his hand swell up so badly that he could not open it or extend the fourth and fifth fingers without excruciating pain. Perry returned to the hospital for treatment of his hand in March 1951. Unable to find the physical cause for the persistence of his condition, doctors diagnosed Perry as suffering from a psychological reaction to the service stress of eight months in battle. They recommended that he be removed from combat duty until his condition improved.[46]

Although he had injured that same hand twice previously as a civilian, it would not be surprising if psychological factors did account for his condition.[47] The things he saw in combat upset him terribly, and left him with nightmares for years. As Perry tells it:

Every now and then I still have a dream. I hear kids crying, babies screaming. You know, we had some real stomp-down racists in the Korean War, officers. I done seen them burning houses up on ladies having babies. We used to tell them, "Captain, there's a lady in there giving birth to a baby." He still burned the house up.[48]

Uncertain about the reasons for the war—"We couldn't tell a North Korean from a South Korean," he remembers[49]—he nonetheless understood that he had to fight in order to survive. During one exchange of grenades and weapons fire, a sudden silence stilled the fighting. Perry figured that the other side had run out of ammunition. Inching closer to the North Koreans' position, he breathed a sigh of relief when they waved a white flag and surrendered. The four men he helped capture in that action made a big impression on Perry because they seemed just like the men fighting alongside him. He remembers talking to the prisoners that day. "One was a sergeant. He used to go to the University of San Francisco. Oh man, he showed me his family's picture. And he could speak very fluent English, speak better English than I can. And we got to know each other while he was a PW in my camp."[50]

American troops suffered terrible casualties from North Korean and Chinese attacks, and prisoners of war faced particularly brutal treatment. The savagery of battle discouraged soldiers on both sides from looking on enemy troops as fellow human beings, and all knew that they could face death at any moment. Many nights, Ivory Perry went out to repair communications wires along with two or three other soldiers, never knowing if the next minute might not be their last. They found their way in the darkness by keeping one hand on the communications wire, oblivious to the land mines that could kill them at any moment.[51]

In the midst of these conditions, Perry found himself compelled to fight an enemy that he had no knowledge of and no personal quarrel with, while on his own side he saw evidence of the hatred he had been subjected to his entire life. He recalls one representative incident:

> I remember one night I was in Korea and a white soldier called me a nigger. And we got into it. I started punching him and he was punching back. I got the best of him and he was bleeding like I don't know what. I busted his lip, his nose, but he was still saying, "You're a nigger, you're gonna always be a nigger; if you kill me you gonna still be a nigger." And I said to myself then, "Now this is a die-hard racist. He's gonna die a racist. Now he's over here fighting too and I'm trying to protect him because we're in the same outfit together." But that kind of did something to me.

Perry remembers white officers like the company commander who "gave me a direct order to get out of my foxhole and let him have it." He gave the officer his foxhole "because I didn't want to get court-mar-tialed," but recalls vividly his disgust for an officer who would not even dig his own shelter. Perry also resented the fact that black soldiers car-ried their own ammunition into battle, while white soldiers had am-munition bearers. His officers called for artillery coverage that never came, and black soldiers received less rest time than did white soldiers. "Every time we got to go up to the rest areas," he says, "they called us back before we even got the chance to take a bath—they put us right back in the front lines."[52]

One person in Korea paid a lot of attention to discrimination against black soldiers—"Seoul City Sue." Her nightly ten o'clock broadcasts for the North Koreans taunted black GIs about defending a country that refused to grant them full rights and privileges as citizens. She reported a steady stream of racist incidents involving blacks in Korea and back in the United States in an attempt to persuade black soldiers to defect. Ivory Perry and Harold Terrell heard her broadcasts, but they rejected her invitation to switch sides. Of her descriptions of racism, Perry says, "I already knew about it, but I had to survive—I was in the front lines." Terrell thought that most of the things she reported were by and large the truth, but he remembers, "I just laughed at her. Because America had to change, and out of all the countries I had been in, America was the best country for a black."[53]

Rather than accept Seoul City Sue's enticement to defect, Perry and Terrell, like other black soldiers, directed their energies toward proving their merits so unambiguously that no one could deny them equal rights in good conscience. They knew that their entire race would be judged by their performance in Korea, so they set out to prove to black and white alike that they could succeed at whatever they tried to do. "They didn't want black folks to know how good they was," Perry remembers feeling, "so we were trying to be the best in everything—the best dressed, the best soldiers, the best combat troops, the best boxers—we had to be better." Perry recalls that black soldiers shined their boots during every free moment and put starch in the creases of their uniforms. They put in extra hours of practice on their own time to win the flag given to the best marchers in the Fourth of July parades. Black soldiers responded to un-fair treatment with exemplary performance. "It was pride," says Harold Terrell; "we had to outdo the white GI in everything we tried to do."[54]

Yet racism persisted. During a brief visit home in 1951, Ivory Perry saw just how little had changed in American race relations while he had been away at war. On a trip to St. Louis, where his sister Kathen and her husband now lived, he and two white soldiers entered a restaurant in Joplin, Missouri. A boy behind the counter poured Perry some coffee in a china cup, but the boy's father came over, poured the coffee into a paper cup, and told Perry to drink it outside. Later that day, the three soldiers entered another restaurant, this one in Springfield, Missouri, only to be informed that the establishment "didn't serve niggers." When the two white soldiers objected, the proprietor offered to let the three of them eat at his restaurant—in a broom closet next to the kitchen. After all he had faced in Korea, these manifestations of racism infuriated Perry. As he remembers:

> I had all my army ribbons and stuff on—combat infantry badge and all. I said I done been over there fighting, and now I come back here, and this is my fight at home. If I can fight for a country and come back and can't enjoy the fruits and the benefits, then there isn't any need of my fighting over there. My fight is here.[55]

But his visit to St. Louis also exposed Perry to the growing problem of black unemployment at home. Deciding that he still had more opportunities in the military than in civilian life, he reenlisted in the army at Fort Lewis, Washington, on November 3, 1951. When he returned to Korea, Perry found that his feelings about the army had undergone some profound changes. He could no longer endure the racism that he previously tolerated in silence. He began to speak out, questioning acts that he perceived as motivated by racial prejudice. The army had disbanded the Twenty-fourth Infantry Regiment as a means of fulfilling its commitment to desegregation, and Perry found himself serving in Japan with an integrated but mostly white unit in the Signal Corps. He felt that he enjoyed better living conditions and received better equipment in his new post, but that racial prejudice still simmered beneath the surface. Perry resented losing a promotion as a result of his transfer to the Signal Corps, and he felt that some of the white noncommissioned officers discriminated against black soldiers under their command. In turn, some of the white officers resented Perry's quickness to criticize them.[56]

In February 1953, Signal Corps Captain David A. Fitzpatrick brought charges against Ivory Perry for two alleged violations of the Uniform Code of Military Justice. The charges specified that on January 10, 1953,

Perry had been found in possession of heroin, and that on January 24, 1953, he had disobeyed an order from a superior officer. Perry insisted on his innocence, but if convicted he faced a possible life sentence in the stockade.

The court-martial convened on March 4, 1953, at Camp Sendai, Japan. Agent John J. Walker of the army's Criminal Investigation Division testified that he encountered Perry during a drug raid at a geisha house at 1-50 Kakyoindori Street in Sendai on January 10 of that year. Another agent tossed Perry's field coat to Walker, who searched its pockets and found "one glassine packet containing traces of a white powder." Under cross-examination, Walker contended that the packet had previously contained a very small trace of the powder, even though none remained when the prosecution introduced it into evidence. Walker also testified that Perry denied any knowledge of the packet when it was found and that the other CID agent had already searched Perry's coat before Walker discovered the packet in it.[57]

The prosecution claimed that the packet had contained less than .005 grams of heroin. Chemical tests conducted under the prosecutor's supervision revealed no presence of the drug in the packet, but reaction tests indicated that the pouch might have contained heroin at one time. The defense responded by emphasizing that no heroin had been found, and that the small amount of powder in the packet constituted an insufficient amount for quantitative analysis. Ivory Perry testified that he had no field coat when he entered the house, that he had purchased one just minutes before the police arrived. He claimed that after the first CID agent searched him, Agent Walker said to Perry, "I know you from San Francisco," and only then pulled the glassine packet out of the field coat. Perry had no idea what Walker meant by that remark, nor did he understand when Walker asked him if he knew that the owner of the geisha house was a Communist and that people transacting business there were helping to buy bullets to kill American soldiers. Bewildered by the accusations, Perry told Walker that he had never seen him in San Francisco, and that as for doing business with a Communist he had served in combat in Korea and "I told him I didn't know anything about that. I wasn't buying anything and all I knew was somebody had already been buying bullets before I got there because they were throwing them at me."[58]

Defense witness Private Donald Hadlock supported a key part of Ivory Perry's testimony when he told the court that he had seen Perry in downtown Sendai two hours before the raid, and that Perry had asked to borrow his overcoat. Since Hadlock intended to remain in town, he did not give his coat to the defendant, establishing corroboration for Perry's contention that he entered the house without a coat and bought one while inside. To rebut that testimony, the prosecution produced Kyo To Kan, the owner of the house at 1-50 Kakyoindori, who said that Perry wore a field coat into his establishment that evening. Under cross-examination, however, Kyo To Kan disclosed that he had been jailed for selling narcotics and stated that he wished to please the authorities with his testimony so that he could get a lighter sentence.[59]

The second charge against Perry stemmed from an incident at Camp Sendai two weeks after his arrest at the geisha house. Sergeant Alex Galbreath testified that he saw Ivory Perry and another soldier walking past the company as it stood in formation on January 24 at eight in the morning. When he realized that the two soldiers should have lined up with the company, Galbreath sent Sergeant Robert Willner to bring them back. Willner stated that he found the two at a bus stop with a third soldier, and that he ordered them to return to the formation but that they refused to comply. Under cross-examination Willner admitted that he did not give the order to Perry directly, but instead "spoke in the direction of the other two men who were with him." The sergeant admitted that he had been with the company only fifteen days at the time of the incident, but insisted that he knew the men well enough to convey the order to the correct soldier. In response, Ivory Perry swore that he never saw Willner at the bus stop, and that he never received any order to return to the company. Private Phillip Braxton testified that he had accompanied Perry and a Private Martinez (who was in the United States at the time and unavailable for testimony) to the bus stop that morning, but that he had not seen Sergeant Willner nor had he heard any order to return to the formation.[60]

In concluding arguments, the defense pointed out that the prosecution had not established that the glassine packet had contained heroin or that Perry had "wrongful" possession of it. Furthermore, two witnesses (Perry and Braxton) stated that Willner never gave the order that Perry stood accused of disobeying. The prosecutor responded that the glassine packet had been found in Perry's coat pocket, and he asserted that Kyo To Kan could be trusted as a witness since the narcotics charges pending against him by Japanese authorities would not be under the jurisdiction or influence of a U.S. military court, giving him no self-serving reason for wanting to please U.S. authorities. In addition, the prosecution noted that Braxton and Hadlock were Perry's friends, while prosecution witnesses had no personal stake in the case.[61]

Faced with conflicting testimony, the court-martial hearing board had to evaluate the credibility of the witnesses, especially Ivory Perry. In his favor, they had his military records demonstrating no previous charges or convictions for any breach of the military justice code, and they had documentation that he had won the Korean Service Medal with five battle stars, the Republic of Korea Presidential Unit Citation, and the Japanese Occupation medal. But his claim to the right to wear a Purple Heart medal proved crucial in turning the verdict against him. Perry testified that he had been wounded twice in Korea and awarded a Purple Heart. But that citation did not appear on the records available to the court-martial board. Confronted with this disparity, he told the court, "They gave me the Purple Heart in the hospital. They had a list on the roster, and they called your name and gave you the medal. My other service record was destroyed in Korea. I had a new record made when I went back to the States."[62]

The service record available to the hearing board did bear the date of his reenlistment at Fort Lewis, Washington, in 1951, and it omitted mention of some of the medals he won, including the Combat Infantry Badge and the United Nations Ribbon. Perry's original service record does not appear in his army files, lending credence to his contention that it was destroyed in Korea. His medical records, which the hearing board evidently did not have, show that he was wounded twice in combat, but they make no mention of a Purple Heart medal. With no evidence that he had been awarded a medal he claimed the right to wear, the court-martial board decided not to trust Perry's credibility as a witness.[63]

After deliberating less than thirty minutes, the court-martial trial board found Ivory Perry guilty on both counts, evidently doubting the veracity of his testimony. But in the hearing conducted immediately after the verdict to determine his sentence, some issues came out that had not surfaced during the trial. After telling the court that he had never used any narcotic drugs (a claim supported by his medical records), Perry talked about his relations with his unit.

I have never had a court-martial before and I always got along alright [sic] but ever since I been in T&T Company I been in trouble. I tried to transfer but they wouldn't let me. They said the only place I can go is back to Korea, and I don't want to do that.[64]

A member of the board challenged his statement. "If you are such a good soldier as you say you are and after all the combat decorations you have why don't they like you?" he asked. "Is it because you are colored?" Perry replied that maybe some of the officers disliked him for that reason. The questioner asked if all the noncommissioned officers in the Telephone and Typewriter Company of the Signal Corps displayed prejudice, and Perry responded, "Not all of them; since I am colored they act like I am a boy and we just can't see eye to eye. I do my job to the best of my ability and knowledge but they just don't like my reaction."[65]

Evidently, the officers on the hearing board did not like his reaction either. They sentenced Ivory Perry to two years at hard labor in the stockade, a dishonorable discharge, and forfeiture of benefits and pay. The lieutenant colonel from the army Judge Advocate General's staff who passed on his appeal, and upheld the conviction, cited doubts about the defendant's character in justifying the verdict. Speaking about Perry, the officer noted that "although he has no record of prior conviction by court-martial his present Company Commander rates him 'poor' as to character and 'satisfactory' as to efficiency." He went on to argue that "although the accused has a comparatively good record up to the present time he apparently has been a troublemaker in his organization."[66]

To this day, Ivory Perry breaks out into a sweat when he talks about his court-martial. "I don't fool with no drugs," he insists; "even in combat I wouldn't take anything to stay awake." In his view, the charges stemmed from his complaints about racism in the company, complaints that got him branded as a "troublemaker" by his superior officers. The verdict left him shattered. "When I got to the stockade," he remembers, "I cried for the first time since my mother died."[67]

He remained in the stockade at Camp Sendai until he had exhausted all his appeals, at which point the army transferred him to confinement at hard labor in the disciplinary barracks at Lompoc, California. With credit for time served while awaiting trial and for good behavior afterward, he was released from prison and received his dishonorable discharge from the service in March 1954.[68] He left the army very much as he had left Arkansas six years earlier—with little to show for years of hardship and sacrifice. Yet just as his experiences in Pine Bluff predisposed him to be critical of his treatment in the army, the community consensus and shared moral stance among black soldiers in Korea laid the groundwork for Ivory Perry's subsequent social activism in civilian life.

Ivory Perry joined the Signal Corps as a veteran of the Twenty-fourth Infantry Regiment, as a black man aware of the declining economic situation facing his race, and as the product of the community in which he was raised. After entering a desegregated unit, he had more contact with white soldiers than before, but he felt keenly the loss of camaraderie and solidarity he had experienced in the Twenty-fourth Infantry Regiment. Having witnessed firsthand during his furlough the disparity between the ideals he fought for in Korea and the racism practiced at home, he resolved to challenge discrimination whenever he could. Small wonder then that his company commander could rate his character "poor" even though there was no record of disciplinary action against him, no record of drug use, no blot on his combat record, and no complaint about the performance of his duties. The officer from the Judge Advocate General's office was not entirely wrong when he described Perry as a troublemaker, but it was troublemaking of a complex and sophisticated kind. Drawing on his own experiences, he fashioned a code of personal behavior that enabled him to endure both the deserved and undeserved consequences of his actions.

Ivory Perry and Harold Terrell both returned home from the war in 1954. Both men noticed that attitudes among white GIs who had served with them overseas changed once they got back home. "If you had been overseas, you could have a white buddy good," relates Terrell; "he'd be your buddy overseas, be friends, stand by you—but by the time you hit stateside, they changed." Perry felt the same change from whites he had known overseas. Yet if the racial climate in America had not changed significantly, Ivory Perry and Harold Terrell felt that they had changed a great deal. They left Pine Bluff as teenagers with limited opportunities and few skills; they returned as combat veterans with a secure sense of purpose.[69]

On his way home to Pine Bluff, Harold Terrell stopped off at the bus station in Fort Smith, Arkansas. Wearing his uniform and accompanied by some white soldiers, he walked to the "whites only" section of the lunch counter. To his amazement, they served him lunch with no argument. Even though he could see other blacks not in uniform still eating in the "colored" section, he felt that real progress had been made, and he felt that it justified his faith in America's ability to change its racial policies.[70]

Ivory Perry's homecoming offered less reason for optimism. As he returned to St. Louis, he did some serious thinking about his future. St.

Louis had attracted thousands of black people from the rural South in the previous decade, and its industries offered the potential for employment and advancement. Perry decided to stay in the city and look for work, and he also decided that he would look for a way to do something about the racism that seemed to be waiting for him around every corner. He remembers thinking: "I shouldn't have been in Korea in the first place because those Korean people they haven't ever did anything to Ivory Perry. I'm over there trying to kill them for something that I don't know what I'm shooting for. I said my fight is here in America."[71] Soon that resolve would take him into the streets as a participant in one of the most important mass movements in modern history.

CHAPTER 3

St. Louis: Civil Rights and the Industrial City

Ivory Perry spent his first six months in St. Louis looking for work. Few job opportunities awaited a twenty-four-year-old semiskilled black worker with a dishonorable discharge from the service and no high school diploma. He knew only three people in the city—his cousin Isaac, his sister Kathen, and her husband Fred—and neither the army nor life in Pine Bluff had prepared him for the congested neighborhoods and busy streets of St. Louis.[1]

"I learned more about street life than you can get out of any book," Perry says about his first months in St. Louis. Landlords and realtors restricted large parts of town for white occupancy, leaving blacks crowded into older, and in many cases, deteriorating housing. Black workers made only 58 percent of the wages paid to whites, and black unemployment outpaced white by a three to one ratio. Discrimination forced skilled black craftsmen to travel as far as Paducah, Kentucky, and Jackson, Mississippi, to secure union cards and steady work. Ivory Perry exhausted his small savings looking for a job in that environment, and eventually he counted himself lucky to get work on a loading dock at Merrill Labs, a cosmetics company, for $1 an hour. "When I came to St. Louis I thought it was gonna be altogether different from what it was in Arkansas," he recalls. "When I got here I found out it was almost worse than down in Arkansas. At least in Arkansas you knew what you could do and what you could not do. But in St. Louis, it said you could do it until you tried to do it, and when you tried to do it, they'd come up with another excuse to keep you from doing it."[2]

Yet for all its problems, St. Louis continued to attract black migrants like Ivory Perry throughout the 1950s. During the 1940s, 38,000 black people had moved into the city, bringing the total local black population to 154,000, or 18 percent of the municipal population. An additional

80,000 black migrants between 1950 and 1955 brought the percentage of blacks in the city to 26. Mechanization of agriculture pushed blacks out of the South, while defense spending for the Korean War and Cold War arms buildups expanded industrial production in the cities, raising the hope, however illusory, of job opportunities for black workers.[3]

The large numbers of blacks who moved to cities like St. Louis in this period did so as individuals, but collective historical circumstances determined the dimensions of their migration. The move to the cities disrupted traditional social patterns in the South and established new ones in the North. Contradictions in the industrial economy and labor market, coupled with racial discrimination in housing and hiring, made the transition to urban life difficult. Yet this social upheaval also enabled people like Ivory Perry to transcend some of the parochial limits of rural life and escape its isolation and dependency. He became part of an urban community with rich historical and cultural resources, and contact with that community helped transform his own world view.

Despite its widespread segregation and discrimination, St. Louis had long enjoyed a reputation as a vital center for Afro-American life and culture. Black settlers helped found the city in 1763, and prominent free blacks like Jacques Clamorgan owned significant amounts of property in its early years.[4] Yet slavery and segregation whittled away at the rights and power of those free blacks and their descendants. By the 1820s, slaves were 18 percent of the local population, free blacks only 1 percent. Slaves performed household labor in fashionable homes while free blacks generally worked on the riverfront docks.[5] The Missouri state constitution made it illegal to educate free or enslaved blacks, and even after the Civil War and emancipation brought an end to that law, state spending on black education significantly lagged behind expenditures on schools for whites.[6] Most unions and guilds denied membership to black workers, financial institutions routinely engaged in discriminatory loan practices, and white supremacist attitudes and institutions permeated the city's political and social life.[7]

In the face of these conditions, the St. Louis black community created institutions of solidarity and struggle. Before the Civil War, the Reverend John Berry Meachum defied the legal ban on black education by running a secret school on a boat in the middle of the Mississippi River. Black parents sued the city school board when it refused to educate their children after the Civil War, and their efforts brought about the establishment of Sumner High School in 1874 as the first comprehensive black high school west of the Mississippi River. In the 1920s, black leaders pressured city officials for a full-service hospital and medical training center for the black community. They overcame delaying tactics and resistance, and forced the opening of Homer G. Phillips Hospital in 1937, a full-care health facility for the black community. It went on to become an important training center for black doctors from all over the United States.[8]

On the basis of its high school and hospital, St. Louis attracted national attention as a center of Afro-American life, but it also gained renown for the rich cultural life in its black neighborhoods. At the turn of the century, Scott Joplin and his contemporaries created ragtime music in the rough taverns and sporting houses of the infamous Chestnut Valley along Market Street. Josephine Baker grew up in the St. Louis slums, and developed agility and strength running away from night watchmen in railroad yards as she stole coal to help keep her family warm. Later, on the stage of the Booker T. Washington Theater, she learned the dance steps and vocal styles that would eventually make her an international star at the Folies Bergère in Paris and in motion pictures. In the juke joints and on the sidewalks along Biddle Street on the north side of town, musicians like Peetie Wheatstraw, Rufus Perrymen, and Henry Townsend nurtured a distinctive blues idiom during the hard years of the Depression.[9]

Black migrants to St. Louis after World War II entered a community with many problems but also with a rich history, a vibrant cultural life, and a tradition of civil rights activism. The city that boasted the birthplace of NAACP Executive Secretary Roy Wilkins had a strong local chapter of that organization, an effective Urban League affiliate headed for many years by the indomitable John T. Clark, and one of the most active CORE groups in the nation. Sharing resources, information, and memberships, these groups provided newcomers with a ready-made forum for racial grievances. Postwar migration exacerbated the housing and hiring problems facing black St. Louisans, but it also brought in a population capable of accelerating the pace of social protest. For the newcomers, migration from the country to the city broke down traditional constraints. They left dispersed communities encircled by white power for cities with large concentrations of blacks living in relative autonomy from white interference—at least on a direct experiential level. Sociologist Aldon D. Morris points out that newcomers often feel grievances more keenly than long-time residents while at the same time showing less deference to local institutions and leaders.[10] In St. Louis where those migrants encountered an already existing network of community organizations capable of providing an institutional basis for social contestation, massive in-migration increased the likelihood of social unrest and encouraged the emergence of a new generation of activists.

But structural forces do not create movements for social change—people do. The strains and tensions of mass migration led to a civil rights movement only because individuals saw political activism as historically sanctioned, politically necessary, and ideologically desirable. In attempting to deal with the conditions of everyday life—unemployment, poor housing, and racism—they overcame external pressures and internal doubts to build a political movement. Some of the individuals in that struggle possessed education and influence, and were able to exercise both individual and institutional resources. Others, like Ivory Perry, had to create their own resources from the everyday experiences of ghetto life.

Shortly after securing employment at Merrill Labs, Ivory Perry got an apartment on Cabanne Avenue in St. Louis's increasingly black West End. His neighborhood consisted of houses once owned by elite families, but recently divided into apartments and rooming houses. The West End had been one of the first St. Louis neighborhoods to desegregate after the Supreme Court's 1948 ruling that restrictive covenants—agreements forcing deedholders to resell their homes to members of the same race—violated the Constitution. But as blacks moved into the neighborhood, whites moved out. Perry remembers being one of the first black people on his block, but within two years only blacks lived on that street.[11]

The magnitude of black migration to St. Louis created an enormous demand for housing. In the 1950s the area of the city open to black residents increased from 500 to 650 square blocks, but all 150 of these new blocks had already been designated as deteriorating or blighted by the City Plan Commission before blacks moved in. Loan agencies refused to extend credit to whites for purchases in those areas, further encouraging white flight. Unscrupulous realtors exploited the black demand for housing (as well as white hostility to blacks) by "blockbusting"—frightening white homeowners about declining property values in order to panic them into selling houses at low prices that realtors could then resell to blacks at inflated prices. Perry decided that he would have to learn to live in a black ghetto because wherever he moved, the ghetto seemed certain to follow him.[12]

Perry operated machines, packed boxes, and loaded trucks for his negligible paycheck. Some days he got so covered by chemicals and powder that it took hours after work to clean up. When he went home, it was to a neighborhood that had plenty of problems of its own. Kathen Wright understood how her brother felt about the city. She had undergone her own difficult transition to urban life in 1950 when she moved to St. Louis from Pine Bluff. Her husband Fred found a good job in the garment industry, but she had a hard time adjusting to the social conditions in the city. "I didn't like it really," she says about her first few months in St. Louis, "because I wasn't used to wineheads lying in the street drunk. I never saw nothing like that before, so I was kind of upset—I really wanted to go back."[13] Yet she stayed because the city seemed to offer better economic opportunities for the future than she had known in Arkansas, and her example encouraged Ivory to stick it out in St. Louis despite his initial discomfort.

Work at Merrill Labs did not pay very much, but it did provide Perry with steady work. He sampled the night life in the North Side taverns and in after-hours clubs on the Illinois side of the river, listening and dancing to rhythm and blues music performed by local favorites like Little Milton Campbell, Ike and Tina Turner, and Albert King. In 1956 a mutual friend introduced him to a young woman named Earline Terry. Terry grew up in Meacham Park, a black suburb in St. Louis County; her family moved to an apartment on Cabanne Avenue in the West End shortly after her high school graduation. She had just returned from a tour with the Wings Over Jordan Choir, a gospel singing group, when she met Ivory Perry. Her sister's boyfriend knew Ivory and arranged a double date. Ivory fell in love with Earline immediately but she had her doubts. "He seemed nice enough," she recalls, "but he seemed a little unstable." Terry felt that Ivory had a chip on his shoulder about race relations, that he had an inordinate hostility to white people. But she also felt that he could be a very kind and generous person, and so, somewhat reluctantly, she continued to date him.[14]

Ivory Perry pursued his relationship with Earline Terry enthusiastically, sometimes more enthusiastically than she wanted. He was extremely possessive and jealous and got angry whenever she dated or even talked to other men. After she had been seeing him for several months, Terry discovered that she was pregnant. Ivory wanted them to get married, but she felt that it wasn't going to work, that the problems between them would just get worse and worse. "He wanted a family life," Terry recalls; "he fought pretty hard for it," but she continued to resist. They lived together for a short while before their son Roger was born in December 1956. They continued to date even after they stopped living together, and in October 1958, their daughter Corliss was born. Ivory kept up the pressure to get married, but Terry felt his efforts only revealed the innate instability that made a marriage between the two of them impossible.[15]

While he was dating Earline Terry, Perry suffered an accident at work. A stack of heavy boxes filled with cosmetics fell on his back as he unloaded a truck; serious injuries sent him to the hospital and kept him out of work for months. Medical bills piled up as he lay on his back unable to work. When he left the hospital to return to his job, his boss told him that the accident made Perry a medical risk and he could not be rehired. Once again, he found himself out of work in St. Louis. Perry drifted from job to job—he worked in a bakery, drove a taxicab, operated a welding torch, ran a spray-painting machine, and did electrical repair work.[16]

Recurrent problems with the police compounded Ivory Perry's other problems. He frequently found himself stopped for questioning "on suspicion" of one offense or another. The police needed no proof to detain Ivory Perry overnight while they searched for evidence linking him to some crime, and they required no real evidence to lodge charges so flimsy that magistrates dismissed them outright. Between 1956 and 1963 police officers arrested him ten times on charges including stealing, robbery, peace disturbance, and carrying a concealed weapon. But the charges always got dropped or dismissed. Like many other urban black males, Ivory Perry acquired a long arrest record even though he had never been convicted of any crime.[17]

Two instances illustrate the nature of Perry's uneasy relationship with the St. Louis police department. On January 7, 1960, the police received a report that a black man wearing a dark gray topcoat attempted to sell two stolen wedding rings to a customer at a fast food restaurant and then hurried into a department store across the street. Two officers searched the store and found Ivory Perry sitting in the shoe department wearing a dark gray topcoat. They arrested him on suspicion of stealing. When the officers frisked Perry they found in his pocket an icepick that he used at work, and added charges of carrying a concealed weapon. When the man who reported the incident arrived at headquarters, officers brought Perry before him. He unhesitatingly said that this was not the man who tried to sell him the rings, and all charges were dropped. But the arrest remained on Perry's record.[18]

A more serious case of mistaken identity led to another arrest later that year. A young white woman from south St. Louis told police officers that she had been abducted by three Negro men in a shiny black car. She alleged that the three took her to a vacant lot and along with two other black men they assaulted her there. Understandably, her charges shocked and frightened St. Louisans, who demanded a thorough search for the perpetrators of this vicious crime. Yet community outrage stemmed in part from the allegation that black men had raped a white woman. One of the local newspapers, the *St. Louis Globe-Democrat*, gave especially inflammatory coverage to the story, relating the incident in one editorial to political violence in the newly independent Congo Republic in Africa. The state circuit attorney received more phone calls about the case than any other in recent memory, and the audience at a candidates forum for the office of state attorney general ignored other topics and insisted on pressing the candidates for their solutions to the rape case.[19]

Police officers rounded up hundreds of black men, including Ivory Perry. The tension increased three days later when two white female high school students reported that five Negro men in a shiny black car tried to kidnap them. But then inconsistencies began to emerge in the first woman's story. She claimed she was returning from the movies when attacked, but she could not remember what film she had seen. Under questioning she changed minor details about her abduction and altered the description of her assailants. Finally she admitted to fabricating the entire incident. Lonely for her soldier husband stationed in Germany, the young woman had spent the entire weekend with a young Coast Guardsman in various taverns, in his automobile, and in a vacant house. Strangers found her wandering the streets on her way home, and a hospital attendant remarked that she looked like she had been raped. Intoxicated and feeling guilty, the young woman made up her story to explain her condition and to win sympathy from the army in the hope that it might bring her husband home. The police charged her with making a false report of a law violation and released all suspects in the case.[20]

Underpaid at work, harassed by the police for crimes that he did not commit, and forced by discrimination to live in substandard housing, Perry seethed with resentment over his treatment in St. Louis. Those frustrations helped drive him into the civil rights movement. "I wasn't getting anything for what I was doing on the job," he remembers. "I had a family to try and support and that caused me another problem. I wasn't making that much, and I was supposed to be a man, but I was a black man and there wasn't no decent jobs."[21] A few months after moving to St. Louis in 1954, Perry watched the city desegregate its public schools in an atmosphere of extraordinary tension as neo-Nazis from the National Christian Socialist party distributed hate literature throughout white neighborhoods.[22] A year later, Perry read newspaper stories detailing the murder of Emmett Till, a black teenager from Chicago lynched while visiting relatives in Mississippi. Eyewitnesses identified Till's abductors, but an all-white jury acquitted the defendants and neither Mississippi nor federal authorities pursued the case. In December 1955, blacks in Montgomery, Alabama, following the example of an earlier successful campaign in Baton Rouge, initiated a bus boycott that demonstrated the efficacy of disciplined nonviolent collective action.[23] Perry felt that something important might be happening in America, and he wanted to participate in it.

Racism seemed to have determined nearly everything in his life. Race accounted for the condition of his neighborhood and explained why he could not move to a better one. It determined the low wages he received at work and the limited range of jobs open to him. It shaped a political system that disenfranchised black voters in the South and diluted the power of their vote in the North. By participating in the civil rights movement in St. Louis, Perry confronted the concrete deprivations of his life, the issues so basic to survival that they could not be avoided. From nine to five, from Monday to Friday, he was just another laborer, but in the civil rights movement he could take concrete actions that addressed the main hurts of his life. He could become a humanitarian helping others, and he could find an outlet for all the accumulated anger that had been building inside him from his experiences in Pine Bluff, in Korea, and in St. Louis. Earline Terry remembers, "When I first met Ivory, he wasn't active in the civil rights movement, but he was kind of a rabble-rouser and I could see he wanted to be into something like that."[24] When a friend told him about the St. Louis chapter of the Congress of Racial Equality (CORE), Perry started to attend their meetings and participate in their demonstrations.

An interracial nonviolent organization, CORE started as a response to the civil rights ferment engendered by the "double victory" movement among black people during World War II. As a dedicated group of activists committed to Gandhian principles of passive resistance, CORE leaders viewed the fight against racism as the appropriate forum for the implementation of their philosophy of nonviolence. Located almost exclusively in northern or border cities, composed largely of white activists, and devoted to the principles of passive resistance, CORE differed markedly from other civil rights organizations like the National Urban League or the NAACP. With fewer resources and a far smaller following in the black community than other civil rights groups, CORE might seem an unlikely outlet for Ivory Perry's activism, but its commitment to direct action held enormous appeal for him and for other blacks in industrial cities in the 1950s and 1960s.[25]

In St. Louis, CORE members tested the parameters of segregation by sending integrated groups into restaurants, theaters, and stores to request service. Storeowners and patrons sometimes responded with hostility, but the demonstrators remained nonviolent at all times and attempted to negotiate changes in a way that did not undermine the dignity of their adversaries. Ivory Perry joined in demonstrations at the popular Fox Theater to pressure the management to admit black customers. Weeks of demonstrations and negotiations focused public attention on the "whites only" policy at the Fox and other local movie houses, but they brought no immediate changes in policy. Charles Oldham, a founding member of St. Louis CORE and at one time the organization's national president, relates one of the demonstration's more ironic incidents: "One of the Fox owners wandered off down to Florida during the wintertime and got himself a beautiful suntan, came back and sat in his own theater. And some lady went in and complained about the dark man sitting in the theater." Eventually CORE worked out an agreement to allow blacks into the theater, but Fox management still insisted that blacks enter only in couples, and only if the men wore jackets and ties.[26]

CORE waged a struggle to secure employment opportunities and access to service in stores and restaurants. Perry threw himself into these campaigns, and they became an increasingly important part of his life. Nobody considered him a leader, but if they wanted a leaflet handed out, or people brought to a demonstration, they could count on him. Long-time CORE activist Marian Oldham recalls that "Ivory as far as I

perceived him was a very nice, sincere, dedicated, really hard worker."
Father John Shocklee adds:

> The interesting thing about Ivory Perry was that he didn't shoot for
> the limelight. You'd always see him in a secondary role getting the
> job done. Ivory was always there, and I always understood that,
> well, this guy's legitimate. He's there because there's a mission to be
> accomplished and he's not hogging the headlines.[27]

Yet at that stage, his civil rights activism coexisted uneasily with the
difficult struggles that made up the rest of his life. He scrambled from
job to job trying to make a living, and he continued his chaotic relationship with Earline Terry.

As part of her effort to break away from Perry, Earline Terry began
dating other men. She appreciated Ivory's devotion to the children; he
came around to see them frequently and often brought them presents.
But she felt that their relationship simply would not improve and she
particularly resented his all-consuming jealousy. "If he could not have
me, no one else could either" is the way she remembers his attitude in
those days. On October 18, 1959, he came by, ostensibly to visit the
children, and found her with another man. Ivory pounded on the door
and broke into the apartment; Earline grabbed a knife from the kitchen
to defend herself. The landlord called the police, who arrested Ivory for
disturbing the peace. In the next two weeks Earline and Ivory lodged
charges and countercharges against each other, but dropped their complaints before they reached the stage of prosecution. The incident ended
their relationship once and for all. "I was too young to see him for the
type of person he was," Terry says about her involvement with Ivory
Perry. But after the incident that caused them to break up for good, their
relationship improved. "He really wanted a family life, and once he met
another girl, then he left me alone. After that I could tolerate it," she
recalls.[28]

The woman Perry met was Anna Cox. Cox grew up in rural Lewisville, Tennessee, and moved to St. Louis in 1960, staying with her brother. She left home with high hopes, expecting everything in her life to
improve once she got to St. Louis. "I thought everything would be
great," she says, "but when I got there people didn't have jobs, and the
discrimination was terrible." At the age of seventeen in a strange city,
she took a minimum-wage job washing dishes at a local restaurant and
wondered whether she had made the right choice in leaving Lewisville.

Anna met Ivory Perry one day while she waited for the bus on her way to work. He drove by and stopped to ask her name and to offer her a ride, but she was suspicious of the invitation and declined. But Perry came back every day to renew his offer, and soon he began driving her to work. He was fourteen years older, but Cox felt a gentleness and consideration from Ivory that made her trust him. They began to see each other frequently and they found that they shared some fundamental attitudes and beliefs, including a commitment to the civil rights movement.[29]

For as long as she could remember, Anna Cox had been asking questions about white racism. When the black and white children in her home town started to attend different schools after having played together when they were younger, she wanted to know why. Her mother shrugged her shoulders and simply said, "That's the way it is," but Cox never believed that it *had* to be that way. Confronted with an active civil rights movement when she got to St. Louis, she instantly joined it. "I knew that what we were doing was right," she relates; "that it might not do anything for us, but it was going to open the door for somebody." The civil rights movement enabled Anna Cox to address some of the unresolved pain of her past just as it had done for Ivory Perry. When the dangers and sacrifices demanded by the movement seemed overwhelming, she thought of her father having to say "yes ma'am" to white women even when he was past fifty years old, and she thought of the times she had seen her mother sick and waiting for the ambulance that might never arrive to pick up a black patient. It felt good to do something to change all that, if not for herself then at least for the next generation.[30]

Ivory Perry and Anna Cox married in 1963, and moved into an apartment on Raymond Avenue in the West End. He drove taxicabs and took other jobs as they became available—spray painting and welding at the American Car Foundry, sand blasting and steam cleaning at Westinghouse, making sewer pipes at Dickey-Clay, and painting electrical equipment at General Cable. She worked cooking hamburgers and busing dishes at restaurants while running her own house. As black workers, they got the lowest pay for the hardest work; they were the last hired and first fired.[31] But in direct-action protests, they participated in important events and made an impact on the entire city. One particular campaign to secure jobs for blacks in the local banking industry had a particularly pronounced effect on their lives, and on the city as a whole.

In the summer of 1963, Ivory and Anna Perry joined in St. Louis's most important civil rights battle, the demonstrations at the Jefferson

Bank. For five years, St. Louis CORE had tried to persuade local bankers to hire black tellers and to open up managerial opportunities to minority employees. Twice they reached agreements with industry representatives, only to have the bankers fail to live up to their promises. CORE focused its campaign on the Jefferson Bank because it served a large black clientele but had no black employees. They presented an ultimatum to the bank's officers: hire four black tellers by the end of August or face mass demonstrations. The bank dismissed the demand. Instead it secured a restraining order from state Circuit Court Judge Michael Scott, prohibiting mass demonstrations or other disruptions of business at the bank.[32]

Early in the afternoon on August 31, 1963, more than 150 demonstrators gathered on the street in front of the Jefferson Bank. Although officially sponsored by CORE, the action drew wide support from many community groups. The picket line included schoolteachers, laborers, students, housewives, and members of the NAACP, Urban League, and CORE. Demonstrators paraded in front of the bank, making entry into the building difficult, and a small contingent went inside to sit on the floor in front of the tellers' windows. They linked arms and sang freedom songs, effectively closing the bank. Police officers arrived quickly and arrested many of those on the picket line and almost everyone inside. Judge Scott responded harshly to the defiance of his injunction. No one at the demonstration expected to escape punishment completely, but the judge shocked defendants and their supporters by meting out jail sentences ranging from sixty days to one year, and by assessing fines of as much as $1,000 apiece. CORE leader Robert Curtis charged that the nonviolent demonstrators received sentences more appropriate for bank robbers than for bank demonstrators. Other civil rights leaders shared the belief that the sentences constituted an attack on the entire movement.[33]

The first large-scale direct-action protest in St. Louis had drawn broad-based support, but it also revealed the stubborn resistance of the courts and the banking industry to civil disobedience and mass protest. CORE elected to stage continued demonstrations until the Jefferson Bank and other financial institutions promised to employ blacks. Ivory Perry enthusiastically participated in the organizing. He helped plan fund-raising activities to pay bail and fines for protesters, and he talked to high school students to try and involve them in the protests. He and Anna joined in the daily demonstrations outside the Jefferson Bank and in marches on City Hall, part of a pressure campaign to convince the city treasurer to withdraw municipal deposits from banks with discriminatory hiring practices.

Every day, people with no previous involvement in the movement appeared on the picket lines to lend a hand. A mass rally at City Hall drew 1,000 people on October 28, and a related demonstration that evening at St. Louis University found a law school professor leading 250 Catholics, most of them white, in "a public confession that we have sinned in the pride of race."[34] Direct-action civil disobedience brought repression, in the form of fines and jail sentences, but it also mobilized support for the movement more effectively than most activists anticipated. The campaign to rally support for the Jefferson Bank demonstrators brought large numbers of people from the black community into the civil rights movement, and their presence helped to propel young rank and file activists like CORE's employment committee chairman, Percy Green, into positions of leadership.

Green began attending CORE meetings in the early 1960s because he thought that they might help him find answers to his many questions about racism. He wondered why his father after thirty years working in the meatpacking industry made less money than Green did as a young worker in the aerospace industry, and he wondered why young white workers with seemingly his same skills and education routinely got access to higher-paying jobs. CORE meetings offered one of the few opportunities to hear those issues discussed. But what Green found there did not put him completely at ease. As he recalls, "I looked around and saw that there were few people there that did not have a degree. I was just coming out of gang fighting and all the regular things in the community so I kind of felt like maybe I was out of place."[35]

Nor did the content of the meetings reassure him. CORE's emphasis on negotiations, cordiality, and incremental change seemed to Percy Green like a capitulation to the status quo, and he campaigned for a more activist approach including civil disobedience and confrontation. In the Jefferson Bank campaign he got his wish, and what he saw there made him more certain than ever about direct-action protest. Writing in *Freedom Now*, St. Louis CORE's newsletter, Green argued that the confrontational nature of the action, coupled with the press's response to it, created preconditions for victory.

It was the nature of our demonstration—blocking doors, singing in the bank—that revealed to the Negro community the unjust employment policies of the Bank. The news media, being a part of the power structure, covered the story and hoped to smear our organization. Instead the articles informed the people of St. Louis that the Jefferson Bank clearly had a discriminatory policy.[36]

Ivory Perry agreed with that analysis, and in the ensuing months worked closely with Green and other advocates of direct action to keep the dispute in the forefront of public attention. Gene Tournour served as St. Louis field representative for the national CORE organization at that time, and he vividly remembers Perry's contributions to direct action. "Ivory was one of the more active leaders in the chapter. He had no official leadership position at that time, but he played a big role in planning and executing strategy. He struck me as completely dedicated. People at that time were jeopardizing their jobs and their livelihoods by demonstrating. Ivory was one of the people you could always count on being there."[37]

On November 21 after an afternoon demonstration at the Jefferson Bank, Perry and thirty CORE demonstrators marched in front of the downtown department stores. They handed out leaflets asking Christmas shoppers to support a CORE boycott of downtown businesses charged with siding with the Jefferson Bank. The marchers then paraded into the Scruggs department store, chanting civil rights slogans and singing freedom songs, before returning to the sidewalks outside. By prearrangement they started out into the streets to try to disrupt traffic. Ivory Perry walked into the intersection of Sixth Street and Washington Boulevard and sat down in front of a municipal bus while Gene Tournour blocked the rear wheels. Tournour remembers getting a mixed response from passers-by, some voiced encouragement, others scorn. But he remembers Ivory Perry's determination under those circumstances. "He was personally courageous, going out and stopping traffic. You have to think of what St. Louis was like at that time. It was essentially a southern city with a lot of virulent racism. I never saw him flinch. I never saw him run from it."[38]

Police officers arrested all the demonstrators on charges of disturbing the peace. On December 4, CORE staged another march through downtown stores, and after being arrested Perry and others sat down in front of the wheels of the police wagons called to take them to jail. Twelve days later, these same demonstrators sat down again, this time in the courtroom. After being fined and sentenced to probation, they refused probation and insisted on going to jail. Seven police cruisers converged on the court building, and officers loaded the uncooperative passively resisting demonstrators onto stretchers to take them into custody. When Ivory Perry got to jail, the booking officer asked him for his middle name. "Freedom," he replied, "Ivory Freedom Perry."[39]

When President Lyndon Johnson came to St. Louis in February 1964 to attend the city's bicentennial anniversary celebration, Perry and eighty-three other demonstrators marched on Johnson's hotel from a nearby park, hoping to draw national attention to the stiff sentences facing Jefferson Bank defendants. Instantly, police officers blocked the march and arrested everyone in it before they had even left their starting point, on the grounds that they posed a threat to the President's safety. Once Johnson left town, the police pressed no charges and released all the demonstrators.[40]

Because of this spate of direct-action protests, the St. Louis news media tended to portray civil rights demonstrators as extremists who tarnished the city's reputation and injured their own cause. But Percy Green recalls that the protests made a quite different impression on the constituencies that he wanted to reach. "If you are nobody, you have to then become somebody," he explains. One way to "become somebody" was to create a disturbance profound enough to attract the attention of adversaries.

> It's a challenge to your ingenuity. If you happen to be oppressed and you don't have the tools to defend yourself with—the same or equal tools to those of the oppressor—then you're forced to use or develop some type of equalizer. If David attempted to fight Goliath with a sword, it wouldn't have been a contest. So therefore he had to use his head to develop an equalizer.[41]

Activists like Percy Green believed that the community they wanted to reach would understand their motives and actions. Father John Shocklee had been assigned to a church near the Jefferson Bank at the time of the demonstrations, and he became acquainted with Percy Green, Ivory Perry, and other CORE activists at that time. He saw that his parishioners liked the very qualities that got civil rights demonstrators criticism from the press. Community people felt pride in the ability of demonstrators to command so much attention from the power elite, and they admired the

ingenuity they displayed in the process. As long as the issues dramatized real problems facing the community, and as long as activists retained personal credibility as sincere and dedicated individuals, bad
publicity did not hurt them. As Shocklee remembers, "They were un-
usual leaders because even when the press tried to harm them with bad
publicity, the people never really did believe it, because they were not
bad guys."[42]

Beyond receiving bad publicity, civil rights demonstrators also received terms in the city jail. For Ivory Perry, going to jail for civil rights
actions carried a mixed meaning. He never liked it, but it held no particular terror for him either. "I'm in jail anyway," he remembers thinking;
"as long as there are places I can't go and things I can't do, I'm already in
jail." As he explains it:

> See, when you're locked up, you got a certain time you can come out
> for recreation, you got a certain time you had to go to lunch, you got
> a certain time that they let you out to go to the library. So you're
> locked up. And that's the same way it is in society. I'm locked up.
> There's certain things I couldn't do. I couldn't go here, I couldn't go
> there. I couldn't do this, I couldn't do that. So I consider myself
> locked up since I've been in this universe.[43]

Ivory Perry felt that the police had been arresting him simply because
he was a black man, not because they had any indication that he had
committed a crime ever since he came to St. Louis. Their behavior made
it easier for him to face the risks of going to jail for political activism. If he
could be picked up and jailed for a crime he did not commit, he might as
well go to jail for a cause. In that way he could turn an indignity into a
badge of honor, transforming incarceration from a random blow of fate
into a conscious strategy to undermine the power of those seeking to
intimidate him. And even in jail he could fight battles for justice; Perry
remembers that while serving one sentence for peace disturbance in
1963 he joined with other CORE members to refuse assignment to segregated cells, forcing the city to desegregate its workhouse.[44]

On the streets of the city in the arena of social contestation, the willingness to go to jail sometimes made a real difference. CORE leaders
served long sentences and paid large fines because of the Jefferson Bank
demonstration, but their efforts won an important victory. In March
1964, management at the bank agreed to hire its first five black employees; in subsequent months eighty-four blacks got jobs in previously

all-white St. Louis banking institutions.[45] Victory at Jefferson Bank confirmed the emerging commitment to direct action among CORE members like Ivory Perry and Percy Green, and it made them eager for more of the same. "Ivory and I became radical," Green recalls, "not only in what we said, but in what we were always advocating—let's do something, let's cut out all the talk, and let's get it on."[46]

When CORE's national leadership asked local chapters for assistance with demonstrations at the 1964 New York World's Fair, Ivory Perry volunteered immediately. CORE wanted to focus attention on the civil rights struggle by challenging the self-congratulatory boosterism about America that characterized the fair. The civil rights group's national secretary, James Farmer, issued a press release timed to coincide with demonstrations at the opening ceremonies, announcing, "We have brought our grievances to the World's Fair to contrast the real world of discrimination and brutality experienced by Negroes north and south with the fantasy world of progress and abundance shown in its official pavilions."[47] Farmer asked demonstrators to concentrate their protests in two spots—at pavilions representing states with particularly poor records on civil rights, and at those sponsored by corporations accused of discriminatory hiring practices.

During preparations for the CORE demonstrations at the fair, Ivory Perry came in contact with militant young activists from the Brooklyn and Harlem chapters. He learned about their efforts to organize rent strikes and school boycotts, and he listened to their descriptions of dramatic confrontations with employers, landlords, and police officers. These militants planned a special disruption for the World's Fair, a "stall-in" orchestrated by allowing their cars to run out of gas at key intersections, highway exits, and bridges. They hoped to prevent the fair from opening by saddling it with the worst traffic tie-up in New York's history. Fair officials, editorial columnists, politicians, and even most civil rights leaders opposed the stall-in, charging that it penalized innocent bystanders and created more resentment than sympathy for the cause of civil rights.

Ivory Perry understood these arguments, but he supported the militants and their plans. To him, the stall-in promised to educate whites and raise the morale of blacks. White people might ignore the brutality directed against nonviolent civil rights demonstrators in the South or the squalor and hopelessness of northern slums, because neither of those conditions touched them personally. The stall-in intruded on the private lives of "innocent bystanders" in hopes of making them face up to their responsibilities as people and citizens. Perry felt that the life-and-death issues facing black people, and their exclusion from access to political power, justified obstructive actions like the stall-in and he fully supported it.[48]

One person who understood the reasoning behind the stall-in was Martin Luther King, Jr. When asked by other civil rights leaders to condemn the stall-in, he refused. Conceding that the action would be a tactical error because it resorted to disruptive civil disobedience before efforts at good-faith negotiations had been exhausted, King nevertheless argued that he would not condemn it. "The World's Fair action must be viewed in the broader context of 20,000,000 Negroes living in an unfair world," King maintained in a letter to civil rights leaders, pointing out that black people faced "grinding poverty, and humiliating denial of access to public accommodation, voting, housing, education, and jobs." Further, he contended that the stall-in at the World's Fair came as a response to the "stall-in" by legislators in Washington who refused to pass civil rights bills, and to "a substantial and growing counter-revolutionary movement" opposed to racial justice, and to the timidity and excessive moderation displayed by people who considered themselves to be allies of black people. Admitting that the stall-in might offend potential friends, King nonetheless insisted:

> We do not need allies who are more devoted to *order* than to *justice*, and who would prefer a negative peace which is the absence of tension, to a positive peace which is the presence of justice. Neither do we need allies who will paternalistically seek to set the timetable for our freedom. I hear a lot of talk these days about our direct action program alienating former friends. I would rather feel that they are bringing to the surface many latent prejudices which were always there. If our direct action programs alienate so-called friends, even if the program happens to be a tactical error like the "Stall-in," they never were real friends.[49]

James Farmer suspended the Brooklyn CORE chapter from membership in the national organization because of its insistence on the stall-in, and the protest failed miserably as only a handful of drivers participated. New York City police officers and tow truck operators tipped off by informants followed the few cars that did stop traffic and cleared them out of the way. But inside the fair, demonstrations proceeded as scheduled, and Ivory Perry joined with other members of St. Louis CORE blocking entry into the Missouri pavilion. Eager to avoid negative publicity, management at the pavilion closed its doors when the protesters arrived, so the CORE demonstrators walked off in search of another target.[50]

Demonstrators from New York protested the employment practices of the Schaefer Beer Company by blocking the entrances to its tent, disrupting sales. The St. Louis group joined them and squared off against angry patrons throwing cups of beer at the protesters and shouting "Ship 'em back to Africa" and "Get the gas ovens ready." When the police arrived to arrest the demonstrators, Ivory Perry and others from St. Louis sat down in front of the police wagon. Officers picked up the protesters and loaded them into the wagon, taking them to jail where they were charged with disturbing the peace. CORE representatives posted bonds of $500 for each demonstrator and secured their release. One month later each of those arrested received suspended sentences of thirty days in jail.[51]

Their experiences at the World's Fair made the St. Louis participants more committed than ever to direct action. They returned home with renewed determination and enthusiasm. But their fervor troubled some in St. Louis CORE who believed that an excessive propensity for action diluted the group's resources and undermined its credibility as a responsible organization. Long-time veterans of nonviolent struggle particularly regretted the militants' tendency to put confrontations at the start, rather than at the conclusion, of negotiations. The Jefferson Bank campaign and the militancy spawned in its wake had transformed St. Louis CORE in significant ways. It brought new faces and new energy into the group, but also changed its practices and philosophy. Charles Oldham had helped start the chapter in 1948 and he took pride in its traditions of nonviolence and reconciliation. "It was amazing," he says of CORE's history; "I can't think of any group of people that we had difficulties with and took direct action against that we did not end up being friendly to." But in the climate emanating from the Jefferson Bank situation, that approach began to change. Oldham welcomed the energies and respected the commitments of many of the new members, but he disagreed with their philosophy. "I think that the people that were involved were very sharp politically," he says of the activists who rose to prominence at that time. "I think they were rather astute, but they obviously didn't believe in nonviolence."[52]

For their part, CORE members favoring a new approach looked with scorn at what they called the "tea and doughnuts" negotiations that they felt characterized too much of CORE's activity. A group centered around Percy Green and chapter chairman Lucien Richards argued that confrontive direct-action protests mobilized the community and forced its adversaries into making concessions. The philosophical disagreement split the chapter into competing factions until Richards and Green resigned from CORE to form the Action Committee to Improve Opportunities for Negroes (known as ACTION). Characteristically, Ivory Perry remained active in both groups. Despite the strains that divided CORE and ACTION, he insists, "We were all like just one big family. The differences was not important because we was trying to get to the same goal. They might have had different philosophies, but when it was goin' on, they was all fighting for the same thing."[53]

Yet one difference did matter to Perry, a difference about leadership. CORE started as an integrated organization, one of the few integrated groups in the city. But Perry and other blacks came to feel that whites monopolized leadership positions and that blacks should be more prominent in the leadership because whites did not really understand the black community's problems. Perry liked and respected white people in the organization and felt that they made important contributions to the cause. Tactically, whites were less likely to get arrested by the police and repression against them was more likely to get publicity. In addition, black separatism did not appeal to Perry; he feared it might lead to a kind of black chauvinism that would be unfair to sincere whites and would deprive the movement of needed allies. But he felt that it was important to have black leadership in the movement, and so he gravitated more toward ACTION and its activities.[54]

CORE and ACTION worked together on projects of mutual interest like freedom rides to rural areas of Missouri to test compliance with the 1964 civil rights law mandating desegregation of public restaurants serving interstate commerce.[55] The groups also set up informational picket lines in downtown St. Louis to protest the exclusion of black workers from skilled jobs in the construction of the Gateway Arch, the centerpiece of the federally funded Jefferson National Expansion Memorial. As CORE pickets paraded in front of the Old Courthouse downtown to draw attention to the expenditure of federal funds on a project that discriminated against black workers, Percy Green and Richard Daly of ACTION made their complaints known in a more dramatic way.[56]

Daly and Green climbed the base of the arch, and Green chained himself to the structure one hundred feet above the ground. They remained there for four hours until the police figured out a way to cut Green's chains and arrested the two demonstrators for trespassing and disturbing the peace. Green and Daly won few friends with their stunt: politicians, editorial writers, and community leaders lambasted them as frivolous publicity seekers. Yet the very vehemence of those condemnations focused attention on the arch and turned that symbol of civic pride into a symbol of civic division over racism. Protests against hiring practices in the construction of the Gateway Arch eventually secured jobs for black workers on future federal projects in St. Louis, and the dispute gave rise to the St. Louis Plan, the first federal affirmative action program. Green and Daly received no credit for these breakthroughs when they came, but it seemed clear to Ivory Perry that their flamboyant demonstration had played a crucial role in bringing about substantive change in employment opportunities for blacks.[57]

Ivory Perry's intense involvement with political activism after the Jefferson Bank demonstration changed him as a person. It activated his long-standing desire to make a statement about racism and brought purpose and meaning to his everyday activities. In the process of social contestation he learned that others felt as he did and that challenges to authority sometimes brought favorable results. Gradually he stopped viewing himself as someone on the margins of society, and more and more he thought of himself as involved in important issues and events. At one point civil rights activism had seemed like little more than an outlet for the frustrations of his everyday life, but eventually it became the central focus of that life. In September 1964 he secured employment as a spot welder at the Chrysler assembly plant in suburban St. Louis. He started at $2.62 per hour and received raises in October and December that brought him up to $2.81 an hour. He was making more money than he had at any previous job and he enjoyed the work, but he risked it all by continuing his political activism. Newspaper stories about his civil rights activities appeared on the bulletin boards at Chrysler as soon as he started work there. Someone posted them all over the plant, adding "KKK" and "Niggers Go Home." Cars came down the assembly line to his section with "KKK—Look Out Perry" written on them, and neither company supervisors nor union committeemen seemed interested in his complaints about this harassment. Perry filed grievances and voiced his objections to the scarcity of black foremen and the dearth of promotion opportunities for black workers, adding to his reputation in the plant as a controversial figure. But he was too committed to the cause at this point to worry about its effect on his employment security.[58] Instead, he was more concerned about what he could do to advance the civil rights movement. That concern brought him to a new level of public notoriety when he engaged in his most provocative and flamboyant direct action to date.

AS COMMUTERS made their way home from downtown St. Louis on a March afternoon in 1965, they faced the usual aggravations of rush-hour driving. Traffic slowed to a crawl at all the major intersections shortly after five o'clock, and most drivers could only curse the congestion and resign themselves to the stops and starts of their trip home. But inside a rented yellow U-Haul truck bearing Missouri license plates LLT-505, two black men surveyed the traffic and smiled quietly to each other. Ivory Perry had spent long months with more than traffic on his mind, and the slow pace of travel on the highway fit his plans perfectly. Along with his companion, Ernest Gilkey, he intended to stop the truck at one of the busiest exit ramps to create a massive traffic tie-up that would paralyze the city.[59]

Perry thought that a traffic jam would be a good way to force people in St. Louis to confront the violence and brutality then being directed against the civil rights movement in the South. Every day he read news accounts of attacks against black people seeking to secure the right to vote in places like Selma, Alabama; lately he had been able to think of little else. In February, an Alabama state trooper had shot twenty-six-year-old Jimmie Lee Jackson in the stomach when the young man tried to protect his mother from a beating by officers attempting to break up a voter registration rally. Jackson died from his wounds eight days later. On March 7, sheriff's deputies and state troopers confronted peaceful marchers on the outskirts of Selma and used tear gas bombs, attack dogs, and riot batons wrapped with barbed wire to inflict injuries on more than one hundred demonstrators. Two days later, vigilantes armed with clubs assaulted James Reeb, a white Unitarian minister from Boston participating in the Selma civil rights campaign; on March 11, he died from the injuries.[60]

So on Monday afternoon, March 15, 1965, as a federal judge deliberated over Martin Luther King, Jr.'s request to lead a protest march from

Selma to the state capitol in Montgomery, and as President Lyndon
Johnson prepared a nationally televised address to Congress about civil
rights, Ivory Perry prepared to tie up traffic in St. Louis in order to focus
attention on the situation in Alabama.

He had now been active in the civil rights movement in St. Louis for
over a decade, and he felt that events in Alabama might prove decisive
for that cause. If black people failed to win even minimal goals in the
South like the right to vote or the freedom to stage peaceful protests, it
would be impossible to challenge the equally oppressive but more subtle
racism facing northern blacks. But if the nation could be made to see the
moral bankruptcy of racism in Alabama, it might help to change conditions that constrained political, social, and economic opportunities elsewhere. Perry knew that many people would be angry with him for tying
up traffic, but he thought that his actions would nonetheless force them
to confront the civil rights struggle in Alabama.

> I wanted to dramatize the need for people from St. Louis to go down
> there and participate in the demonstrations, because different
> churches in St. Louis at that time was setting up workshops and
> conferences about racism, and certain white preachers were talking
> about what they wanted to do to try to help. And I thought it was a
> good time to try and dramatize that we needed their help in Selma.[61]

Steering the truck onto the Highway 40 exit ramp at Kingshighway
Boulevard, Ivory Perry eased it at an angle across the traffic lane, stepped
on the brake, and turned off the ignition. He left the vehicle and locked its
doors, pausing only to remove the distributor cap from the engine, while
Ernest Gilkey let the air out of the right front tire. When a black and red
taxi tried to pass the truck by driving on the grass shoulder, Perry threw
himself into the path of the cab, directly in front of the wheels. The cab
driver slammed on his brakes. Angry motorists got out of their vehicles,
shaking their fists and shouting obscenities at the man lying calmly in the
road. The cab driver demanded that the truck be moved and clenched his
fists to square off with Ernest Gilkey. From the ground Perry ordered
Gilkey to put down his fists, insisting that there be no violence. He
explained to the cab driver and to the other motorists that he and Gilkey
had stopped their truck as a protest against violence in Alabama. About
fifteen or twenty cars backed up on the exit ramp, and most of the drivers
got out of their vehicles and gathered around Perry, shouting at him to
move the truck.[62]

As Ivory Perry stretched out in front of the wheels of the taxi cab, a black motorist walked up. When he found out what had happened to block his path, he became so angry that he told the cab driver to back up because he wanted to run over Perry himself. But then two young white boys, who seemed to Perry to be about eight or nine years old, spoke up. "Well mister, if you're gonna run over him, you're gonna have to run over us too. Because he's right." The black man retreated to his car without saying another word.[63]

At the same time that Perry and Gilkey blocked the Kingshighway exit, other civil rights demonstrators stalled vehicles at two congested locations in other parts of St. Louis. Police officers found themselves confronted with three simultaneous traffic emergencies. It took them almost twenty minutes to make their way to the Kingshighway exit ramp, where they found Ivory Perry on the ground, blocking an entire lane of traffic. They asked him to get up and move his truck, but Perry told them that he intended to remain where he was until five-thirty "to draw attention to the Negro cause in Selma, Alabama," according to one policeman's official report on the incident. Newspaper reporters arrived and asked Perry if his actions wouldn't make more enemies than friends for his cause by angering innocent bystanders. He replied, "I want people to be mad at me." Turning to the police officers, he challenged, "Why don't you arrest me? I'm a freedom fighter." By this time, the police were only too happy to comply, but first they wanted him to move the truck. At exactly five-thirty—as planned—Perry and Gilkey pushed the truck onto the shoulder of the exit ramp, leaving enough room for one lane of cars to pass. But when officers informed Perry that he was under arrest, he sat down in the street again—blocking traffic once more—and told policemen that they would have to carry him away.[64]

His actions that day cost Ivory Perry thirty days in the city workhouse and a $250 fine for disturbing the peace. But as he had hoped, the news media reported his arrest and his reasons. His demonstration helped bring the situation in Alabama to the forefront of local consciousness. Perry spent the next ten days trying to line up volunteers from St. Louis to join the Selma to Montgomery march, and he found that most of the people that he talked with had heard of the stall-in on Highway 40. On March 25, Ivory Perry and nineteen busloads of demonstrators assembled by the St. Louis Conference on Religion and Race traveled to Alabama to join the march. The mass rally of some 25,000 people helped convince Congress to pass the Voting Rights Act of 1965.[65]

Ivory Perry became a front-page figure with this traffic tie-up on Highway 40. Drawing on lessons learned at the World's Fair in New York the previous year, St. Louis CORE kept its plans secret to prevent informants from tipping off the police. Each new experience with direct action sharpened the sophistication of Perry's strategy and accelerated his desire to push the cause as publicly as he could. Less than two months after stopping traffic on Highway 40, Perry made front-page news once again, this time with an obstructive sit-in at the Laclede Gas Company headquarters.

That demonstration had its roots in long efforts by St. Louis civil rights groups to persuade public utilities to hire more black employees. A 1958 NAACP press release complained that Southwestern Bell Telephone Company hired only 121 Negroes out of a work force of more than 7,000, and that 92 percent of the firm's black workers held custodial positions. CORE and ACTION kept up the pressure on Southwestern Bell, Union Electric, and Laclede Gas in subsequent years, but won no concessions. Percy Green believed that those companies made perfect targets for direct-action protests because they had high visibility in the community. Everyone who had contact with a lineman, meter reader, or repairman could see who did and did not work for those companies. They also had the size to absorb an attack; they would not be put out of business by protests. So Green mounted a campaign against the utilities, beginning with a demonstration by ACTION and CORE members, including Ivory Perry, on May 12, 1965.[66]

At half past four in the afternoon, a small group of pickets began to march in front of the main entrance to Southwestern Bell's headquarters on Pine Street in downtown St. Louis. They carried signs condemning the firm's reluctance to hire black telephone operators, installers, and repair personnel. Fifteen minutes later they marched into the street and blocked traffic. Police cruisers converged on the scene, and officers moved quickly to end the disturbance and clear the streets for rush-hour traffic. At that very moment, Ivory Perry and Marvin Moseby stood two blocks away, outside the headquarters of Laclede Gas on Olive Street. When alerted by walkie-talkie that the action at the phone company had attracted the police, they draped chains through the handles of the doors leading into the gas company, snapping them shut with padlocks. They signaled to the demonstrators on Pine Street who then marched toward the gas company building, bringing the police along with them. Five hundred Laclede Gas employees trying to leave work for the day found themselves trapped inside the building (although another exit remained open, most inside the building were not aware of it) as demonstrators blocked the sidewalks with linked arms and large signs accusing Laclede Gas of closing the doors on black employment and of perpetuating the "chains" of slavery.[67]

Security officers inside the building called on the police to arrest Moseby and Perry. The demonstrators had gummed up the padlock so that it could not be opened by a key, forcing the police to find bolt cutters. Police officers took Perry and Moseby into custody and handcuffed them back-to-back around a parking meter while detectives went to a squad car to get the bolt cutters. But when the police directed their attention to the chains on the doors, Perry and Moseby stood up and worked their arms over the meter and walked out into the middle of the street, where they sat down to block traffic. Lieutenant Donald Rankins, a detective attached to the department's unit in charge of monitoring protest activities, finally opened the chains. People from the building streamed out, running toward Perry and Moseby, venting their rage at the demonstrators by shouting obscenities and attempting to kick the two handcuffed men lying on the ground. Police officers called for reinforcements to disperse the crowd, and they dragged Perry and Moseby off to jail. When the case came to court, the judge sentenced Perry and Moseby to sixty days in the city workhouse and a $400 fine, but that failed to deter them from subsequent political activism.[68]

Donald Rankins still has the padlock that Perry and Moseby used to close the doors at Laclede Gas in 1965. He keeps it as a souvenir of his days in the police department's intelligence unit, the Red Squad. In that capacity, he came to know many of the city's political activists quite well. Rankins saw his role in demonstrations as providing a buffer between activists and their opponents, protecting the rights of each side. The department wanted to avoid violence, and when things got heated it was Rankins's job to defuse the situations. He remembers that Perry sometimes posed problems for him. "He could get heated up pretty well in the midst of any given situation. When Ivory was in the middle of things, he'd get very heated; at those times he could seem fanatical." Yet over the course of hundreds of demonstrations Rankins developed a singular respect for Perry. "I don't think he was crazy; he was involved. When they needed someone to be arrested, he was elected. I admired him because he was sincere. He was dedicated to the cause of the time. Other people were there for who knows what reasons; people used it for their own personal gain. But not Ivory."[69]

The same qualities in Perry that earned Rankins's respect made him an important figure in the protest community. He had come to St. Louis in 1954 as an unemployed high school dropout with a dishonorable discharge from the army, and his subsequent experiences as a semiskilled black worker living in a deteriorated neighborhood left him facing the hardships of life without any particular distinction or recognition. Political activism gave him an opportunity to "become somebody"; it soothed the anxieties and strains of marginality by involving Perry in collective purposeful work. Direct-action protests addressed the accumulated grievances of his life while at the same time transforming his everyday experience. Through social contestation he became connected to other people in an atmosphere of mutuality and respect.

But activism amounted to more than an exotic form of therapy; it imposed responsibilities and obligations on him as well. Through exposure to protest actions and their ramifications, Perry began to take on the tasks of the organic intellectual. He studied the problems facing his community, developed his understanding of them, and devised tactics and strategies to educate and agitate others for social change. He developed a reputation as someone who did the things that needed to be done, a man who displayed leadership—not through verbal eloquence or bureaucratic in-fighting, but through the public exposure of a sincere and unrelenting commitment.

Less than a month after the demonstration at Laclede Gas, Perry confronted one of the consequences of his devotion to political struggle. Chrysler management fired him from his job, allegedly because on his job application he failed to mention a hand injury suffered at a previous job. Yet he had worked there almost a year without taking sick leave or filing any medical claims about injuries. It seemed clear to Perry that he was fired for his willingness to voice complaints about racism inside the plant and his notoriety outside it. Yet he had no intention of abandoning his political work.

Shortly after he lost his job at Chrysler, Perry attended a CORE meeting about the ongoing civil rights struggle in Bogalusa, Louisiana. The things he heard that night brought back memories of his years growing up in the South. Perry felt that he knew exactly what black people in Bogalusa were facing in their campaign for jobs, access to service in stores, and their fair share of city services. He listened to accounts of demonstrators being attacked by thugs from the Ku Klux Klan, civil rights workers being beaten and shot, and city officials failing to protect the black community from racist violence. A year earlier he had been asked by some of the CORE members he met at the World's Fair to go to Mississippi to help with the voter registration and community organizing drives. He wanted to go, but his son Reggie had just been born. A year later his daughter Angie arrived and he now had two infants at home. He felt bad about leaving them and their mother alone, but Perry's commitment to the civil rights movement had deepened. He felt an urgency about what was happening, and he felt that he had to be part of it. Now CORE was again asking for volunteers to go south. That night, Ivory Perry left St. Louis for Bogalusa.[70]

CHAPTER 4

Bogalusa: Civil Rights in a
Southern City

Ivory Perry rode a bus to Bogalusa, the most violent city in the South in the summer of 1965. Many southern towns experienced conflict over civil rights issues in that year, but in few were the combatants as sharply polarized, or as heavily armed, as in that Louisiana city of 25,000 inhabitants. For six months, attempts by the black Civic and Voters League to secure jobs, voting rights, and desegregated service in stores and restaurants met with fierce resistance from local officials and provoked violent reprisals by the Ku Klux Klan. When law enforcement officers proved themselves unable—or unwilling—to prevent that violence, young black workers formed an armed self-defense group, the Deacons for Defense and Justice. Perry could feel the tension as soon as he stepped off the bus. Along with other CORE volunteers, he made his way to the home of A. Z. Young, the leader of the Civic and Voters League, where he learned about the local situation and the role he was expected to play in it.[1]

Every day, Ivory Perry and other CORE volunteers manned picket lines alongside activists from the Civic and Voters League. They asked black people (who made up 40 percent of the local population) to boycott businesses that hired or served only whites, and they distributed leaflets outlining black grievances against segregation in Bogalusa. Sharp exchanges between picketers and white shoppers led to many tense moments and helped set the stage for even more violence in the future.[2]

Perry's introduction to the violence in Bogalusa came during a civil rights march from a black neighborhood to the downtown shopping district. As soon as the marchers reached the downtown streets, Perry could see the hostile mob waiting for them—whites perched on cars on both sides of the street, sitting on top of their cars with the rebel flags and making those remarks like "niggers go home," drinking Pepsi-Colas and throwing the bottles and throwing eggs. One fella had some fish hooks. He had about eight or ten of them tied in one line. And they'd snatch, they'd just snatch plugs out of the demonstrators. I was hit a couple of times with eggs and rotten oranges and a rock.[3]

By the light of day on marches and picket lines, and under cover of darkness in high-speed chases on back roads, civil rights demonstrators in Bogalusa lived with constant threats and abuse. Perry remembers counterdemonstrators on picket lines screaming "Nigger go home" and spitting in his face. On more than one occasion automobiles with one high-beam headlight, purportedly a secret sign of the Ku Klux Klan, forced him off the road. He remembers thinking that he had more in common with these "enemies" than they knew, that like them he had grown up poor in the South. He knew something about the frustrations and anger that lay behind their behavior, and he suspected that they probably shared many of his own grievances with the economic system. Yet racism made it impossible for them to see that. "They was poor," he recalls, "but they was stomp-down racists from the heart."[4]

The main source of protection for civil rights workers in Bogalusa came from the Deacons for Defense and Justice. Louisiana law barred citizens from carrying concealed weapons, but it allowed open display of firearms. The Deacons expressed their intention to defend their community by carrying guns out in the open and using them in response to violent attacks against civil rights workers or community people. Charles Sims organized the Deacons in Bogalusa after two civil rights workers were attacked by six white thugs. Sims and some friends rescued the two CORE representatives and detained their attackers until the police arrived. When officers refused to press charges against the six men, Sims concluded that black people had to rely on their own resources for self-defense and he organized a local chapter of the Deacons.[5]

An insurance agent and collector with twenty-one arrests over the previous eight years, Sims did not exactly fit the typical profile of a southern civil rights leader. In most southern cities, church leaders and the educated middle class played prominent roles in civil rights activity and generally advocated conciliatory and nonviolent methods. In Bogalusa, articulate and politically astute black workers took the lead in shaping strategy and planning confrontations with the white power structure. But if Bogalusa's civil rights leaders differed from those in other cities, Sims was an exception even within Bogalusa because of his concentration on armed self-defense.

Explaining his transformation into an activist, Sims told an interviewer:

> I liked to play. That's all I done, just party and wear pretty clothes. But, when the Civil Rights Movement came about and we had the day of testing public accommodation, had so much trouble, that day I made up my mind that we was gon' have to fight, whether people saw it or not. And I made up my mind that this is where I'll be able to be found, because at least I know what I'm fighting for.

Sims explained that his willingness to use firearms in pursuit of his goals stemmed from his military experience.

> I went to World II. I helped train a thousand men to kill . . . and I didn't know what the hell I was teaching 'em for. Went in behind the Civil Rights Act, I knew what the hell I was fightin'; I was fightin' for equal rights that Roosevelt promised us before he died. Didn't do a damn thing about it. Truman, he promised . . . he didn't do a damn thing.[6]

Ivory Perry understood those sentiments from his own experiences in the Korean War, and he appreciated the presence of the Deacons in Bogalusa. "Having these young brothers all up in trees, on rooftops, everywhere, made it easier to get people involved in demonstrations and picket lines." In Perry's judgment it also reduced the likelihood of actual violence. "When you confront one on one, they have a weapon and you have a weapon, most of the time they gonna back down because they can get killed the same as you. But when it's the other way around," he cautions, "they have a gun and you don't have anything, they're not gonna back down."[7]

Bogalusa Civic and Voters League president A. Z. Young also welcomed protection from the Deacons; in fact, he considered it essential. "I know the Klan would already have come in here and killed or whipped the leaders of the movement if it weren't for the Deacons; the Deacons give them something to think about."[8] Even CORE staff members, steeped in the philosophy and practice of nonviolence, welcomed the support of Sims and his group. Richard Haley served as southern regional director of CORE in 1965, and he recalls that "black men in

Bogalusa made it clear that they had no intention of taking a Gandhian stance while these people with a killer mentality would be moving among them." He notes that "CORE was in a peculiar position; . . . the truth is that most of us were grateful that there was a Deacons for Defense around. CORE couldn't walk around with guns, but the Deacons could."[9]

The Deacons for Defense and Justice made Bogalusa one of the places in the South where armed self-defense supplemented tactical nonviolent direct action in the civil rights movement. Sims boasted of the effectiveness of his group when he told a reporter:

> Martin Luther King and me have never seen eye to eye. He has never been to Bogalusa. If we didn't have the Deacons here there is no telling how many killings there would have been. We stand guard here in the Negro Quarters. We are the defense team. But if the Klan or anybody else comes in here to hit us, I guarantee they will get hit back.[10]

But Ivory Perry noticed an equally important side effect of the Deacons' commitment to armed self-defense. Their discipline and dedication inspired the community, their very existence made black people in Bogalusa think more of themselves as people who could not be pushed around. CORE national director James Farmer identified those virtues in response to criticisms for allying with a group uncommitted to nonviolence.

> We believe nonviolence still has much tactical validity in the Civil Rights Revolution and many of us are philosophically committed to nonviolence as a way of life. . . . But this movement is about people, not philosophies and it is people that we must move, ally ourselves with, and ultimately sway. And the kind of people who would prefer to die than see their families outraged are the kind of people we mean to live and work with until we turn this thing around. And that means poor people and that means Deacons.[11]

Armed self-defense bolstered spirits and saved lives, but even at best it could play only a supporting role in a larger drama. The courage of men and women on the picket lines, their resolve to persevere in the face of violent provocations, and their ability to sustain disciplined collective protest defined the true nature of the movement in Bogalusa. For Ivory Perry, the struggle in Bogalusa provided an education, an object lesson in the complexity of social contestation and a model for his future activism.

> Bogalusa was very educational, very enlightening. It showed me another side of America: violence and hatred that I couldn't believe could happen here. But there was also a damn good organization there—CORE people who could get the community organized and keep it organized. They connected the concerns of the people in the street to the causes of their problems in the higher circles of society.[12]

That ability to link the problems of everyday life with their underlying societal causes characterized the protest movement in Bogalusa, and it taught grass roots activists and organizers like Ivory Perry important lessons about social contestation. From the Civic and Voters League and CORE strategists Perry discovered significant ways of analyzing problems and shaping protests toward addressing the causes of injustice and exploitation.

JUST AS mechanization of agriculture and wartime industrial expansion helped create the preconditions for the civil rights movement in St. Louis, technological changes and economic growth set the stage for contestation in Bogalusa. In the early 1960s, the giant Crown Zellerbach paper company, which dominated the city's economy, spent $35 million to modernize its plant and equipment in Bogalusa. That modernization increased productivity but also led to a decrease in the work force. Five hundred black workers lost their jobs, and whites and blacks competed for a declining number of employment opportunities in the local paper mills. At the same time, developments in national politics had an effect on race relations in Bogalusa. The national civil rights movement placed pressure on elected officials to respond to the economic problems confronting the black community. Large concentrations of black voters in highly populated and politically important states could not be ignored by candidates for national office, particularly within the Democratic party. President Kennedy won the 1960 election over Richard Nixon on the margin of black voters who expected him to support federal assistance to distressed black communities. Yet Kennedy moved slowly on civil rights and antipoverty initiatives for fear of alienating southern white voters who also contributed important strength to his party. The President did issue Executive Order 10925 designed to encourage equal employment opportunities in firms with federal contracts, firms like Crown Zellerbach, and his order had a pronounced impact on race relations in Bogalusa.[13]

Executive Order 10925 induced Crown Zellerbach management to eliminate separate plant entrances for black and white workers and to end provisions for segregated drinking fountains and restrooms. Crown Zellerbach pledged to adhere to fair employment practices, a pledge that drew careful scrutiny from black workers. They complained that Crown Zellerbach management divided black and white workers into separate job classifications and promoted them only within their race, rather than across the board by seniority or merit. No black worker could advance more than one step above general laborer, and the firm had no black supervisors. Contracts for ancillary services like timber cutting went exclusively to white contractors, even those that had their black employees do all the actual cutting and hauling. The company hired hundreds of women workers, but all of them were white—with the single exception of a black woman hired to clean the apartment suites reserved for visiting executives. And even she got fired.[14]

Crown Zellerbach provided 70 percent of Bogalusa's income in 1964, with its $19 million payroll, and company-backed candidates dominated local politics. Two of the four city council commissioners worked for the firm directly, and all the other elected officials maintained cordial relations with top management. With that kind of power, Crown Zellerbach could influence a whole range of government decisions in town that adversely affected blacks. So Executive Order 10925 raised black hopes that changes might be made not only inside the paper mills but outside them as well. The city had no black doctors or nurses; the local medical facilities treated black patients only on Thursdays and even then only after whites. Tax money for street repairs and sewer construction went disproportionately to white neighborhoods, while black taxpayers received little in the way of city services. Only 1,500 blacks had succeeded in registering to vote in Bogalusa and surrounding areas of Washington Parish, although the population contained nearly 7,000 potential black voters.[15]

National ferment over civil rights issues and the passage of the 1964 Civil Rights Act further encouraged the black community in Bogalusa to believe that changes might be possible. Yet the same forces that encouraged black hopes terrified many Bogalusa whites. Kennedy's executive order threatened to undercut white access to the declining number of paper-mill jobs, and every step toward desegregation undermined social traditions and privileges long taken for granted by white southerners. When two twelve-year-old black girls walked up to the Woolworth's lunch counter (where blacks had traditionally been denied service) in downtown Bogalusa on July 3, 1964, word spread quickly throughout the white community. A mob of more than one hundred white men chased the girls from the store and remained outside it until after sundown, long after the girls had left. Any civil rights activity in Bogalusa seemed certain to meet with ferocious resistance from the white population.[16]

Unlike other southern cities, the civil rights movement in Bogalusa had little significant connection to the black church, the NAACP, or a black college. Young workers in the local paper mills formed the Civic and Voters League to address the city's racial problems, and they drew support from blue-collar workers and small-business owners. Without access to the resources of the church-oriented Southern Christian Leadership Conference, they turned to CORE for assistance.[17] The national CORE leadership wanted to increase its influence in the South and had targeted Louisiana for special attention. They sent two staff organizers to Bogalusa and called for volunteers from other chapters to join them. The presence of CORE workers promised to bring national attention to Bogalusa, stimulating outside pressure for change while adding to the organizational resources of the local movement.

According to Richard Haley, southern regional director in 1965, CORE's officers viewed Bogalusa as a small country town with connections at very high corporate levels because of Crown Zellerbach. The corporation followed local customs on racial issues, and consequently functioned to reinforce institutionalized racism in the city. CORE strategists hoped that direct-action pressure against Crown Zellerbach would educate the rest of the nation about conditions in Bogalusa, and induce the company to use its influence to change race relations there. In 1960 and 1961, CORE staff member James Peck had great success using Woolworth's stockholders meetings as forums for exposing that company's collusion with segregation in its southern stores. CORE leaders saw a similar opportunity with Crown Zellerbach. They felt that inviting volunteers to Bogalusa from all over the nation would help broaden the pressure on the company to help end discriminatory practices in Bogalusa.[18]

Yet CORE officials agonized over the decision to invite volunteers to Bogalusa. They had seen all too clearly that violence could be expected there as a matter of course. Among the young men drawn to the paper mills from rural Louisiana and Mississippi were some members of the Ku Klux Klan, individuals whom CORE leaders knew to be both violent and vile. But precisely because hatred and racism took such crude forms in Bogalusa, it became essential for CORE to show the rest of America what was happening there. As Richard Haley recalls, "CORE recognized that the exposure of this mentality would mean something, not only to the matter of Bogalusa, but to the matter of making America take a look at itself." For those reasons, "CORE both invited and feared the possibility that Bogalusa could be a monstrous situation."[19]

CORE organizers Bill Yates and Steve Miller went to Bogalusa in January 1965 to join the Civic and Voters League in nonviolent action to test compliance with the Civil Rights Act of 1964. The league received assurances from Mayor Jesse Cutrer that the local police would protect their right to request service at lunch counters and restaurants, and when they entered eighteen local establishments on January 28, they received service without incident at eleven of them. Yet these tests provoked an immediate and ugly response by segregationists. Several dozen whites, some affiliated with the Klan, confronted the protesters. They surrounded Bill Yates as he sat in his car outside the Plaza Restaurant. Some shouted threats, others drew their index fingers across their throats in a threatening gesture. Still others called Yates a "Hebrew." At the Redwood Inn, a mob gathered around an automobile containing CORE organizer Steve Miller and Civic and Voters League official Robert Hicks, threatening them for forty-five minutes before police officers sent the crowd away. Two days later, Robert Hicks found tacks in his driveway, evidently in retaliation for allowing CORE staffers to stay at his house. Officers of the black labor union representing employees at Crown Zellerbach also discovered tacks in the driveway of the union hall after it had been used for a Civic and Voters League meeting.[20]

On February 1, the Civic and Voters League held a mass meeting in the union hall at eight in the evening. Shortly after midnight, Chief of Police Claxton Knight and Deputy Sheriff Doyle Holliday came to the home of Robert Hicks and informed CORE organizers Yates and Miller that a mob of two hundred people had gathered downtown with the intention of lynching them. Knight and Holliday offered to escort Yates and Miller out of town, but Hicks invited them to remain in his home. When they accepted, Knight and Holliday left in disgust, warning that they had better things to do "than to protect people who aren't wanted here."[21]

Overt acts of violence escalated on February 3. Yates and Miller noticed a police car tailing them that afternoon, but suddenly a car with six white men pulled up behind them while the police car drove away. The frightened civil rights workers took off for the nearest black neighborhood, the other car pursuing them at high speed. Miller stopped his vehicle so that Yates could run into a black-owned restaurant to call for help. Before Yates could get in the door, two white men from the other car caught him and beat him severely, breaking his hand. As Miller drove around the corner, his pursuers fired a shot at his car and hit the door with a rock. Yates and Miller made their way into a black establishment, Audry's Bar. They stayed there for six hours while carloads of taunting white men circled the block and shouted threats.[22]

Bogalusa city police officers did nothing to break up the mobs of whites roaming the streets near the bar, but they did disperse a group of blacks who had gathered nearby. Someone cut off telephone service for the entire block, and eyewitnesses reported seeing a local Ku Klux Klan leader sitting in a police car and conversing with a deputy sheriff just two blocks from the besieged building. After more than six hours of this tense confrontation, police officers intervened, escorting Yates and Miller from the bar, driving them to Baton Rouge, some sixty miles west.[23]

During the next two weeks, white thugs made repeated attacks on blacks. On February 5, a black man driving on a lonely road outside Bogalusa stopped to give assistance to a white man who had flagged him down, ostensibly for help with car trouble. As soon as the black man stepped out of his vehicle, a group of whites jumped out of a ditch and beat him with their fists. Three carloads of white men stopped an automobile belonging to one of the men most active in the Civic and Voters League on February 10, only to find a teenager inside instead of the activist. One man showed the teenager a badge and threatened to take him to jail and beat him up "like any common nigger." On February 14, a bottle thrown from a car of white youths struck a black boy in the eye. Two days later, a group of white men with chains chased another black youth in downtown Bogalusa, but he escaped before they could catch him.[24]

Other incidents stemmed directly from civil rights activity. On February 1 two white men with clubs drove five black customers out of the recently desegregated Landry's Restaurant; later that evening a white customer put a gun to the head of a black diner and told him to leave. One day later, a Bogalusa telephone operator prevented Robert Hicks from informing the FBI about a bomb threat by cutting off the connection and refusing to put through any more calls. Police officers followed, stopped, and searched automobiles belonging to Civic and Voters League activists on numerous occasions. On February 21, three CORE workers and two local activists found themselves pursued by a car filled with whites for 29 miles at speeds of up to 110 miles per hour. Two days later, a car occupied by six whites chased a cab driver prominent in civil rights activities. When he stopped his car and pulled out a gun, the other car sped away.[25]

Despite the obvious repression, the Civic and Voters League received little sympathy or support from outsiders, and secured few concessions from the local power structure. Governor John McKeithen of Louisiana claimed that he knew of no circumstances that would cause Negroes in Bogalusa to stage demonstrations; Richard Haley of CORE sent him a polite but pointed note detailing beatings of civil rights workers, refusals to comply with the Civil Rights Act, and an attack on a Civic and Voters League meeting that included a tear gas grenade thrown through an open window. When members of the city council asserted that race relations in Bogalusa had always been harmonious until the recent civil rights protests polarized the city, the Civic and Voters League issued an eloquent response: "Negroes are not interested in 'race relations.' We speak of freedom, justice, and equality. We are citizens, not 'race relations'; and we assert our citizenship."[26]

In April, the Civic and Voters League compiled a comprehensive list of demands that united the black community as thoroughly as they frightened the city's diehard segregationists. The league defined "full citizenship" as

1. Equal economic opportunity in public and private employment and in city licensing practices.
2. Equal educational opportunities.
3. Desegregation of all public accommodations facilities.
4. Extension to all of the community of sewers, paved roads, bright street lights, and adequate enforced housing codes.

5. Inclusion of Negro leaders in a decision making level on City and Parish general and industrial development planning boards.

6. Employment of Negro city policemen with all proper police power to help insure the equal enforcement of laws.[27]

A voter registration clinic on April 7, designed to mobilize the community on behalf of the "full citizenship" demands, provoked more vigilante violence. Bill Yates saw some sixty to seventy Klansmen massed outside the black union hall where the clinic was taking place, and he called the FBI and the Justice Department requesting protection. Federal agents prevented violence at the meeting, but later that night the Ku Klux Klan burned a ten-foot cross in front of the union hall, placing two coffins under it. Early the next morning, Klansmen began circling Robert Hicks's home in their cars and trucks as a threat against the CORE organizers inside. Blacks began converging on the house from all directions in anticipation of a full-scale Klan attack, but when Mrs. Hicks walked outside her front door carrying a shotgun, the Klan members fled.[28]

On April 9, CORE brought its national director, James Farmer, to the black high school in Bogalusa for a rally. Because of the tensions generated by that visit, Crown Zellerbach closed operations for the day, as did all downtown stores. Black schoolchildren walked out of their classrooms and began to march downtown, but police officers intercepted them. The students changed course and headed for the black union hall, where they joined a meeting planning a mass march on City Hall the next day. Farmer spoke to a crowd of about five hundred Civic and Voters League members and supporters in the high school gym, while outside, city and state police officers turned away thirty-two cars of Klan members. After the march on City Hall, Mayor Jesse Cutrer told the marchers that there was no reason they could not settle their grievances through direct negotiations with him.[29]

Black leaders interpreted the mayor's statement as a major concession, but Cutrer began to hedge on the commitment almost as soon as he made it. He claimed that he could negotiate only with the legitimate representatives of the black community, and he had trouble understanding who those representatives might be. With an executive committee that included twenty-two black leaders and a record of mass mobilization stretching back to January, the Civic and Voters League naturally thought that it had earned the right to represent the black community. Cutrer's refusal to negotiate with them seemed an evasion of his earlier pledge. James Farmer returned to Bogalusa to lead another march on April 20, and he announced that picketing would be expanded to include demonstrations at City Hall.[30]

The Civic and Voters League continued to press for meetings with the mayor as incidents on the picket lines took on a more hostile tone than ever before. When black demonstrators marched in front of downtown stores with placards reading "We don't buy where we can't work," counterpicketers displayed signs that said "Nigras will be niggers won't they?" "Join CORE—$10.00 a day, three meals, plenty free mates," and "Support this business place—fight communism." During one picket line incident, a heckler rubbed live snakes in the faces of demonstrators outside the J. C. Penney store. A force of 350 state troopers stood guard over the potentially explosive situation on downtown picket lines, while negotiators for the city and for the Civic and Voters League worked to set up a meeting.[31]

On May 16, Mayor Cutrer finally met with representatives from the Civic and Voters League. He announced a new city policy on desegregation, promising repeal of all city ordinances mandating segregation of the races. He vowed to hire black police officers and to encourage the city council to comply with requests for sewers and water mains in black neighborhoods. The mayor added that anyone violating the rights of other citizens would face immediate arrest and prosecution.[32]

These concessions encouraged the Civic and Voters League to renew their tests of public facilities. Three days after Cutrer's proclamation, they notified state and local police officers of their intention to enter a city park previously reserved for white use only. When they arrived at the park, they found a mob of whites determined to drive them from the area. White thugs attacked men, women, and children for several minutes until the police finally appeared. But the police officers used their clubs and police dogs to clear blacks from the park, while taking no action against the whites.[33]

IT WAS then that the Civic and Voters League and CORE stepped up their efforts to get help from outside volunteers. Five months of sustained and disciplined struggle had proved that they could carry on the fight by themselves, but intervention from outside might supply the extra bit of pressure necessary to end the bloodshed and terror. Like the Freedom Summer Project in Mississippi in 1964, the CORE campaign in

Louisiana in 1965 attracted college students and social activists from other states. CORE volunteers like Ivory Perry helped bolster the morale of the local movement simply by showing up and proving that the struggle had been noticed elsewhere. In addition, national contacts broadened the struggle and brought increased pressure on the U.S. Justice Department and on Crown Zellerbach to intervene in Bogalusa. But the volunteers profited from the experience as well. They learned about social contestation from a community movement that had refined its theories and practices to an extremely sophisticated level, and they brought that knowledge back to their home communities when they left Bogalusa.

Ivory Perry knew that he might be killed in the "monstrous situation" prevailing in Bogalusa, but he had to go anyway. "What's one life to give if you can save hundreds of thousands of people?" he remembers asking himself. "I'm gonna die anyway, so I might as well go for a good cause." Besides, not going also exacted a price. "I couldn't have no peace of mind if I stayed home. I knew people was dying every day, but I was proud because I knew I was another number, another person that was gonna be there."[34]

Other volunteers had equally compelling reasons. Jacquelyn Butler had attended the same St. Louis CORE meeting about the situation in Bogalusa, and like Perry, she felt obligated to put herself on the line. Butler had become active in CORE during the Jefferson Bank demonstrations two years earlier when she was a high school senior. She had helped organize caravans after school to take demonstrators to the bank, and she had done her best to get arrested on the picket lines. Whenever the police refused to press charges against her because she was too young, she went right back to the picket lines to try to get arrested again. "I was actually upset because I couldn't go to jail with the rest of the people," she remembers. When the police discharged her, Butler's family and friends supported her completely. "My mother was one hundred percent behind me," she relates, recalling the night she looked out of the window of her jail cell and saw her mother across the street leading a group of demonstrators singing freedom songs. Butler participated in the St. Louis CORE actions at the 1964 New York World's Fair, and when CORE asked for volunteers to go to Bogalusa, she put up her hand immediately.[35]

To finance her trip to Louisiana, Butler telephoned Dr. George Mann, who had been her principal at Washington Grade School in St. Louis.

She had not spoken to him since the eighth grade, but she thought he would understand why she had to go to Bogalusa. He came over to her house immediately and wrote out a $200 check. "I can't really get out there with you all," she remembers him telling her, "but I'm with you." Supported by that kind of community consensus, Jacquelyn Butler, Ivory Perry, and other organic intellectuals and social activists from across the nation hastened to Bogalusa. They were young and old, black and white, rich and poor. "We asked people to walk into a life-threatening situation," Richard Haley emphasizes, "and it's remarkable to me that people did."[36]

"We didn't just picket and demonstrate in Bogalusa," Ivory Perry points out; "we'd go to classes and discussions about tactics and strategy for the movement; I learned a lot of things from those talks."[37] CORE organizers and Civic and Voters League members wanted the volunteers to be able to think for themselves, to reach the community on the basis of a thorough understanding of local problems. They also knew that many confrontations would allow precious little time for internal discussion, and that meant that picketers would have to know in advance what to do if provoked. Under those circumstances, activism involved more than determination and discipline; it required a critical and creative consciousness as well. Talks and discussions made for better actions, and actions led to new reflections and analyses.

The combination of racist provocations and black self-defense made it necessary for CORE volunteers to be prepared for violence at all times. On July 9, counterdemonstrators attacked marchers with rocks and bottles. One projectile struck seventeen-year-old Hattie May Hill of Bogalusa in the face. Demonstrators tried to help her into a car to take her to a doctor, but counterdemonstrators blocked their path. A scuffle broke out, and one or more of the demonstrators fired shots to disperse the crowd blocking their way to the automobile. A bullet struck a white counterdemonstrator, and police officers arrested two black men and charged them with assault.[38] One week later, violence erupted again. A white man walked up to two picketers in front of the A&P supermarket and cursed them. Sixteen-year-old Marvin Austin, the Civic and Voters League picket captain for the day, came over to see what was wrong. The man swore at Austin and punched him in the jaw; the youth struck back, knocking the man to the ground. At that point, two state police officers who had been watching the entire incident ran over and arrested both men. They handcuffed Austin's wrists behind his back but let his assailant walk to the squad car unconstrained.[39]

On July 17, Ivory Perry found himself in the middle of the picket-line violence.

> We was trying to integrate this supermarket because it didn't have any black employees. I don't know if it was the store manager or who, but they hooked up some fire hoses to a water hydrant. But they hooked it up to hot water like they was going to wash off the sidewalk and they started spraying that hot water on the demonstrators.

He recalls city police officers, state troopers, and U.S. Department of Justice special representative John Doar standing by passively, watching the incident without taking measures to stop it.[40]

In an affidavit later filed in federal court, another CORE volunteer described that same incident. Victor Levine remembered a man in a white jacket walking out of a barbershop next to the supermarket. The man carried a hose and, as Levine recalled:

> He said "I've got to clear this trash off the sidewalk" and sprayed the water into our faces. The water was very hot, but not scalding. He played the hose on us for about twenty minutes. Someone in the barbershop produced a bar of soap, and the first man began soaping our bodies and our faces. He stuck his fingers in our ears and put soap in our eyes.

A crowd of about fifty hostile counterdemonstrators gathered around the picketers during this incident, shouting insults and threats, while state troopers stood by idly. Carolyn Bryant, a demonstrator, later filed an affidavit swearing that two large groups of state policemen did nothing to stop three separate assaults on demonstrator John Hamilton. The last blow against Hamilton knocked him to the ground, apparently unconscious. When the picketers finally tried to leave after forty minutes of abuse, city police officers drove up and started arresting the picketers, some of whom had already entered their cars to leave. Bryant saw no arrests of counterdemonstrators.[41]

Ivory Perry escaped arrest and serious injury that day, but Jacquelyn Butler was not as fortunate. Police officers took her to jail in one of the "K-9" cars, and as they threw her into the vehicle, she struck her head against a metal cage that contained one of the police dogs. At the station, officers pulled her out of the car and slammed her against the wall so that she hit her head against it. Dazed from the blows, Butler sat in her cell until the Civic and Voters League arranged bail for her. Then officers told her that she had to leave the station immediately, and pointed her in the direction of the street where a mob waving Confederate flags and making threats waited for her. Her affidavit for the federal court alleged:

> There were four or five officers sitting around in the office, Bozo [John "Bozo" Riley, a police officer] kept telling me that I had to leave, since I had been bonded. A mob of about thirty whites were standing outside hollering. They seemed to be shouting at me. They were shouting threats to rape me and to kill me. Bozo opened the door and ordered me to go out. I pleaded with him to let me make a telephone call, and one of the other officers said "Let the nigger make a call." . . . I was afraid that he would push me into the mob, but finally Gail came in her car and picked me up.

"I just knew they were going to kill me," Butler remembers thinking that night, but then her friend came to pick her up, and a car filled with Deacons pulled up behind them to escort her home safely.[42]

The violence that day at the shopping plaza and at the jail afterward further exacerbated racial tensions in Bogalusa. At a mass rally called by the Civic and Voters League the next night, the organization's president, A. Z. Young, expressed the anger and frustration that had been building inside the black community for months. Young warned, "If blood is going to be shed, we are going to let it rain down Columbia Road—all kinds, both black and white." Ivory Perry could understand Young's anger and his willingness to fight back. The incident at the shopping plaza seemed particularly inexplicable to him. "I saw John Doar of the Department of Justice standing inside the doors of the supermarket watching them spraying water on us. All he did was take notes, when there was FBI, state troopers, and police officers all around." If a racial powderkeg did explode in Bogalusa, it seemed to Perry that the federal government had to bear some direct responsibility because of its inaction in the face of flagrant civil rights violations.[43]

Doar's conduct at the supermarket came into somewhat clearer focus later that week when the Justice Department took legal action to halt the violence in Bogalusa. Relying on evidence supplied by John Doar about the shopping center incidents on July 17, the Department of Justice requested judicial intervention in Bogalusa from Judge Herbert W. Christenberry of the U.S. Fifth District Court in New Orleans. Previously the department had played a more timid role in Bogalusa, filing suit in April against restaurants violating the 1964 Civil Rights Law and dispatching Doar to the city to monitor police behavior. It fell to members of the Civic and Voters League to file suit in New Orleans in late June charging Bogalusa city officials with condoning civil rights violations.

On July 10, Judge Christenberry had issued an injunction obliging the city public safety director, police chief, and mayor to protect the rights of all citizens. After the attacks at the shopping center, and fully conscious of the presence of the Deacons for Defense, the Justice Department joined the Civic and Voters League suit and offered evidence to the judge that his orders had been violated. Christenberry heard testimony about repeated acts of violence and intimidation on the picket lines that police officers refused to control. Jacquelyn Butler testified about her experiences, and other demonstrators talked about their perceptions of police misconduct. Testimony by police officers, however, painted an entirely different picture. They claimed to have handled Butler gently, alleging that she faked her injuries. And they insisted that they arrested and prosecuted all lawbreakers regardless of race.[44]

Judge Christenberry found it difficult to accept the police officers' version of events. He expressed particular skepticism about testimony that the police had no knowledge of any Ku Klux Klan activities or members in Bogalusa. Officers claimed that they had never heard any shouting, threats, or insults on the picket lines, so all the outbreaks of violence took them by surprise. The more testimony he heard, the more Christenberry felt compelled to question the quality of law enforcement in Bogalusa. At one point he interrupted a witness to remark, "Apparently the pattern is to have civilians attack the pickets and then for the police to arrest the picket." When an activist connected with the Deacons testified that jailers at the Washington Parish jail paid inmates $1 apiece to whip him with a belt, an inmate in the jail took the stand to refute the testimony. He countered that the guards had nothing to do with the beating and that the inmates had planned it on their own as part of their routine hazing of new prisoners. But Christenberry replied tartly, "I know that they wouldn't dare come in here and testify otherwise and then go back to that jail."[45]

On July 30, Christenberry found Bogalusa Public Safety Director Arnold Spiers, Police Chief Claxton Knight, and Patrolman Donald Penton guilty of civil contempt for violating his injunction. He threatened the three offenders with fines up to $100 per day and jail sentences of an unspecified length if they failed to design and adhere to plans for enforcing the civil rights of all citizens in their city. Christenberry ruled that he had insufficient evidence to convict the officers charged with mistreating Jacquelyn Butler, and he found no fault with the performance of the state police. Blaming the trouble in Bogalusa on a small group "of white persons who simply will not recognize that Washington Parish is part of the United States and that its inhabitants are subject to the laws of the United States," the judge went on to observe, "I'm afraid I've discovered a desire on the part of the local police to remain in the good graces of some of the people they should be controlling."[46]

Although his ruling fell short of securing the aims of the Civic and Voters League, Judge Christenberry's action did protect civil rights workers in Bogalusa and encourage peaceful resolution of grievances there. The plaintiffs and defendants returned to the Fifth District Court numerous times over the next six years with a series of charges and countercharges about racial incidents, but by imposing a single standard of behavior applicable to all parties, the ruling constrained vigilantes, emboldened moderates, and provided a peaceful means of resolving racial disputes.[47] In making his ruling, Christenberry responded to the dictates of law and conscience that mandated equal protection for all citizens. But he also responded to the accumulated pressures of the Bogalusa campaign, pressures generated by a grass roots group that succeeded in bringing their grievances to the attention of national leaders. Had it not been for sustained direct-action protest and comprehensive community mobilization at the grass roots, the injustices perpetrated in Bogalusa might never have come to the attention of the Department of Justice or a federal judge.

From its inception, the Bogalusa campaign attempted to exert maximum pressure on those who benefited from the status quo. The boycotts of downtown business establishments imposed a financial penalty for complicity with segregation, while the national educational campaign against Crown Zellerbach brought its behavior in Bogalusa to the attention of customers and stockholders nationwide. With its $100 million investment in Bogalusa, Crown Zellerbach management accepted segregation because it could not afford to disrupt the status quo. But civil rights turmoil disrupted production, hurt the company's image, made it harder to attract executive talent, and threatened the corporation's lucrative government contracts. Eager to avoid public controversy, top management worked quietly to pressure local moderates to bring an end to the disturbances in Bogalusa.

Mayor Cutrer, himself a small-businessman, consistently pledged to enforce the law, and his administration did institute limited reforms like hiring a few black city employees and paving streets in black neighborhoods for the first time. Newspaper editor Lou Major used his columns in the *Bogalusa Daily News* to condemn both CORE and the Klan as outsiders exploiting the crisis in Bogalusa for their own purposes, a stand that made him a target for Klan harassment. Radio station owner Ralph Blumberg aired editorials criticizing the Klan, only to find advertisers canceling their accounts. A group of local professionals and clergymen had attempted to moderate tensions as soon as the public accomodations tests started in January. They invited Baptist leader and former Arkansas congressman Brooks Hays to speak on behalf of the moderate view, but Klan threats forced cancellation of his visit.[48] Yet despite their many failures, the moderates nonetheless continued to pressure others for a peaceful settlement based on concessions to the Civic and Voters League.

By themselves, the moderates could not secure the peace in Bogalusa. They watched CORE bring in strangers from all across the country to provoke their city's most virulent racists into violent reaction, and they saw those racists import their own outsiders. The National States Rights party brought the Reverend Connie Lynch from Riverside, California, to Bogalusa. He told a white supremacist rally, "We're gonna clean the niggers out of these streets. . . . That means bashing heads or anything else it takes. There's lots of trees around here and we don't mind hangin' em."[49]

Outsiders did not create the trouble in Bogalusa; real and longstanding grievances guided local blacks to form the Civic and Voters League, and they turned to outside help only when that became necessary to break the hegemony of white racist violence. But outside pressures made Bogalusa's problems visible, public, and a threat to the interests of other outsiders, most notably the Democratic party and the Crown Zellerbach Corporation.

Polarization in Bogalusa threatened the coalition within the Democratic party that had elected Lyndon Johnson President in 1964 and pushed civil rights legislation through Congress in 1964 and 1965. In April, when

Louisiana's governor John McKeithen disdainfully announced that blacks in Bogalusa had no reason to demonstrate, he also bent to pressure from Vice President Hubert Humphrey to send state troopers to Bogalusa to keep order and to use his offices to bring about meetings between city leaders and Civic and Voters League representatives. Demonstrations at stockholders meetings and in front of Crown Zellerbach plants and offices across the country pushed the corporation into a defensive posture that made it eager to see civil rights conflicts ended in Bogalusa. Consequently, when Department of Justice officials intervened on behalf of the Civic and Voters League lawsuit in July, they could be assured of important support from local and national business and political leaders, even if that support could not be expressed openly.[50]

For Ivory Perry, the struggle in Bogalusa offered an education in the techniques and philosophy of social contestation. No one tactic ensured victory, but a willingness to explore all possible forms of pressure and protest set in motion a process that brought real change. Faced with brutal oppression and powerful enemies, black people in Bogalusa manned picket lines, sustained an economic boycott, and organized for armed self-defense. Disciplined mobilization of community resources created a crisis that provoked intervention by outside parties—CORE, the National States Rights party, Crown Zellerbach, Democratic party officials, the Department of Justice, and the U.S. Fifth District Court. By broadening the conflict and involving previously detached bystanders, the Civic and Voters League won important victories.[51]

That capacity to draw outsiders into their dispute struck Ivory Perry as one of the most important accomplishments of the Bogalusa movement. "Everyone is involved in institutionalized racism, and everyone is affected by it," he maintains. "If they're not directly involved, they're indirectly involved. But what was so good about Bogalusa was the way that they got to all the people that were indirectly involved."[52] He admired their tactics and the way they had transformed a relatively powerless community into an important force for social change. They made their grievances known to businessmen, politicians, and government officials, and they also assembled a coalition of people from very different backgrounds.

In Bogalusa, Perry met CORE volunteers from both the North and the South. They were black and white, male and female, young and old, educated and uneducated. He participated in a movement that blended the contributions of sharecroppers with those of middle-class students, that brought lawyers and doctors halfway across the country to work in a coalition directed by black paper-mill workers and cab drivers. The coalition did not always run smoothly; conflicting interests, mutual suspicions, and petty jealousies created tensions and disagreements. But in the end, this eclectic group held together under great stress and won some important victories. In subsequent campaigns, when Ivory Perry put together unlikely coalitions, he always remembered his experiences in Bogalusa as a model of what could be done. "You know, that summer in Bogalusa was just like going to a school. You can learn some things in the streets with the people that you can't ever learn from books or in a classroom," he insists.[53]

The campaign in Bogalusa also helped Perry clarify his thinking about nonviolence and social change. The armed self-defense practiced by the Deacons for Defense and Justice won some breathing room for the movement and raised the morale and courage of the civil rights activists. Certainly the presence of the Deacons and the potential for massive black armed resistance helped galvanize the Justice Department into action. But once the conflict drew nationwide attention, nonviolence proved itself an important tactic for winning the sympathy of public opinion and federal authorities. If Perry and the other shopping mall demonstrators on July 17 had resorted to violent self-defense, they would have provoked massive repression and rendered Justice Department intervention on their behalf unlikely. Reluctantly, Perry accepted the utility of tactical nonviolence in most situations of social contestation.

He felt that people had a right to defend themselves, especially in situations like Bogalusa where inadequate publicity, collusion between police officers and vigilantes, and a widely dispersed population made violent repression effective. But in most cases, he felt that nonviolence worked better to focus popular attention on the injustices of racism. "If I'd gone out there violent and something happened," he explains, "they'd say he should have known better, he shouldn't have gone out that way." Besides, his support for armed self-defense as a necessity never turned into an enthusiasm for violence itself.

I ain't never liked no guns. See, I don't like killing and I don't like violence. You know, I was in Korea, and a lot of people say guns don't kill, that people kill. But guns do kill, because if you don't have a gun you wouldn't be able to kill nobody. I know it takes a person to pull the trigger, but I just don't like to spill no blood. I don't even hate the Ku Klux Klan. I don't like what they stand for, but to just come out and say I hate them and I wish all of them was dead, it just ain't me.[54]

Perry's admiration for the Deacons and his somewhat grudging acceptance of tactical nonviolence may seem out of step with the civil rights movement at large, with its well-known devotion to nonviolent principles. But recent research indicates that Perry's view of nonviolence as a tactical rather than an absolute principle held true for many other activists. In his investigation into the origins of the civil rights movement, sociologist Aldon D. Morris quotes Hosea Williams, an officer of the Southern Christian Leadership Conference and a close aide of Martin Luther King:

I'm not ashamed to say that I've never believed in nonviolence as a philosophy of life. And I don't know anybody else who did but Martin Luther King, Jr. Andy [Young] jumped on me one day, physically—knew he couldn't whip me—and if you think Ralph [Abernathy] is nonviolent, back him up. I don't believe I ever met but one man in my life that believed in nonviolence, accepted it totally as a philosophy and that was Martin Luther King, Jr.[55]

Similarly, historian Clayborne Carson's study of the Student Nonviolent Coordinating Committee reveals a consensus within that group after 1962 that nonviolence was primarily tactical. Nonviolence won sympathy for the movement and undermined the legitimacy of its opponents, but grass-roots activists and community residents still maintained high regard for their legitimate right to defend themselves by whatever means necessary.

For Ivory Perry, the issue of nonviolence seemed less important than other lessons he learned in Bogalusa. He had seen direct-action protests alter existing power relations. The physical presence of picket lines and mass marches provoked repression, but that very repression educated the black community about the necessity for united action and it also helped win allies for the black cause. Once people participated in demonstrations, they had a stake in the struggle. As long as they remained willing to come back out into the streets, they had the capacity to influence powerful individuals and institutions. Action had its own momentum, and Perry came to feel that determination and collective effort could overcome seemingly insurmountable barriers.

But he had his doubts too. His more pessimistic moments found him reflecting on the futility of the struggle in Bogalusa. All the risks taken by the brave men and women he met seemed to have won only modest gains. Despite Judge Christenberry's intervention, black people in Bogalusa remained poor, underrepresented in government, and subject to random acts of brutality and hatred. The rest of the country had been exposed to the cancer of racism in Bogalusa and had responded with more apathy than opposition. Unlike the incidents in Selma in the spring of 1965, no coordinated national action addressed the problems dramatized by the violence in Bogalusa. Perry hoped that the melioristic gains made by the Civic and Voters League would lead to more improvements in the future, but he worried about the seeming indifference to injustice and racism manifested by most Americans. Nevertheless, he felt committed to doing his share to bring about some of the changes he believed necessary.

The things he had learned in Bogalusa made Ivory Perry eager to return to St. Louis. He felt lucky to be alive, and he felt an obligation to carry on the fight in his own community.

> I spent about ninety days in Bogalusa, but it seemed like ninety years. Toward the end I started thinking about all that had to be done in St. Louis, and all the ways that I could use the things I learned in Bogalusa back there. So I went back home, knowing that I had to be in the thick of things.[56]

Bogalusa had provided him with important lessons in strategy and tactics. St. Louis offered immediate opportunities to put that knowledge into practice. Almost before he knew it, Ivory Perry found himself involved in community mobilizations and street demonstrations once again, this time over the issue of police brutality in St. Louis.

CHAPTER 5

The War on Poverty: The Emergence of
an Organic Intellectual

Bogalusa and other southern cities had no monopoly on racial violence during the summer of 1965. In the crowded ghettos of northern and western cities, the accumulated frustrations of poverty and racism erupted into rage. Violent insurrections marked by arson, looting, and rioting swept the country. During the second week in August, a routine arrest for drunk driving escalated into a six-day confrontation between ghetto residents and law enforcement officials in the Watts section of Los Angeles. Some 14,000 National Guardsmen and 1,500 policemen occupied southcentral Los Angeles in an attempt to quell the disturbance, but rioters still destroyed $30 million worth of property. The police and National Guard troops arrested 4,000 people and shot more than 900 alleged snipers, killing 34. That same week, civil disorders brought sniping, looting. and burning to Chicago, Philadelphia, and Springfield, Massachusetts.[1]

As soon as he returned home from Bogalusa in late August, Ivory Perry noticed how the riots in Watts and other cities had contributed to increased racial tension in St. Louis. From friends in CORE he learned about the activities of the Nineteenth Ward Improvement Association, a coalition of neighborhood businessmen, community residents, and political activists trying to address problems in a deteriorated part of the city. Perry volunteered his services to that group, and as he canvassed their neighborhood he found that the issue most on the minds of the residents was one that had often sparked riots in other cities: police brutality.[2]

A series of incidents in which St. Louis police officers fired on fleeing suspects provoked a bitter reaction in the black community. On June 12, 1965, St. Louis police officers shot seventeen-year-old Melvin Cravens in the back and killed him. They claimed that the handcuffed youth had kicked one of the officers and attempted to flee from custody. Twenty-eight-year-old Willie Lee Harris died from gunshot wounds inflicted by police officers when he attempted to run away from his damaged automobile after a high-speed chase on August 7. On September 8, fifteen-year-old Melvin Childs fled from a policeman who encountered him at the site of a reported burglary. The officer fired at the youth, who suffered serious injuries from bullets lodged in his back. On September 13, policemen shot and killed nineteen-year-old Robert Robinson as he ran away from them when they tried to question him on suspicion of stealing a car. The next night, officers shot and wounded Dwight Hill, a twenty-one-year-old wanted by authorities in a nearby municipality on charges of stealing. In each of these cases, the suspects were black and the police officers were white.[3]

Spokesmen for the police department defended the right of officers to shoot at fleeing suspects, reminding the public about the many acts of violence perpetrated against policemen by criminals. The department representatives also pointed to the prior criminal records of several of those shot in the recent incidents. Yet these claims seemed like feeble excuses to the people that Ivory Perry spoke with in the ghetto. They viewed the shootings as an unprovoked attack on their community, and they demanded remedial action. On September 15, in the wake of three serious shootings in a six-day period, leaders of the major civil rights organizations in St. Louis announced a coordinated campaign against police brutality. They called for disciplinary action against officers who discharged their weapons at unarmed suspects, for the creation of a civilian review board to monitor complaints about brutality, and for a police department effort to employ more black officers.[4]

When Ivory Perry talked to people on street corners, in their homes, and in the offices of the Nineteenth Ward Improvement Association, again and again they brought up the hostility between the community and the police. Perry took it upon himself to transform community concern into concerted action. He knocked on doors, informing people about a mass march on City Hall to protest the shootings. Asking people to think about the young men killed by the police as if they were family members, he warned them that the next victim might be their own son, brother, or father. Late in the afternoon on September 16, he led about one hundred demonstrators into the streets outside the Improvement Association headquarters. One marcher carried a sign reading "Chief Brostron—Stop Shooting Negro Children." Another warned ominously, "I Want the One That Shot My Friend."[5]

Parading through the streets of the North Side ghetto on their way downtown, the marchers chanted, "Police Brutality Must Go." People from the sidewalks and homes along the line of march joined them. Ivory Perry, wearing the straw hat and white T-shirt with "Freedom Now" stenciled on the back that he had worn in Bogalusa, guided the demonstration through the walkways around the Pruitt-Igoe housing project. By the time the marchers arrived in the central business district, the crowd had grown to more than 250 demonstrators, snaking through the streets and blocking both vehicle and pedestrian traffic. At City Hall, Macler Shepard, the Nineteenth Ward Improvement Association founder and an upholstery shop owner in the neighborhood, addressed the marchers. He recited a list of grievances against the police and warned that the day's demonstration represented "just a beginning to the way that we are going to call attention to what is going on in the Nineteenth."[6] Several speakers echoed Shepard's warning, and when the last one finished, Ivory Perry sprang to action.

Turning to the crowd with arms raised to request quiet, Perry asked, "Are we going to stand back and let white police and the Ku Klux Klan kill our brothers?" "No!" roared the crowd in response. Perry turned toward City Hall and led the entire group into the building and up to the mayor's office. Discovering that the mayor was not in, they walked out of City Hall and moved across the street to police headquarters, where they demanded a meeting with Chief Curtis Brostron. Police officials said that they would allow only six representatives of the crowd into the station, but nine, including Ivory Perry, entered the building. Once they got inside, they found out that the chief would not meet with them because they had not made an appointment. Outside, 250 angry people waited for some response to their protest.[7]

Ivory Perry immediately walked out of the police station into the street and organized the demonstrators into a circular picket line designed to obstruct traffic. A little red car got caught inside the circle and its driver guided it slowly toward the demonstrators in order to get away. Ivory Perry threw himself onto the asphalt in the path of that car, and when it stopped, he stretched out in front of the wheels. Police officers rushed over to drag him out from under the automobile, but demonstrators encircled the policemen and tried to prevent them from reaching Perry. In the crush, a demonstrator fell on top of Perry, and as officers attempted to pull her away, they provoked an outbreak of pushing and shoving between demonstrators and police officers. Eventually two detectives succeeded in dragging Perry away, and arrested him for general peace disturbance. As other officers dispersed the crowd, Perry explained to the detectives that he had come downtown to discuss police brutality with Chief Brostron, but since the chief would not see him, he felt that he had to bring the situation to the chief's attention by other means.[8]

The demonstration at police headquarters and the near riot that accompanied Ivory Perry's arrest focused public attention on police-community relations in dramatic ways. Church and civic groups added their names to the list of those sponsoring the reform proposals, and the police department itself promised that it would soon release the results of its internal investigation into the recent shootings. Renewed demonstrations in the next few days brought more citizens into the streets, and the local news media gave extensive coverage to the charges against the police department. Yet the ferment won no real gains. The internal police department investigation cleared all officers of any wrongdoing in the shootings, and the police board of commissioners joined with the chief in rejecting the proposals for a civilian review board and for hiring additional black officers.[9] Perry saw the demonstrations as important evidence of the community's willingness to act on its own behalf, but to others, failure to win changes in police procedures revealed the counterproductive nature of social protest that appeared to be out of control.

The pushing and shoving that followed the September 16 rally proved particularly troubling to some of the moderates in the civil rights movement, who feared that any unruly behavior by blacks would be used to undermine the legitimacy of their cause. They reasoned that if protests remained peaceful, pressure would build on the police to come through with reforms. But if the protests erupted into violent confrontations, then the police would have an excuse to brand their opponents as enemies of all police behavior, not merely police brutality. With these considerations in mind, the executive committee of St. Louis CORE publicly reprimanded Ivory Perry for his role in the September 16 demonstration, charging that his decision to lie down in the street evidenced a "lack of propriety."[10] Perry defended his actions, insisting that only direct action could bring about the changes needed to prevent violence, but the CORE membership voted to uphold the board's censure.

"That vote didn't mean nothing to me," he recalls defiantly, alleging that the reprimand was engineered by two CORE organizers from New York who had just arrived and knew nothing about the local situation. Perry found it useful to work through CORE, but not essential—his primary loyalties lay with the community itself. If CORE found it useful to reprimand him, that was their business, but Perry felt that he did not necessarily need their approval for every action. "The organization didn't make me," he remembers thinking; "I made the organization."[11]

Perry's attitude created problems for people trying to work within the confines of institutions and organizations. They worried that his proclivity for hasty individual action might someday jeopardize the interests of the group. But his willingness to act also won him the admiration of others in the community who saw him as more devoted to advancing their interests than the institutional goals of any formal organization. Maurice Williamson, a tavern owner and friend of Perry's, remembers Perry's flamboyant use of direct-action confrontations: "Ivory is the type of person who will do whatever it takes. Ivory's no dummy, but he'll do whatever it is. I'll tell you, I would never lay down in the street and take a chance on getting run over—somebody just might do it. But somebody has to do it, and Ivory did."[12]

Opinions like Williamson's helped build a community reputation for Ivory Perry that proved instrumental in finding him a job after he was fired at Chrysler. Anna Cox had heard from a friend that the local antipoverty program, the Human Development Corporation (HDC), needed community organizers. At first she toyed with the idea of applying herself, since it seemed more interesting and constructive than her current job "busing dishes and cooking hamburgers." But she decided to tell Ivory about it instead because he had been out of work since June and "because he was the man in the family." Perry feared that his activism might disqualify him for the job, but it turned out that his activism actually helped him get the position. The person in charge of hiring organizers for HDC was Howard Buchbinder, a psychiatric social worker who had been in the Jefferson Bank demonstrations himself and who had a high regard for people involved in direct-action protest. Buchbinder believed that the War on Poverty could succeed only if it involved poor people in the process of solving their own problems. He felt that someone like Ivory Perry could make a great contribution to that process. "What Ivory had to offer," Buchbinder recalls, "was what he was and who he was, his whole experience and his anger."[13]

Perry wanted to be sure that his employers at HDC understood exactly who he was and what he might do as a community organizer before he accepted the job. An interview with Howard Buchbinder put him completely at ease. "I didn't know much about the program," Ivory re-

members, "but he said I looked like the type of fellow he had been looking for to organize the community." For his part, Buchbinder knew little
about Ivory Perry, but he liked the things he had heard. "I knew he had
been lying down in front of cars," Buchbinder confides with a smile,
"and I thought that was terrific."[14]

Pearlie Evans served on the board of directors of HDC at the time. She
was a graduate of the George Warren Brown School of Social Work at
Washington University, and had participated in drawing up the original
plans for St. Louis's antipoverty program. She had known Perry for
years from a variety of community contexts and strongly supported him
for the position of neighborhood district worker. Some board members
complained about Perry's irregular work history, his lack of education,
and his record of civil rights activism. They feared that he would be
irresponsible, that he would not come to work, and that he would not
take directions. But Evans disagreed. "Ivory's main credential was his
extensive contact with grass-roots people because of his civil rights activities," she recalls. "As a member of the board I spoke up and heavily
endorsed his name for consideration as a neighborhood district worker.
I felt he had not really had a job of any import before, but that once
given the opportunity, he would do the job."[15]

HDC could offer only twenty hours of paid work per week at first, but
Perry threw himself into full-time organizing anyway, working as much
as eighty hours a week for his twenty hours' pay. Finally he was doing
work he loved to do—it brought him into contact with the community
and its problems, gave him access to information and resources previously unavailable, and enabled him to cultivate an extraordinary expertise about the city. "I always saw the civil rights movement as connected
to housing and health and job issues," Perry remembers. "So working for
the War on Poverty just seemed like a natural extension of the organizing I
was doing anyway. Besides, I could get paid to be an organizer for the
HDC and I couldn't get paid to be a civil rights worker."[16]

As he began to talk to people in the neighborhoods in his new capacity as an antipoverty worker, he found that many in the community felt
the same as he did. "Housing and employment were big concerns for
the people, and because of discrimination, housing and employment
were not just economic issues to most black people; they were civil
rights issues too." Others within the agency shared Perry's perception
about the relationship between the civil rights movement and the war
on poverty. Mickey Rosen was a social worker at the Jewish Community

Center in the spring of 1965 when Dr. Wayne Vasey asked him to come work for the Human Development Corporation. Rosen remembers that "we kind of rode the coattails of the civil rights movement. We all felt part of that revolution, even the nonblacks. The government was supporting our antipoverty efforts and the country seemed ready for a change. Things had been static for a long period of time, and it was just time for things to change."[17]

For Ivory Perry, employment at HDC provided one more surprise in a year of frenetic activity and unexpected changes. In March he had been arrested for stopping traffic on Highway 40. In May he had blocked the doors at the Laclede Gas Company building. In June he had been fired at Chrysler. In July he had confronted the threats and assaults in Bogalusa. In September he had been involved in an obstructive demonstration in front of police headquarters that led to a reprimand from CORE. Then in October, a year characterized by arrests, firings, and volatile confrontations culminated in his appointment to a job with HDC—precisely because of his activist credentials.

INSIDE THE antipoverty program, Ivory Perry quickly earned respect for his ability and dedication. Mickey Rosen recalls:

Ivory was an activist. He was one who could not really sit by idly. He was able to point out a lot of really terrible housing conditions in his area, and in other parts of the city as well. On many occasions he was able to coerce or negotiate landlords into fixing up some of their property.[18]

Judge Theodore McMillian, currently a federal Judge, then served as an officer of the Human Development Corporation, and he recalls Perry's impact on the agency. McMillian remembers with admiration how Ivory Perry canvassed dangerous neighborhoods to find out what was on the minds of the poorest and least represented parts of the community, and how his persistence won respect from co-workers. "Really, when you get someone who's not too well lettered, people have a tendency to look away from him and not pay too much attention," McMillian observes, "but Ivory got people to listen to him because he's such a great organizer." Judge Clyde Cahill, also currently a federal judge, served as the chief executive officer of HDC during the years that Perry worked there, and his recollections correspond with Judge McMillian's. Cahill remembers that Perry had "a determination, an ability to converse and be understood." Perry sometimes used that ability to mobilize the community into actions that conflicted with the policies and goals of Cahill and HDC, but although the judge often disagreed with Perry's judgment, he never questioned his integrity. As Cahill explains, "No one conveyed the idea of sincerity more than Ivory Perry; he was willing to go to any length and suffer any pain for his beliefs."[19]

Work in the antipoverty campaign brought unprecedented opportunities to Ivory Perry, but it posed some new problems as well. In the past, he had acted on his own or under the auspices of civil rights groups, and he answered to no one but the community he wanted to mobilize. As a paid government official at HDC, he ran the risks of having an entire bureaucratic apparatus passing judgment on his actions. The War on Poverty's enabling legislation specifically called for "maximum feasible participation of the poor" in community action programs, but the poor gained no significant economic or political resources to make that "participation" meaningful. Designed at least in part as a response to the civil insurrections in the ghettos, the structure of the antipoverty program might just as easily tranquilize as mobilize poor people, depending on its implementation at the local level. Ivory Perry ran the risk of squandering his reputation and prestige in the community on tokenistic efforts to draw poor people into programs with neither the will nor the resources to meaningfully address their grievances.

Howard Buchbinder understood the dilemmas facing the activists like Ivory Perry that he hired as community organizers. The government offered them careers in the program to make it possible for them to work full time on social problems. But as full-time employees, the organizers became separated from the people that they sought to mobilize. Government employment might coopt and dilute radical dissent, and it might subtly transform community leaders for change into harried bureaucrats, caught between the needs of their constituents and the limited resources and potentially conservative goals of their employer. Buchbinder feared that the organizers would become alienated from the community, and so he tried to hire outreach workers with deep commitments and ties to others that might enable them to withstand institutional pressures.

Antipoverty workers also confronted numerous demands for immediate assistance that conflicted with their own long-range political goal of empowering the poor. People could not participate in the tedious process of improving their communities if they had no jobs or no food. But an antipoverty program that spent all its time tending to the immediate needs of individuals would quickly exhaust its resources treating the symptoms of poverty without addressing the systemic economic and political problems that caused poverty in the first place. Workers for HDC had to balance the immediate survival needs of their constituents with the long-range goal of eliminating poverty. "We had to solve problems without becoming a service organization," explains Howard Buchbinder.[20]

Activists also had to strike a balance between low-key community organizing and sensational direct action confrontations. Block-by-block organizing and small discussion groups laid the groundwork for collective action, but excessively lengthy planning meetings and deliberations could discourage community militancy. Cathartic confrontations that boldly proclaimed the legitimacy of poor people's demands fanned the flames of militancy, but without a carefully prepared base they too could become counterproductive. Antipoverty organizers could not be too far ahead of the community; they had to gauge accurately which issues would mobilize people to action. But once they did organize a confrontation, organizers had to ensure adequate media coverage and appropriate official responses to convince participants that their voices were being heard. "People had to see that what they were doing was being noticed," Buchbinder observes; they had to be convinced "that if you rocked the boat, someone got seasick."[21]

Perry negotiated the difficulties of organizing in a manner that preserved both his integrity and his effectiveness. He accepted a career job, but devoted his time and energy to getting out into the community rather than trying to rise within the HDC organization by pleasing his supervisors. When people in the neighborhoods had questions that he could not answer, Ivory brought them back with him to ask officers at HDC. When their responses dissatisfied community residents, he organized demonstrations against the antipoverty agency itself. If there were individuals who needed jobs or food and he could not help them any other way, Perry brought them down to the meetings of the HDC board of directors and urged them to stay until they got what they needed.[22]

Fortunately, some HDC officials understood and appreciated Perry's role. "They were always trying to get me to fire Ivory, but I wouldn't stand for it," Judge McMillian recalls. Board members and politicians particularly resented Perry's actions against the agency itself, but

McMillian reasoned that "when you've got somebody in the community organizing and telling people what their rights are—even if they make the same demands on you—at least we did our job."[23]

On at least one occasion, a local minister affiliated with the Citizens' Council—an avowed white supremacist group—complained to the Office of Economic Opportunity headquarters in Washington that the St. Louis agency employed "Communist" organizers, including Ivory Perry. Nobody said anything to Perry at the time; he later learned that his supervisor had simply put the complaint in her desk drawer and forgotten it because she found the charge so absurd. Even if she had been inclined to believe the accusation, Perry's reputation in the community would have made it difficult to fire him. Poor people in the neighborhoods appreciated his political acumen, but they also respected his many quiet acts of kindness.

"Ivory helped a lot of people with their problems," says Anna Cox. "He did a lot of things for people that only I knew about." Kathen Wright corroborates Cox's perception, remembering that her brother would habitually go out of his way to help strangers. "If he saw somebody sitting out on the street, he'd go rent a truck and find them a place to move and get them off the street before it got dark. He did that many a time." A co-worker at HDC told a reporter researching a story on the St. Louis civil rights movement, "I have seen Ivory coming out of a hardware store at closing time with light bulbs he has bought out of his own pocket for some poor family that couldn't afford them."[24]

When people needed to get their children to a doctor, when they needed blankets or food, Ivory Perry would come through for them. But even when he engaged in direct-action protests that brought HDC negative publicity, many of Perry's co-workers still supported his actions. Mickey Rosen remembers:

> At that point, the national mandate was that we were going to have a war on poverty. We're going to do something about the terrible conditions. One of the reasons that poverty was allowed to exist up to that point was that it was hidden. . . . Here in St. Louis many of us travel over Highway 40 or Highway 70 from suburbia into the inner city going right over and right by some of the most deplorable housing conditions in the country. We're not aware of it. So these kinds of demonstrations spotlighting conditions and circumstances facing the poor were very important in those days.[25]

The Human Development Corporation assigned Perry to its first neighborhood project at the Union-Sarah Gateway Center. Thirty thousand people lived on the 133 city blocks that made up the Union-Sarah neighborhood. Established as a middle-class white section late in the nineteenth century, Union-Sarah became 90 percent black and overwhelmingly working class and poor in the years after World War II. By 1965 when Ivory Perry started working there, almost half of the neighborhood's 6,984 families earned less than the poverty-level income of $6,000 per year; about one in every six residents received some form of public assistance, and almost 30 percent of the housing could not meet minimum city health and safety standards.[26]

As housing coordinator for the Union-Sarah Center, Perry organized tenants' groups, led demonstrations against landlords who refused to make needed repairs, and conducted rent strikes when other methods of pressure failed. He learned which complaints struck a resonant chord in the neighborhood, and he devised tactics capable of bringing people out to meetings and protest actions. Yet he did not let his new position totally define his relationship to direct-action demonstrations or to the civil rights movement. When the St. Louis chapter of the white supremacist Citizens' Council invited Sheriff Jim Clark of Selma, Alabama, to speak in St. Louis on November 20, 1965, Perry and other civil rights activists prepared a special welcome for him.

As Clark made his way into the hall, two hundred demonstrators greeted him with signs protesting his role in the brutal suppression of civil rights marches in his city. When the sheriff began his remarks, demonstrators tried to enter the auditorium. Citizens' Council members rushed to bar them, and police officers had to separate the two groups. Ivory Perry and a white college student active in CORE, Ron Landberg, led the charge into the meeting. Police officers arrested Perry and Landberg for disturbing the peace, and as they took them to jail in a police cruiser, the demonstrators marched and chanted outside the hall. Inside, Sheriff Clark denounced Martin Luther King, Jr., as a man "determined to promote violence at any cost," and he described civil rights demonstrators as "beatniks, misfits, and garbage trying to produce a coffee colored nation."[27]

Ivory Perry drew a sentence of ninety days in jail, his fourth peace-disturbance conviction that year but his first while working for HDC. Although his sentence was reduced on appeal, his conviction could not have pleased people at high levels in the antipoverty program. But at the same time, it served notice to people in the community that employment at HDC would not deter Perry from taking to the streets in protest demonstrations.[28]

While employed at HDC, Perry remained prominent in St. Louis CORE and ACTION. Dorie Ladner became active in the same organizations shortly after moving to St. Louis in 1966, after years of civil rights activism in Mississippi. She recalls that "CORE was the type of organization that I liked. These were young people and old people, people of all age categories and racial groups, who were very active. You had intellectuals, and you had people who didn't have degrees. But they all had a serious commitment." For Ladner, CORE and ACTION provided the means for continuing the resistance to racism she had learned growing up in a black family in the deep South. As she viewed it, "You either fought or you surrendered. You survived or you perished. You had a choice; it was either black or white. You could stay there and not fight. You could stay there and surrender and be humiliated with no self-respect or dignity. I elected to fight." Ladner saw Perry as somebody who waged that same kind of a fight and who did it effectively. "I think a lot of people wanted to disregard him because he didn't have a formal education and his use of the language might not have been as formal as a lot of people would have wanted. But the messages always got across."[29]

By going to Bogalusa, stopping traffic on Highway 40 at the time of the Selma march, and demonstrating against Sheriff Clark, Ivory Perry expressed solidarity with the civil rights movement in the South. But Perry—whose own life had brought him from the plantation to the ghetto—believed that racism in the North created even more problems than it did in the South. White southerners enacted discriminatory laws and openly proclaimed their commitment to white supremacy, but in the process provided a clear and unambiguous target for those determined to bring about change. Perry found that northerners generally spoke in more conciliatory language but still engaged in discriminatory, exploitative, and repressive actions against black people. Thus when Dr. Martin Luther King, Jr.'s open-housing campaign in Chicago in 1966 attempted to address the complex racial problems facing northern cities, his crusade attracted Perry's attention immediately.[30]

King's Southern Christian Leadership Conference (SCLC) sought to mobilize slum dwellers in the North into a disciplined collective movement for change, just as it had done for sharecroppers and laborers in the South. Yet Chicago's landlords, realtors, building inspectors, and

politicians proved to be more elusive targets than bigoted southern sher-
iffs and storekeepers. To further complicate the problems facing SCLC
organizers, northern slum dwellers proved less enthusiastic about direct-action protests than their southern counterparts. Northern blacks
already had the legal right to jobs and education, but had inferior opportunities to obtain them. They had the right to vote, but little to vote for.
Tactics designed to end legal discrimination appeared to have little to
offer those who suffered from an equally oppressive but more indirect
racism.

The SCLC sent out a call for organizers familiar with the problems of
northern ghettos to aid in the Chicago campaign. Excited by King's decision to focus on circumstances confronting black people in the North,
Perry spent his vacation time during the summer of 1966 working with
the SCLC in Chicago. He helped organize tenant groups and he helped
operate public address systems during small marches in neighborhoods
and at a mass rally in Soldier's Field. He marched with the Reverend Dr.
King and his followers through all-white areas like Cicero and Marquette
Park, where they encountered hatred so venomous that Dr. King said that
it exceeded anything that he had seen in Mississippi or Alabama.[31]

The Chicago open-housing campaign won some minor concessions,
but for a variety of reasons failed to capture the imagination of the city
and the nation in the way that previous successful civil rights campaigns
had done. Yet Perry felt that the SCLC and Dr. King had understood
correctly the need for a new direction in the civil rights movement—to
go beyond ending discriminatory laws and to start ending discriminatory practices. Especially in northern industrial cities like Chicago and St.
Louis, civil rights issues transcended legal issues and involved concrete
acts of economic and political oppression ranging from poor housing to
police brutality. Perry felt that the movement had to become more oriented toward what he called the survival issues of jobs, housing, and
health.

When he returned to St. Louis, Ivory Perry found one of those issues
confronting him in a dramatic way. On Saturday night, September 24,
1966, police officers arrested Russell Hayes, a nineteen-year-old black
youth, on suspicion of burglary. According to the police, Hayes made a
suspicious movement and appeared to be reaching into his back pocket
for a gun, so the arresting officers shot and killed him. To support their
contention, the officers produced a tear gas gun they said had been
found in Hayes's back pocket. Three days later, a coroner's report en-

dorsed the officers' version of events, ruling the shooting a "justifiable homicide."[32]

Yet some aspects of the police account raised doubts among citizens. The shooting took place in the courtyard of the police station while Hayes sat in the back seat of a squad car with his wrists cuffed behind his back. Police officers generally searched black suspects thoroughly, and it seemed unlikely that they would fail to notice a tear gas gun in the back pocket of a burglary suspect. The back doors of police cars opened only from the outside and a partition divided the front seats from the back. Many wondered how a young man in the back seat with his hands cuffed behind him could pose a threat to police officers sufficient to make them shoot him at close range.[33]

Remembering Ivory Perry's role at the forefront of demonstrations against police brutality a year earlier, a number of community people asked him what they could do to express their anger. Perry helped plan a march on police headquarters and a demonstration outside the home of the chairman of the board of police commissioners. On September 28, four days after the shooting, another demonstration against the coroner's verdict erupted into violence. At the conclusion of a protest rally, one hundred people roamed through the downtown business district, smashing store windows and damaging parked cars in a violent spree that left ten police officers and two firemen injured. Ivory Perry had no part in the violence, but he understood the anger that lay behind it, and he attempted to channel that anger into political pressure on the police department to secure a change in its policies.[34]

Three weeks after the Hayes shooting, St. Louis police officers killed another suspect, this time a sixteen-year-old white youth named Timothy Walsh. Police spokesmen contended that officers were questioning Walsh inside the police station about a shooting incident when the young man jumped up from his chair, ran through a window, and climbed a fence outside the station. They explained that one of the policemen aimed a shot below the suspect while Walsh stood on top of the fence, but that when Walsh jumped down, the bullet struck him in the back. Perry learned that Timothy Walsh had been enrolled in HDC's Neighborhood Youth Corps program, and he mobilized the resources of HDC to protest the shooting. He paid a visit to the Walsh home. The youth's mother and brother talked about "being poor and having no one to stand up for you and about their anger at people in power," and Perry pledged to help them. They agreed to organize a picket line that night outside the police station, and to work together to demand an investigation of the incident.[35]

His visit to the Walsh home provided Ivory Perry with a rare opportunity. He believed that poor and working-class whites had extensive grievances that never got aired, and that under the right circumstances they might become firm allies of poor and working-class blacks. But in all his organizing, he found white people extraordinarily resistant to cooperation with blacks. "A lot of times I used to go into the white South Side and try to organize. And the first thing they want to know is 'what's this nigger doing at the meeting?' They was hostile over there." White antipoverty workers also noted the difficulties. Mickey Rosen recalls:

We could never establish anything in far south St. Louis. There was quite a bit of racial hostility. . . . People thought the antipoverty program would bring the ghetto with them. I worked in south St. Louis with some black staff in an area that was one of the worst ones over there. It was all white and our social service staff or health staff or whatever were black staff. I recall receiving phone calls at home, hate phone calls, threatening my family if I didn't stop trying to create a revolution and stop trying to mix the races.[36]

Ivory Perry brought thirty demonstrators, most of them blacks, to the Lucas Avenue police station to protest the Walsh shooting. One week later, two groups of marchers—blacks from the North Side and whites from the South Side—converged on police headquarters where the coroner's inquest was being held. Perry led the demonstrators into the hearing room: some carried cardboard coffins with the names of Walsh and Hayes on them; others held signs reading, "The Police Are Hired to Protect, Not to Shoot." When the coroner declared the shooting a justifiable homicide, Walsh's father pointed to an off-center clock on the wall and said bitterly, "Even the clock is crooked."[37]

From the inquest, the integrated group of marchers accompanied the Walsh family to a City Hall meeting with Mayor A. J. Cervantes. The mayor expressed his regret over the shootings of Walsh and Hayes and threw his support behind moderate proposals to revise police procedures about fleeing suspects. Both St. Louis daily newspapers editorialized about the need for better relations between the police department and the poor, and at least for a time after this demonstration the police did act with more restraint. Perhaps more significantly, for the first time in recent memory, a civil rights issue in St. Louis united poor whites and poor blacks in a common political protest action.[38]

Perry used his position at HDC to respond to a variety of challenges to the interests of poor people. In March 1967, the U.S. Chamber of Commerce printed an article in their national magazine titled "We Can Get Jobs for Anyone." The article blamed unemployment on the laziness of the poor, and boasted that the chamber could find employment for anyone willing to work. Ivory Perry gathered fifteen unemployed black and white workers and called a press conference, challenging the chamber, Mayor Cervantes, and the press to find jobs for them. Cervantes promised to help, but although the men all expressed willingness to work, prospective employers concluded that they lacked the skills or work experience necessary to fill vacant positions, and they hired none of them. Five months later, the city secured a large federal grant to train the hardcore unemployed, and Perry made sure that the fifteen men would be among those benefiting from that training.[39]

Throughout 1966 and 1967, Ivory Perry used his base at the Union-Sarah Gateway Center as way of intervening in countless disputes and struggles affecting poor people. Housing issues formed the core of his concerns and he instigated a variety of actions designed to address the housing crisis facing poor people. In 1966 he organized the Metropolitan Tenants Organization (MTO) in St. Louis to unite tenants in slum housing in a common effort to secure better housing at affordable rents. The MTO staged Missouri's first rent strike that year, and it encouraged people to think of housing as a community issue rather than a private problem.

On May 8, 1967, Ivory Perry attacked urban renewal as the cause of many housing problems in St. Louis when he testified before the National Commission on Urban Problems. After sitting through optimistic descriptions of St. Louis's urban renewal record by the mayor, civic leaders, and distinguished social scientists, Ivory Perry took the stand and told the commission simply and directly, "This urban renewal is Negro removal. They are knocking down the houses and they have no place to relocate the families. These people can not take too much more." Perry's description contradicted all the previous testimony and it dissented from the assessments of urban renewal presented by architects, urban planners, social scientists, and other traditional intellectuals. But it reflected the things he had learned from daily contact with poor people and from his own research, and he felt confident that he was right and the experts were wrong.[40]

Issues like unemployment, police brutality, and substandard housing occupied the bulk of Ivory Perry's attention at HDC, and those very issues became the focus of the national civil rights movement as well. In late 1967, Dr. King announced a "poor people's movement" to march on Washington the next spring to demand jobs and justice for the poor. Perry became one of the movement's coordinators in St. Louis, using his experience and contacts to mobilize its natural constituency. He was working on that project when he heard over the radio that Dr. King had been shot. "I just went to pieces," he recalls. "I couldn't believe it. I cried. This was our leader, the only black leader I know of, and someone done killed him. It looked like we were gonna go down the road of destruction, but I still didn't want to get violent."[41]

To prevent destruction and violence, Perry stayed up all night long, talking to people on the streets in an attempt to channel their rage into something constructive. He asked storeowners in the ghetto to close their doors in honor of Dr. King, but most refused—at least until reports of riots in black ghettos all across the country convinced them of the dangers of remaining open. After hours of tedious negotiations, Perry and other civil rights activists persuaded storeowners to close in honor of Dr. King, at least for one day.[42]

No riot took place in St. Louis. Yet in helping to spare the city, Ivory Perry failed to protect himself. He had been under enormous pressures for hours, without sleep, and the shock of King's assassination led to a nervous collapse. "They say I had a nervous breakdown," he says about that day, but adds regretfully, "I don't remember." He does remember going without sleep for two days, trying to deal with the horror of King's death, and thinking about the possibility that it might set off a race war in America. He also remembers his hallucination. "I got home about nine-thirty or ten, and I decided I wanted to use the bathroom. I went up there, and I could hear some voices, and I could see his picture [Dr. King] and Malcolm's picture [Malcolm X], and they said some things and I told my wife about it."[43]

Perry believed that Dr. King and Malcolm X were talking to him, demanding that he carry on the struggle that took their lives. Anna Cox remembers the pain of that day. "We were hurt," she says about the assassination. "Gosh, it was like losing a member of the family."[44] Late into the night Perry ranted about "what he had to do." When he went back upstairs where he kept a gun, Cox called Kathen Wright. She tried to calm her brother, and alerted the police and Perry's landlord that there might be trouble. When the police officers arrived at four in the morning they convinced Ivory that he needed a rest in the hospital. Doctors diagnosed him as manic depressive and kept him in the hospital for about a month. On Sunday morning, April 8, when St. Louisans staged a memorial march in honor of Dr. King, Ivory Perry could participate only by watching the procession as it passed beneath the window of his hospital room.[45]

Anna Cox understood the pressures that helped precipitate his collapse.

> Ivory had been under a lot of pressure, because sometimes he would feel like "Well, what am I doing? All these things I've done and they were supposed to make things better, and there are still people out there who will take a life, take the life of Dr. King? I mean, what am I doing that's not reaching those kind of people?"

She also felt that the intensity of his activism made it easy for her husband to lose perspective.

> He had been on this high of activity. Ivory had this driving force—he was going to change the whole world, he was going to do it or be damned, because things were not right. And he felt he had been called to make things right. . . . He got to the point where he couldn't eat, his whole conversation was civil rights.[46]

Father John Shocklee knew Ivory Perry well at the time of King's murder and recognized the extraordinary pressures on him. "Ivory was not a mean guy," Shocklee recalls; "he got harmed, people hurt him more than he hurt anybody else, I'll tell you that." As an organizer and activist, Perry repeatedly found himself in circumstances that made it possible for him to get hurt. People in power blamed him for calling attention to social problems and "stirring up" the poor; poor people held him responsible when his tactics failed to bring positive results. "He paid the price," Shocklee says. "It was very hard just day after day being attacked and defending yourself, pushing a cause—that would take anybody, I don't care how sound your mind is, you will have a breakdown. The frustration, overwork, fatigue, you break down for a while." While aspects of his life history obviously made Perry a candidate for a nervous breakdown, the pressures of activism clearly contributed to his emotional problems. "I paid dearly for what I did," Perry concedes, "paid in blood and sweat and my nerves."[47]

Pearlie Evans felt that working in the antipoverty program had something to do with Ivory Perry's mental breakdown.

> He had traumatic experiences at HDC. It may have been too much too fast. He had been kind of a street guy who wanted to become a professional. He wanted to do something to contribute. I had great respect for that. But despite his great desire to be a professional, he didn't get much guidance. All of a sudden he was wearing a suit and carrying a briefcase and being told to get to it.

Evans also felt that Perry's all-consuming involvement in his work hurt him in the long run. "It is not exciting to work with the poor," she explains. "It is just a job. Ivory did an excellent job, but he'd be furious and hurt if poor people didn't take some initiative after all he had done for them. He had a romanticism about situations that have very little romantic about them."[48]

Yet the pressures that drove Perry to a nervous breakdown emanated from more than his personal psychological makeup and the pressures of political activism. They stemmed, at least in part, from the specific contradictions built into trying to function as an organic intellectual within the context of the War on Poverty. Organizers like Ivory Perry had to deal with the consequences of conflicting attitudes among Americans about poverty and its causes that imposed in-built constraints on antipoverty work. The federal effort to combat poverty in America enabled Ivory Perry to emerge as an organic intellectual, to secure an economic base and a receptive constituency for direct action protests. But it also trapped him in the contradictions of American politics, imposing significant limits on his attempts to build a coalition capable of solving the problems of his community.

In 1964, President Lyndon Johnson called on Americans to wage a campaign for the elimination of poverty as part of his agenda of building a Great Society. Congress translated that ambition into action on August 20, 1964, when it established the Office of Economic Opportunity (OEO) to supervise programs intended to ameliorate the living conditions of the more than 40 million poor people in America. Yet public opinion contained deeply ambivalent feelings about poverty that constrained the efforts of the OEO from the start.[49]

A Gallup poll taken in March 1964 showed that 83 percent of Americans felt that poverty would never be eliminated in the United States. Thirty-three percent claimed that poor people brought misery on themselves through lack of effort, 29 percent blamed circumstances beyond their control, and 32 percent said that laziness and outside circumstances bore equal responsibility for the plight of the poor. Most Americans supported efforts to help individuals victimized by external conditions, but stereotypes about the poor as indolent and immoral worked against a concerted national commitment to eradicate the systemic causes of poverty. Another poll, conducted in October 1964, disclosed that 68 percent of respondents supported government action to guarantee adequate food and shelter to all, but 64 percent also agreed that "welfare and relief make people lazy."[50]

The unprecedented economic expansion and general prosperity that followed World War II added to public confusion about poverty. Increases in the gross national product and declining levels of unemployment brought extraordinary material gains to working-class and middle-class families between 1947 and 1962, but they did little to alter the distribution of wealth in America. The bottom fifth of income earners received 5 percent of the total income in 1947, but by 1962 only 4.6 percent. In 1947, the lowest two-fifths of income earners accounted for 16 percent of national income, but for only 15.5 percent in 1962. In contrast, the wealthiest fifth of income earners received a steady 46 percent of national income throughout the period. While the percentage of Americans living in poverty declined gradually over that decade and a half, the emergence of a "new hard-core" poor population—minority groups, female-headed households, and the elderly—coupled with the rising expectations engendered by economic growth kept poverty a real and potentially explosive social issue.[51]

A large part of the public believed that individuals who remained poor in such a wealthy country had to have internal character failings that kept them from the rewards of economic growth. Yet structural changes in the economy clearly provided an important variable in determining who would be among the poor. Those who entered the work force during and immediately after World War II, and who kept their jobs in the postwar era, benefited from the high wages and full production during wartime and postwar expansion, and they also derived the most benefit from government programs like FHA loans and the GI Bill. Conversely, those workers displaced from rural labor by mechanization, those who arrived in industrial cities too late to become part of political machines in control of patronage jobs, or those who had been expelled from high-paying jobs after the war (especially women and blacks) had a greater likelihood of being poor.[52]

Structural factors clearly played the dominant role in black poverty during the postwar years. At a time when white unemployment hovered between 3 and 6 percent, black unemployment stayed above 10 percent. A survey of selected census tracts in northern ghetto areas in 1960 showed black unemployment ranging from 23 to 41 percent. Black workers came to industrial cities at a time when automation reduced rather than expanded the number of production jobs, when unions and political machines dominated by other ethnic groups dispensed political patronage positions, and when capital flight and deindustrialization began to transform centers of high-paying industrial labor to centers of low-paying service work. Public and private home loan policies denied blacks access to expanding suburbs, while urban renewal programs built up central business districts at the expense of black homeowners and renters. Structural factors explained most of the causes for poverty among whites as well. Trapped in declining rural areas or competing with blacks for unskilled positions in decaying cities, poor whites faced historical and economic transformations similar to those facing many blacks. Sixty percent of poor people could not compete in the labor market because of their age or disabilities, and almost half of the households headed by female or elderly wage earners lived in poverty in the early 1960s. Whatever the quality of their internal moral resources, most poor people faced deprivation because of the nature of jobs open to them in an expanding economy with an inequitable distribution of wealth.[53]

Yet neither the dominant American ideology nor the prevailing American political culture could address these structural inequities. Transfer payments or economic reorganization might have ended poverty, but both demanded sacrifices from the nonpoor. It was easier to blame the victims of this system—the poor people themselves—than to undertake the expense of guaranteed annual income or full-employment policies. A program of self-help aimed at changing the poor themselves by inculcating them with middle-class values required no prohibitive expense, and at the same time helped maintain the fiction that poverty stemmed from the character deficiencies among the impoverished.

Consequently, the War on Poverty emerged as a confused mixture of programs—education, job training, and citizenship instruction, most of which helped prepare poor people for opportunities that did not exist. Low-income people certainly needed literacy, marketable skills, and access to political channels, but without major expenditures on housing, health, transportation, and employment opportunities, the antipoverty program could do little more than raise false hopes for most of the poor.

Even as meliorative self-help, the program spent too little to realize even its own modest goals. Between 1965 and 1970, the Office of Economic Opportunity received only 1.5 percent of the federal budget, a figure amounting to one third of 1 percent of the gross national product. While still large in dollar amounts (federal spending on the poor increased from $12 billion to $27 billion in six years, although the War on Poverty itself received only about $1.7 billion per year between 1965 and 1970), spending on the War on Poverty did not even exceed the amount of money the poor paid in taxes, much less approach the size of the massive subsidies and incentives given to middle-class and wealthy citizens through pensions, investment credits, Social Security, or the home mortgage deduction. Had the money spent on poor people during the War on Poverty been parceled out as cash grants, each poor person in America would have received only $50 to $70 per year. As it was, most of the aid came in the form of federal payment for services that actually enriched doctors, school districts, and realtors more than the poor.[54]

In retrospect, the inadequacies of the War on Poverty raise questions about how the program came into existence at all. Certainly journalistic exposés like Edward R. Murrow's television documentary "Harvest of Shame" and Michael Harrington's book *The Other America* directed the nation's attention toward the persistence of poverty in an affluent economy. Coupled with Cold War pressures that made any failure of the American system an apparent de facto propaganda victory for the Soviet Union, these accounts mobilized public opinion on behalf of the poor.[55] Yet pragmatic political considerations also lay behind the antipoverty program.

Growing Republican voting strength in the South and West threatened traditional electoral support for the Democratic party, and made the Kennedy administration eager to devise programs that would mobilize potential Democratic voters in the rural South and industrial North. Challenges from the civil rights movement and the outbreak of urban riots made government officials sensitive to potential criticisms from the margins of society and posed the spector of a mass movement independent of the control mechanisms of the New Deal coalition. A concerted government program to aid the poor might preempt some of the more radical tendencies of the civil rights movement by drawing activists into government positions where change could be regulated and monitored in ways that prevented radical disruption. Finally, the national Democratic party and pro-growth coalitions coalesced around Democratic big-city mayors depended on an electoral coalition that included poor and black people, and the War on Poverty seemed to offer a vehicle for strengthening those ties.[56]

The diverse political motivations behind the antipoverty program meant that it could succeed in the eyes of some of its proponents, even if it did nothing to improve the lot of the poor. Yet the measure also created an enhanced opportunity structure for activists and organic intellectuals active in oppositional movements. Social service professionals, civil rights activists, community organizers, and traditional and organic intellectuals viewed the War on Poverty as a vehicle for social change. They understood the limits imposed on OEO by politics, but they also felt that the larger social movement emerging out of the ferment of civil rights activity could exert pressures of its own to turn the antipoverty effort in a more radical direction.

Politicians and social reformers found common, if shaky, ground in the program's legal mandate to encourage the maximum feasible participation of the poor in OEO activities. Historian Allen J. Matusow alleges that crafty social scientists slipped the term "maximum feasible participation" past uncomprehending bureaucrats and politicians as a way of insinuating their radical agenda into an essentially reformist program, but the phrase had something to offer the old-line politicians and bureaucrats as well.[57] For politicians, maximum feasible participation held out the promise of fighting poverty at bargain rates by pawning off a lot of antipoverty activity on volunteer boards and committees. Such participation drew poor people into federally funded but locally controlled patronage networks without yielding to them control of existing patronage institutions like school boards, unions, welfare systems, police boards, and housing authorities. In addition, "community" representatives from business, labor, and government also served on OEO boards under the aegis of localism, and they acted as moderating influences on any radical tendencies voiced by the poor themselves.[58]

For their part, the social service professionals and activists that staffed local agencies saw a different potential in maximum feasible participation. In their view, antipoverty organizations could start poor people talking about their problems and begin drawing them into political activism. Once initiated, that process of involvement might break the hold that fear and pessimism had on the poor, a hold that often discouraged aggrieved groups from joining social movements. Maximum feasible participation might mobilize the poor to action, educate them about who really held economic and political power, and alert them to the possibilities of social contestation as a cure for their problems.

In addition, the very delicate national and local coalitions that backed the War on Poverty revealed serious divisions in the rest of the society— between Democrats and Republicans, between northerners and southerners, between competing economic interests. If politicians and pro-growth businessmen needed the votes of poor people for their own purposes, they might be susceptible to grass-roots pressure for concessions that aided the poor. If the credibility of the antipoverty program depended upon coopting and calming potentially disruptive elements, the threat of disruption might win desired advances. In this way, those in the historical bloc coalescing around the War on Poverty felt that their new-found opportunity had been generated from within, that it was a fruit of the civil rights struggle and its ability to focus attention on the living conditions of ghetto blacks. Consequently, they sought to accelerate the pressure to consolidate past gains and to pursue new ones.

Ivory Perry stepped into the middle of this complicated historical battle when he became housing coordinator for the Human Development Corporation at Union-Sarah. His interpretation of "maximum feasible participation" of the poor included rent strikes, obstructive demonstrations, and a fusing of the antipoverty program with the civil rights movement. He assumed that disruption worked in his favor, that the poor would make gains only when they became enough of a nuisance, or enough of a threat, to make people in power decide that it was less expensive to meet their demands than to continue to resist them.[59]

Understandably enough, Perry's activist stance made him a focal point of controversy within HDC. Landlords, employers, and realtors wondered why their tax dollars went to finance obstructive demonstrations against them and their way of doing business. Politicians questioned the wisdom of a federal program that mobilized poor people around the shortcomings of municipal building inspectors or the failings of the police review process. Businessmen willing to tolerate an antipoverty program as a necessary antidote to riots and disruptive protests failed to see why the Human Development Corporation would support an individual who constantly appeared at the forefront of explosive confrontations.[60]

Even within the agency itself, many felt that Ivory Perry's activities jeopardized their own efforts. With hundreds of jobs and a $35 million budget at stake, HDC could ill afford powerful enemies, but Perry seemed to specialize in tactics that antagonized its enemies. While serving as director of HDC, Clyde Cahill often received requests from both inside and outside the agency to fire Perry, but he refused to go along with them. Cahill did not want outside pressure to determine personnel decisions within the organization; he also felt that Perry served a useful function, alerting everyone to real grievances that might otherwise be ignored.[61]

Yet Cahill had serious disagreements with Perry over tactics and strategy. From his perspective as an administrator, the poor needed allies from business, government, and labor; aggressive confrontations turned some of these potential friends into enemies. It seemed to Cahill that Ivory Perry relied too much on emotion and impatience; that it was one thing to organize marches and demonstrations, but quite another to fashion long-range solutions to structural social problems. Cahill favored a more disciplined approach, acting in structured steps to enable the poor to win control over resources. He feared that the antagonisms stirred up by militant direct action might actually retard progress by isolating the poor from potential friends and the resources they controlled. For his part, Perry felt that his constituents had no time to wait for phased-in solutions, that they needed help immediately. In addition, he mistrusted the levels of bureaucracy implicit in Cahill's structured approach because he feared that they would take on an institutional life of their own and lose contact with the constituency they presumably served.[62]

Disagreements with Perry over strategy and tactics did not prevent Cahill from seeing that Perry often was an object of unfair criticism and abuse. He remembers that people outside the ghetto saw Perry as half crazy and totally threatening, that he became a symbol of all their fears about the social ferment of the day. "He became the target," Cahill recalls; "it was easy for the newspapers to paint him as an ogre."[63] Rather than viewing him as a spokesman who channeled the resentment and rage of aggrieved people into constructive protest, many important St. Louisans saw Ivory Perry as the source of social unrest, a man devoted to making trouble for its own sake.

Hated outside his community and barraged by constant requests for assistance from within it, Perry exposed himself to extraordinary pressures working for HDC. The very perceptions and actions that won him credibility within his community made him enemies outside of it. The very actions that to him held the most promise for ending poverty often threatened the institutional survival of the antipoverty program itself. Had he been willing to take a more moderate and conciliatory approach, he might have made fewer enemies, but also fewer friends. By engaging in confontational direct-action protests, Ivory Perry stretched the internal contradictions of the War on Poverty to the breaking point. Every time he took to the streets, every time he organized actions against realtors, building inspectors, or the police, he made a statement about poverty and its causes.

His actions proceeded from the assumption that an unjust system oppressed the poor, and from the belief that specific individuals and institutions profited from poverty. He rejected the idea of poverty as a paradox, as an ironic juxtaposition of deprivation within an affluent society. Instead, he argued for a causal relationship: some people remained poor because the structural systemic workings of the economy benefited the rich. By taking direct action he challenged the idea that poverty stemmed from the character flaws of the poor; he placed the blame instead on the inequitable distribution of wealth and opportunity in American society. In the process, he exposed the deep antagonisms simmering beneath the surface harmony within the coalition supporting the antipoverty program.

More often than not, he found himself the focal point of those antagonisms. But he felt that he had no choice. His own actions and views were not entirely his own. His position at HDC and his influence in the community depended upon reflecting back to the community its own submerged views. The awkward coalition behind the dominant strain of the antipoverty effort handed him an impossible task—to fight poverty without seriously disrupting the vested interests of the status quo. But the oppositional coalition, the historical bloc coalesced around the War on Poverty, also exerted pressure on him, pressure to represent the interests and ideas of the poor themselves.[64]

The nervous breakdown that Ivory Perry suffered when Martin Luther King was killed had many causes. Long-standing personal psychological problems, overwork, fatigue, and the demands of activism all played a part. But the structural tensions built into the role of organic intellectual in the antipoverty program trapped him inside some painful contradictions that also contributed to his collapse. As a social activist, he worked long hours trying to persuade people that their personal problems had structural and systemic causes. Much to his pain, he found that was true of him as well one April night when the accumulated tensions and frustrations of his life became too great to endure. Had he let himself be controlled by people in power, his stint at the antipoverty agency would have undercut his credibility and ended his militancy. But because social contestation could not easily be orchestrated from above, because the War on Poverty existed as the contested terrain of competing constituencies, Perry found a way to survive as a militant and as an organic intellectual.

AFTER HIS nervous breakdown, Ivory Perry remained in the hospital for about a month. He knew that he had subjected himself to too much tension and too much fatigue in the preceding months, but he could not convince himself to slow down. He could not imagine quitting the struggle while so many important things remained to be accomplished. "If you truly devoted, that's your life," he remembers thinking at the time. "You be looking for better things, a better life like other people, a nice house, a nice car, a nice income—but when you devoted, you give up all that."[65] That philosophy compelled him to resume his community organizing shortly after his release from the hospital. Perry continued to work on the Poor People's March in an effort to carry on Dr. King's vision of a broad-based multiracial coalition to press for economic and social justice. Marchers from all across the country made their way to Washington, stopping along the way to publicize their cause and pick up new recruits.

In St. Louis, Perry led a committee seeking a campsite for the Poor People's March on federally owned park land underneath the Gateway Arch. He selected that site because it had been a slave market years ago and because he felt that focusing attention on the arch would enable the marchers to "show how the city has progressed in two hundred years and how the black people have not." He lost that fight, but succeeded in obtaining camping space for the march elsewhere in the city. In midsummer, Perry welcomed the Poor People's March to town with a mass rally of poor people and their allies.[66]

Resuming his work with the Human Development Corporation, Perry once again focused on the problems of slum housing. His campaigns among tenants led to rent strikes, court battles, and confrontations against realtors over conditions in the slums. Those battles would take on added significance in 1969 when tenants in St. Louis public housing projects staged a nine-month rent strike to win basic reforms in federal and local housing policies. Not surprisingly, Ivory Perry's strategy, tactics, analysis, and organizational skills played an important role in that strike, helping to win immediate, tangible victories for one of the poorest and most oppressed sections of the community.

CHAPTER 6

The Rent Strike: Housing Issues and
Social Protest

In the summer of 1968, Ivory Perry returned to his job at Human Development Corporation and resumed his activism in the community. Housing issues provided the core of his concerns, and he spent long hours organizing tenants' groups and pressuring city officials to enforce the municipal building codes. Racial discrimination and poverty left black people in St. Louis with limited housing options, while inflation and rising utility costs further undermined the ability of the poor to pay for adequate shelter. Perry sensed a genuine crisis brewing over housing issues, and it did not surprise him when a citywide rent strike by public-housing tenants made the shelter needs of the poor the most volatile public issue in St. Louis in 1969.[1]

"You have to know what you're talking about when you're out organizing in the community," Perry maintains; "you got to be speaking to the real things that are bothering people." To do his job well he had to pay attention to their lives, to listen carefully to things they told him, and to come back to them with information that spoke to their most pressing needs and concerns. "I did a lot of research," he remembers. "If a building caused trouble for the tenants, I looked up who owned it, and when they bought it, and what permits had been issued on it."[2] His research helped Perry understand how profits were made from slum housing, but it also alerted him to patterns that went beyond the manipulations of individual landlords, that stemmed from government policies about urban renewal and public housing.

Ivory Perry knew about the dreadful living conditions in the inner city firsthand. He had become accustomed to seeing children sleeping next to walls about to collapse, to landlords who refused to make simple repairs, and to the severe shortage of available housing for families with children. He knew that the city lacked adequate housing for its poor population, and it seemed inescapable to him that the reasons stemmed from the combination of urban renewal programs that knocked down poor people's houses and tax abatement for downtown corporate rede-velopment projects that increased taxes for poor and working-class peo-ple while subsidizing the construction of large office buildings.

He saw how urban renewal projects bulldozed blocks of deteriorated but salvageable housing (780 acres bulldozed in St. Louis between 1950 and 1969 involving the destruction of 33,000 dwelling units) while new construction downtown concentrated on commerical development and luxury housing. Office buildings, light industry, and high-income hous-ing not only failed to add to the local housing stock, but they also all received generous tax breaks that worked a hardship on homeowners called upon to compensate for the resulting decline in city revenues. Faced with high taxes and declining services, homeowners and land-lords fled to the suburbs, often abandoning housing that could no long-er be operated profitably.[3]

Federal law required urban renewal plans to include provisions for relocating those displaced by new construction, but St. Louis authorities did a poor job adhering to that mandate. A General Accounting Office (GAO) report in 1964 charged that piecemeal destruction of St. Louis neighborhoods forced many residents to move out before the land clear-ance authorities were required to take responsibility for resettlement. Even those families designated for relocation often found themselves moved to substandard housing or offered no relocation possibilities at all. A GAO spot check of relocation sites deemed standard by the St. Louis Land Clearance and Redevelopment Authority found that 60 per-cent actually deserved a rating of substandard.[4] The city and its defend-ers in the academic world challenged the GAO report, but Perry believed it reflected the things he had witnessed firsthand. Similarly, his experi-ences with public housing made him distrustful of its practical capacity to serve the housing needs of the poor.

In theory, public housing projects could have provided the dislocated poor with shelter, but a variety of constraints doomed their operation from the start. Federal officials attempted to calm the fears of private builders by making sure that public housing would not compete with the apartments offered on the private market, and that it would not drain off surplus capital that might be better used in profit-making ven-tures. Consequently, government regulations required local housing au-thorities to meet operating expenses out of current rents, leaving public housing with inadequate capital reserves and insufficient maintenance budgets. Expensive building and land acquisition costs, aided and abetted by local corruption, saddled public housing projects with heavy debts. Undesirable locations made public housing a poor competitor with private-sector housing. In addition, requirements that tenants pay at least 20 percent of their adjusted income for rent discouraged some of the more solvent tenants, who could find more economical housing on the private market, leaving public housing projects populated by those with the least resources and the greatest needs for subsidy.[5]

Federal home loan policies further compounded the problem by encouraging construction of single-family suburban homes while neglecting preservation and renovation of older multi-family dwellings in central cities. As Senator Joseph Clark of Pennsylvania pointed out in 1966 during hearings on the federal role in urban affairs, programs like the Federal Housing Agency and Veterans Administration loans

> worked out to be a subsidy for the suburb. There was no counter-vailing program which would have induced moderate and high-income families to remain in the cities. They have to finance their homes almost entirely by conventional mortgages without any government guarantee. As a result, there are few middle-income families indeed who can afford the kind of housing they want within the city limits.

Those policies increased the supply of housing for whites in segregated suburbs while diminishing the number of dwellings available to blacks because those homes tended to be in central city areas denied adequate credit support.[6]

For people living in St. Louis public housing projects in 1969, the accumulated legacy of federal urban renewal and public housing policies made for desperate living conditions. Black families displaced from slums by urban renewal found few relocation opportunities on the private market and consequently flocked into public housing. Inadequate capital reserves for public housing meant high rents and poor maintenance. The housing authority had to raise rents to meet operating costs and to subsidize the increasingly indigent population living in the projects. Officials of the St. Louis Housing and Land Clearance Authority admitted as early as 1966 that they faced "a definite breakdown in the relationship between management and tenants" in public housing. Increased utility costs and declining revenues forced the authority to raise rents in 1967, causing tenants from two North Side projects to warn the mayor that low-income families in public housing faced "an increasingly hopeless situation." Another hike in electric utility costs in 1968 led to the rent increases that compelled tenants to strike in 1969.[7]

On February 3, 1969, tenants at the Carr Square Village housing project began a rent strike against the St. Louis housing authority. Faced with a series of rent increases that forced one out of every four tenants to pay more than 50 percent of income for rent, and worked almost as severe hardships on many others, the tenants vowed to withhold rental payments until they secured rent reductions, repairs and maintenance improvements, action to stop crime in project buildings, and increased tenant involvement in public housing management. Soon tenants from the other six housing projects in St. Louis joined the strike. For nine months, tenants and the housing authority waged a bitter struggle marked by threats and intimidation that depleted the resources of both sides. What began as a localized protest by the poorest and least influential segment of the city's population grew into a major dispute that shook the local power structure and eventually involved leaders of all major interest groups in the final settlement.[8]

The Reverend Buck Jones organized the strike at Carr Square Village. A community organizer for the United Church of Christ's Plymouth House settlement near the projects, Jones provided leadership during the early stages of the dispute, and remained an important spokesman even after tenants took over the direction of the struggle themselves. Jones expressly rejected the traditional role of religious ministries in settlement houses, dismissing them as "soup kitchen ministries" that treated the symptoms of poverty while ignoring its causes. Instead, he favored the "willful use of conflict," mobilizing the poor to demand concessions from those with money and power. The rent strike provided an opportunity for that kind of conflict. It violated Missouri law, exposed tenants to the risk of eviction, and defied the authority of elected officials. But if the tenants could organize themselves into a disciplined power bloc, Jones believed that they could bring about meaningful improvements in their living conditions.[9]

Tenants emerged as leaders of strike activities in each of the projects, and women with experience in civil rights and welfare reform organizations played a particularly prominent role. Jean King from the Webbe-Darst projects on the city's South Side served as chairman of the City Wide Strike Committee, drawing on the expertise she had acquired as a leader in the local chapter of the National Welfare Rights Organization. Loretta Hall led the strike in Carr Square Village, helped by the sophisticated sense of strategy she learned in the civil rights movement as an activist with CORE. These tenants, and others like them, did the hard work of persuading their neighbors to withhold rents from the housing authority and to pay them instead into an escrow account. In February 15 percent of all tenants contributed to that account; by October participation reached 35 percent. Many tenants paid no rent at all, and at no point did a majority of the tenants pay into the escrow account. Yet the strikers enjoyed widespread support and faced almost no opposition from other tenants. They became the uncontested representatives of the tenants, both during and after the strike.[10]

Ivory Perry knew many of the rent strikers well. He had worked with Jean King in building the National Welfare Rights Organization chapter in St. Louis, and he knew Loretta Hall from their days together in CORE. Supporting the rent strikers' demands while respecting their internal organization and leadership, Perry searched for ways to mobilize broad community support behind them. "I thought the rent strike was a good idea," Perry recalls, "not just for the people in public housing, but for all tenants. Once the public's attention got focused on housing problems, it had to help people in all kinds of low income housing. The problem was how to focus more attention on their demands and get them more leverage."[11]

During the first few weeks of the strike, Perry went to each of St. Louis's militant black organizations to line them up behind the strikers. In March he called a press conference at an inner-city community center to announce that CORE, the Black Liberators, the Zulu 1000s, the Black Nationalists, and ACTION all endorsed the rent strike. Coming from groups better known for paramilitary organization and armed self-defense than for melioristic reform, that endorsement served to embolden the tenants, worry city officials, and increase the negotiating leverage of the strikers.[12]

At the same time, Perry stepped up his efforts with the Metropolitan Tenants Organization (MTO) to pressure landlords for reforms in private housing. Affiliated with the National Tenants Organization, which grew out of CORE-sponsored rent strikes in New York City in the mid-1960s, the MTO kept housing issues in the forefront of public attention during the rent strike. It also attempted to call attention to the relationship between the problems of public housing and the pervasive slum conditions in much inner-city private housing. MTO argued that only an adequate supply of affordable decent housing could lessen the pressures facing public housing.[13]

But while its formal positions addressed the long-range housing issues confronting the city, MTO's immediate focus was on direct action in support of the rent strike. "We believe in direct action," Perry proclaims in describing the goals of MTO. "When we sit around and discuss a problem, we don't just discuss it—we take action to alleviate the problem."[14]

In response to the rent strike, MTO resorted to direct action repeatedly. When an officer of the National Association of Real Estate Boards spoke to a group of St. Louis realtors in April, Perry brought demonstrators from MTO to the meeting. As twenty pickets paraded outside, he presented the realtors with a list of demands that included support for laws forcing landlords to make needed repairs and for statutes allowing tenants to stage rent strikes in public and private housing.[15] Perry also kept a watchful eye on rent-strike negotiations between city officials and public housing tenants. When Mayor Cervantes asked representatives of a prominent businessmen's organization to lobby the Department of Housing and Urban Development for funds to settle the rent strike, tenants feared a deal that would bypass their demands. To prevent that, Perry and a dozen demonstrators from MTO and ACTION greeted the business delegation at the airport with signs that accused them of siding with the housing authority and of seeking to settle the strike without involving the tenants in the final settlement. Embarrassed by the resulting publicity, and unable to demonstrate solid community backing for their initiative to HUD, the businessmen returned to St. Louis from Washington empty-handed. They turned the burdens of negotiating a settlement back to the housing authority and the tenants.[16]

Ivory Perry began to show up at sessions of the St. Louis housing court with MTO picketers to challenge judges who refused to require slum landlords to bring their buildings up to code. At the same time, he organized two highly publicized rent strikes in private housing, bringing together tenants from different buildings with the same landlord. He represented these tenants in negotiations for lower rents and improved building maintenance, serving notice to other slumlords that the same thing might happen to them.

Most individual landlords had relatively few tenants. The public housing rent strike held center stage because it involved thousands of tenants whose demands called into question a whole series of public policy decisions about land use and housing issues.[17] Perry and the rent strikers understood the importance of the dispute in public housing for the future of their city, and they worked hard to publicize their complaints among the community at large. The legitimacy of their demands won sympathy from people who recognized that the tenants simply could not afford to pay the rents demanded by the housing authority and still feed their families. In addition, fears of urban insurrection and mass violence gave civic leaders a distinct interest in resolving the dispute peacefully. Tenants and their supporters took advantage of the factors in their favor in an effort to build a coalition powerful enough to secure their objectives.

The president of the St. Louis board of aldermen, a Republican and a major opponent of the city's Democratic party establishment, used the rent strike to chide his opponents, contrasting the deprivation of the strikers with the riches expended on downtown urban redevelopment projects. In a speech to the Downtown Rotary Club early in May he argued that "there is a need for brotherhood and sharing that should overshadow, for the moment at least, a desire for new buildings and malls, tourist attractions and bric-a-brac." In mid-May, the Catholic archdiocese announced its support for the rent strike in response to a challenge by civil rights groups. Two weeks later, a Baptist clergyman wrote to the mayor:

> I have observed over the years that it is hard for a leader to resist
> indefinitely the moral and spiritual impulses of the people and from
> my observation for the past several months, it seems like the senti-
> ment of the people is sympathetic toward the rent strikers. My ad-
> vise [sic] to you is to heed the impulse of the people.[18]

Later that week, powerful local labor leader Harold Gibbons of the Teamsters Union added his voice to those urging the mayor to resolve the strike.

None of these people indicated to the mayor where he could get the money to meet the housing authority's needs if it rolled back rents, nor did they have any useful suggestions for lessening tensions arising from the strike itself. Up to that point St. Louis had escaped the conflagrations and civil insurrections that demolished central areas in New York, Los Angeles, Newark, Detroit, and other cities. But with black unemployment at 13 percent, and black underemployment at 39 percent, in a

city where 45 percent of the black population lived in substandard housing, few could discount the possibility of violence.

Jean King of the City Wide Strike Committee played on the prospect
of violence in a letter to Mayor Cervantes early in May. Noting the opening of the Spanish Pavilion from the New York World's Fair (which the
mayor brought to St. Louis as a tourist attraction) she observed:

> We the city wide rent strikers of your city would like to congratulate
> you for your interest in everything but the poor people's plight in
> your fine city. However, we also feel that the poor people in your
> city should be congratulated for their fine behavior and nonviolent
> acts all during this time that you have taxed them to death in order
> that you might provide a happy and wealthy life for yourself and
> your henchmen. We wonder why you are playing a game with us. It
> is a very dangerous one you know. We didn't have to plead with you
> and we won't plead any longer.[19]

The mayor could not have been happy with the tone of King's letter,
but he knew that the strikers had valid complaints. In April, Cervantes
received a memo from an aide outlining the problem posed by the rent
strike.

> The dilemma we face is that the tenants are absolutely right when
> they say they cannot feed and clothe their children if they must pay
> the bulk of their small incomes for rent. At the same time, the St.
> Louis Housing Authority is right when it says that its sole source of
> income for the operation of public housing must come from the
> tenants.[20]

Caught between moral suasion and the threat of violence, trapped between public pressure for a settlement and legal barriers to funding public
housing from any source other than rental income, the mayor remained
powerless to end the stalemate.

Ivory Perry stepped up the pressure on the city in late June and early
July when he participated in a series of demonstrations at the St. Louis
Cathedral. Coinciding with a national campaign by black activists seeking "reparations" from American churches for their complicity with centuries of racism, the St. Louis demonstrations concentrated exclusively
on local housing issues.[21] After a month of passing out leaflets before
Sunday-morning services at the cathedral, the demonstrators took more
dramatic action.

Ivory Perry wearing his politics on his vest in 1971. Courtesy of the Collections of the St. Louis Mercantile Library Association.

Ivory Perry and Gene Tournour under the wheels of a police cruiser after a downtown demonstration on December 5, 1963. Courtesy of the *St. Louis Post-Dispatch*.

Ivory Perry at a 1965 demonstration by ACTION protesting newspaper coverage of incidents where police officers shot fleeing suspects. Courtesy of Ivory Perry.

Demonstrators calling for a Christmas boycott of downtown stores march through a department store on December 5, 1963. Courtesy of the *St. Louis Post-Dispatch*.

The Reverend Jesse Jackson and St. Louis politician Bennie Goins campaigning at the Pruitt-Igoe housing project in 1968. Perry (center top) helped bring Jackson to St. Louis. Courtesy of Ivory Perry.

Ivory Perry lies down in front of an automobile to stop traffic during a demonstration against police brutality in St. Louis on September 16, 1965. Courtesy of the Missouri Historical Society.

Ivory Perry and Marvin Moseby handcuffed to a parking meter outside the Laclede Gas Company headquarters on May 13, 1965. Courtesy of the *St. Louis Post-Dispatch*.

Ivory Perry (front right) in CORE picket line outside the federal courthouse in St. Louis protesting the murders of civil rights workers Michael Schwerner, James Chaney, and Andrew Goodman in Mississippi in July 1964. Courtesy of the Missouri Historical Society.

Ivory Perry (front right) in an ACTION picket line charging employment discrimination against black men by the Southwestern Bell Telephone Company in 1965. Courtesy of Ivory Perry.

Ivory Perry and other antipoverty officials bringing hard-core unemployed to meet with Mayor Cervantes on March 25, 1967. Courtesy of the *St. Louis Post-Dispatch*.

Ivory Perry blocks traffic on a highway ramp in St. Louis on March 15, 1965, to call attention to the civil rights struggle in Selma, Alabama. Courtesy of the Collections of the St. Louis Mercantile Library Association.

Ivory Perry demonstrates against newspaper coverage of police shootings of fleeing suspects in 1965. Courtesy of Ivory Perry.

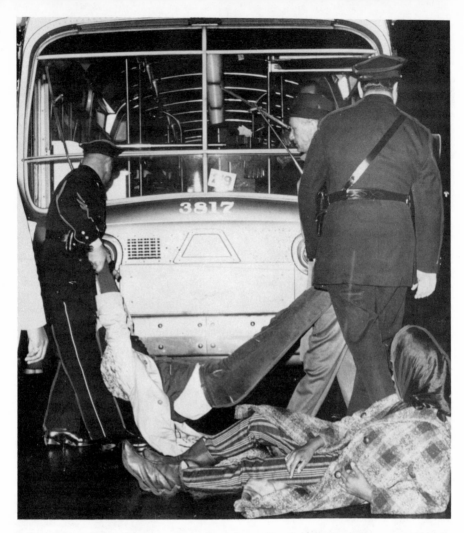

Police officers removing Ivory Perry from beneath a bus during a demonstration in support of the Jefferson Bank protests in St. Louis on November 21, 1963. Courtesy of the Collections of the St. Louis Mercantile Library Association.

On July 6, Ivory Perry and other members of ACTION greeted worshippers at the noon mass with a "black paper" manifesto charging the Roman Catholic archdiocese in St. Louis with owning slum property. By prearrangement, a spokesman for sympathetic parishioners read a statement denouncing racism to the congregation, but before he could finish, shouts and exchanges of insults between demonstrators and church members directed attention to the back of the cathedral. Police officers intervened and arrested some of the demonstrators, including one in uniform similar to that worn by Catholic cardinals except that his robes and hat were black. The demonstrator carried a sign proclaiming that "Carberry [the cardinal of the archdiocese] makes a mockery of the true Church."[22]

Television news accounts and the next day's newspapers carried pictures of the demonstration at the cathedral. One parishioner involved in a scuffle with the demonstrators told a reporter:

> They're trying to start a race riot. That's what they want. That's the communist method—divide and conquer. I saw something on television the other night about American concentration camps. They were wondering what to do with them. I think they should keep them a while and put some of these people in.[23]

Father John Shocklee remembers the demonstration at the cathedral as an effective tactical move. He notes that it called attention to housing conditions in the city in a way that previous efforts had failed to do. "Sometimes you have to shock people into realizing that change is necessary." As to the charges of fomenting a race riot and trying to "divide and conquer," Shocklee observes that the demonstrators "were more patriotic than the people who were benefiting from the system, because they saw the weaknesses of it and were trying to make it perfect."[24]

Like Perry's other direct-action protests over housing issues, the demonstration at the cathedral helped build pressure on the housing authority to settle the strike. When the Department of Housing and Urban Development issued a special report in July supporting the strikers' demands, Mayor Cervantes decided to give in. He announced his willingness to meet all the requests made by the tenants in their February strike statement. To the mayor's shock, the tenants refused to accept his concessions. The strikers had taken great risks and gained a new sense of their own power during the dispute. They believed (correctly) that the mayor lacked access to the finances necessary to meet their demands, and they now wanted tenant management boards running the projects, not just token representation in housing policy decisions. They wanted guarantees against future rent hikes and an autonomous base of power to end what they viewed as the paternalism of the housing authority.[25]

Ivory Perry quickly grasped the significance of the tenants' refusal to end the rent strike. "When it started out, the tenants wanted a little better conditions and a little lower rent. But when they saw how they could make people listen to their demands, they wanted something better," he remembers.[26] Perry realized that issues of power, dignity, and the right to decent housing transcended the original dispute over rent increases. He knew that tenants in private housing throughout the ghetto looked to the rent strikers as an important example of seemingly powerless people making gains. As he talked to the people in the neighborhoods, to displaced victims of urban renewal, to tenants paying high rents for substandard dwellings, to families unable to find adequate shelter on the private market, he sensed a new consciousness about housing issues throughout the community. Once again, he resorted to direct action as a means of translating that consciousness into meaningful pressure for social change.

"I wanted to help the rent strikers and the people out in private housing," he recalls, "but in the MTO we didn't have no money, we didn't have no influence with the politicians—all we had were warm bodies and picket signs. So we used what we had." Throughout the rent strike, the MTO picketed the homes and offices of realtors who refused to maintain their property adequately. Perry led regular protest demonstrations outside City Hall and brought groups of chanting tenants to night court sessions in protest against the light sentences meted out to violators of the municipal housing codes. Early in September, he organized a picket line with some forty demonstrators outside the housing court. They carried signs and chanted slogans about slumlords. One sign taunted "Here comes the Hop! Hop! Hop! Kangaroo Judge."[27]

Late in September, Ivory Perry found an opportunity for his most important intervention in the rent strike. All year he had been building support for the tenants, but his efforts culminated when he secured for St. Louis the annual convention of the National Tenants Organization. St. Louis labor leader Harold Gibbons contributed $5,000 to underwrite the convention, bringing tenant leaders from all over the country to the site of public housing's most volatile dispute. National Tenants Organization president Jesse Gray declared his support for the rent strike and suggested that his organization might consider spreading the strike to public housing in other cities. In a welcoming speech to the delegates, Ivory Perry directed their attention, and that of the national media, to the heightened consciousness about housing issues brought on by the rent strike. Perry declared, "For the first time tenants have organized themselves and are doing something constructive and working toward a solution to our many problems."[28]

Perry's enthusiasm for the rent strike sent an important signal to the housing authority, private realtors, HUD officials, and local business leaders. Their hope that a long strike would discourage and demoralize tenants disappeared. Instead, they faced the prospect of an ever-escalating conflict all across the country. That extraordinary threat added a powerful incentive to efforts by community leaders to end the rent strike before it got completely out of control.

Harold Gibbons used the concerns generated by the strike and exacerbated by the NTO convention to his own advantage. For years he had dreamed of playing a powerful role in local politics like his counterparts from business, and the rent strike provided an opportunity to realize that dream.[29] Gibbons contacted August A. Busch, Jr., the chief executive officer of the Anheuser Busch brewery and the most powerful businessman in St. Louis, with a proposal for ending the strike. Appealing to Busch's sense of civic duty and his fear of civil insurrection, Gibbons proposed an alliance of business, labor, and community leaders to raise additional funds for public housing and to oversee an end to the dispute. With Busch's endorsement and enthusiastic participation, Harold Gibbons convened the first meeting of the Civic Alliance for Housing on October 10. The coalition secured funds for public housing from the Department of Housing and Urban Development and helped negotiate a strike settlement that implemented all the strikers' main demands, including tenant management boards to run some of the projects.

Businessmen supported the coalition largely because of their fear of violence. General Leif J. Sverdrup, one of the most influential business leaders in the city, coaxed Emerson Electric chief executive officer W. R. "Buck" Persons to join the coalition by confiding:

I frankly am not happy about serving on this committee myself. I have neither the time or the inclination for this sort of thing, however I do know it is a damn explosive situation and someone has to do it so I agreed to try it out at least for a time.

Another businessman made a similar point in a letter soliciting continued business support for the coalition after the rent strike ended. International Shoe Company chief executive officer Maurice Chambers wrote:

> The Alliance for Housing relieved the community of a potentially explosive issue when it was able to settle the rent strike, and it appears to have a good chance of going on from there to bring about real improvements in the physical condition of the housing projects and the attitude of the tenants. As businessmen with interests in this area, we certainly want to see something positive done about public housing. Pruitt-Igoe and some of the other projects have been constant sources of violence and social unrest.[30]

Businessmen felt that the settlement avoided violence and helped protect their investments. Harold Gibbons viewed his enhanced reputation as a problem solver and community leader as the key to his future influence over civic affairs. Mayor Cervantes emerged from the strike with his reputation and future political ambitions unscathed, and of course he welcomed the influx of federal money for public housing that the coalition secured. For tenants, the strike resulted in tangible but limited gains. It averted disaster for thousands of families facing homelessness, provoked needed reforms in the operation of public housing, and forced business, labor, and government leaders to come up with funds to improve the living conditions of the poor. Residents of housing projects won lower rents, better maintenance and police protection, and a voice in housing management. The St. Louis dispute helped pressure the U.S. Congress to pass a law limiting rent in public housing to one quarter of the tenant's income, a change that helped public housing residents nationwide.[31]

In St. Louis, tenants' experiences working together to sustain the strike promoted a greater sense of community in public housing and encouraged the development of indigenous leadership among the tenants. Yet within two years, the Civic Alliance for Housing collapsed and most of the chronic problems facing tenants remained unresolved. Without a crisis like the rent strike, businessmen had little interest in the housing problems of the poor, and neither they nor labor and government leaders had devised methods for raising the large sums of money needed to create a decent living environment in public housing. The "willful use of conflict" prescribed by Rev. Buck Jones produced victory for the tenants, but they would have to struggle again and again in the future merely to retain what they had won.[32]

Ivory Perry's role in the rent strike appeared to be small compared to the rent-strike leaders, the mayor, housing authority officials, Harold Gibbons, or businessmen like Busch and Sverdrup. Operating on the periphery of the dispute, he devised no strike strategy, found no money to finance the settlement, and carried no messages between the feuding parties. But his presence acted like a wild card, cautioning all players to realities beyond their control. Ivory Perry's direct-action protests during the rent strike may have seemed like random or desperate bids for attention in the midst of a volatile crisis, but in reality they reflected a sophisticated understanding of the housing crisis in St. Louis and the interests affected by it. Most of all, they reflected the insights of an organic intellectual whose life experiences led him to a refined understanding of urban issues and a determined certainty about how best to apply what he had learned.

BEFORE THE rent strike, Ivory Perry had been intimately involved with the housing grievances of tenants in public and private housing for years. His work as housing chairman for CORE and as an outreach worker for HDC helped tenants articulate their needs and circulate their complaints. But his function in the community served a larger purpose than articulation and circulation of ideas: Ivory Perry's organizing and demonstrating helped poor and black people in St. Louis see their needs as legitimate, and those drawn into his protests provided the cadre organization for other struggles. They engaged in what sociologist Michael Schwartz calls "organizational learning"—a process of struggle in which each stage of contestation creates new resources for the next one. Individuals and groups adapt to events and crises on the basis of immediate needs and interests, but they also draw on the lessons of the past, on the ways their previous encounters with politics educated them about what to do in the present.

One example of this "organizational learning" came in the prominence of welfare rights activists in the St. Louis public housing rent strike. In 1967, Perry had traveled to Chicago to attend the founding convention of the National Welfare Rights Organization (NWRO), and on his return to St. Louis he helped establish the local chapter. Many of the women who assumed important leadership roles in the rent strike got their first taste of political activism in the NWRO, and the organization played an important role in mobilizing the poor and predisposing them for the kinds of contestation manifested in the rent strike. The St. Louis NWRO concentrated on winning increased benefits for welfare recipients, securing clothing allowances for schoolchildren, and arranging extended-payment plans to lessen the burden of high utility bills in winter. The organization also worked to dispel the public's image of people on welfare as lazy people unwilling to work. According to one study, 86 percent of welfare recipients in St. Louis at that time were either disabled, blind, younger than eighteen, or older than sixty-five. At a time when the U.S. government's poverty line stood at $5,500 for a family of four, St. Louis families of four receiving Aid to Dependent Children received a maximum of $1,440 per year.[33] In addition, the NWRO tried to change the image that welfare recipients held of themselves, encouraging them to view an adequate income as their right rather than as a favor extended by a benevolent outside authority.

Ivory Perry viewed NWRO as an important vehicle for the poor in a nation that refused to provide jobs for all. "If they had employment for everyone, they wouldn't need to have no welfare. The way society's structured in this country everybody doesn't have a job, and the people that want work, can't work, most of them." Even if welfare payments provided an adequate income, Perry viewed them as less desirable than full employment. It troubled him that welfare sapped people of their self-confidence and ambition.

> People on welfare, most of them, don't have no motivation. . . . It makes welfare recipients complacent. They know what they got coming on the second of every month so most of them don't go looking for no job. And they know often if they get a job they got to hire a baby-sitter, they got to have carfare, they got to have clothes, they got to be prepared to meet the public every day where they're working. . . . I have been in quite a few welfare recipients' homes. I have never heard one mother say what they want little Johnny or Mary to be when they grow up; or what she wanted to be.[34]

In contrast to the lessons taught by the welfare system, the NWRO offered a process of struggle and "organizational learning." It mobilized welfare recipients to take action around basic survival needs. As an organization, NWRO did not survive the 1970s, but it played an important role in bringing a new consciousness to large numbers of poor people, affirming their legitimacy and encouraging them to analyze, interpret, and act on their status in society.[35]

The increasing number of welfare recipients in the 1960s reflected both the changing structure of poverty and the politicization of the poor in the wake of the civil rights movement. In 1960, 745,000 American families received a total of $1 billion through Aid to Dependent Children (ADC). By 1972, 3 million families received ADC payments totaling $6 billion. More than 70 percent of this expansion took place between 1964 and 1969, less a response to increasing poverty than to changes in attitudes among the poor. As Frances Fox Piven and Richard Cloward note in their important studies of poor people's movements, the raised expectations and consciousness of the civil rights movement convinced poor people that the system that denied them jobs owed them—at the very least—a living wage. Social service personnel in poverty-stricken areas responded to the civil insurrections and riots in the 1960s by securing increased welfare benefits for those eligible. They found that many more people qualified for benefits than had previously been recognized, and that the changed political climate made the poor more likely to claim benefits to which they were entitled.[36]

The declining economic position of women within the American economy also contributed to the rising numbers of people on welfare. Low wages in traditionally female occupations, the dearth of affordable child care centers, and increasing rates of male desertion left women with no source of support for themselves and their children other than the government. The number of households headed by women under the age of fifty-five amounted to 2.5 million in 1940, but reached 4.4 million by 1960. The percentage of white women heading households rose from 3 to 6 percent over those decades, while the proportion of black households headed by women increased from 7 to 20 percent.[37] NWRO responded to the problems facing these women, and its successes mobilized poor people for a variety of political actions in the 1960s and 1970s, including the St. Louis public housing rent strike.

Through his work with NWRO and his experiences at HDC, Ivory Perry realized that the rent strike had deep structural roots. It came out of years of suffering by people displaced from homes in previously stable neighborhoods, out of the misery of unemployment and poverty, and out of the awakened consciousness of 1960s activism. The problems facing tenants could not be traced to one or two bad decisions; they stemmed from the whole direction of the urban economy over the preceding decades. For those reasons, the rent strike held significance for the entire community, not just for the residents of public housing. By addressing the unresolved questions raised by urban renewal, black displacement, and poverty, the rent strike spoke to the core experiences of black St. Louisans. But it also exposed the false promises and tragic costs of urban renewal and the urban economy in general as never before.

For almost thirty years, St. Louis taxpayers had been pouring millions of dollars into a redevelopment plan that promised a better city for all. Yet the disparity between the plight of the rent strikers and the opulence of newly constructed downtown office buildings and tourist attractions called into question the moral and practical priorities of redevelopment. Just as the rent strike provided a focal point for the experiences and needs of the poor, it also drew public scrutiny to the practices and interests of the rich.[38]

Ivory Perry's task as an organic intellectual was to devise methods of contestation that would reveal the hidden antagonisms beneath the surface unity of urban renewal. He had to encourage those parts of the rent strikers' experience that made them see themselves as legitimate, and he had to fight against their tendencies to expect to fail. He had to help build a viable coalition in support of the strikers by identifying groups and individuals with interests harmonious to those of the poor. And he had to help create situations where it became easier for those in power to grant the tenants' demands than to incur the costs of continued struggle.

Basic to his understanding of his task was an acceptance of the inevitability of conflict. Perry viewed the existence of poverty in a wealthy country like the United States as more than a paradox, it seemed to him that the luxury of the rich depended upon the misery of the poor. Slumlords and corporate redevelopers profited from housing shortages created by urban renewal, and they deliberately underfinanced public housing in order to reserve more capital for profit-making ventures. But because redevelopment meant so much to the rich, the organized protest of the poor could be quite effective if it threatened the legitimacy and access to future tax dollars of redevelopment programs. A confrontational strategy seemed to him the best way to force the elite to make concessions to the poor. "I knew that my tactics might make some enemies," he recalls, "but it's not my intention to make enemies. It's just that when you're involved with the struggle you're going to step on a lot of people's toes."[39] One of Perry's tasks as an organic intellectual was to step on enough toes to be noticed, but softly enough to provide incentives for his foes to cooperate on long-range reforms of mutual interest.

Drawing on years of experience with social protest, Ivory Perry responded to the rent strike with four distinct approaches. First, he respected the indigenous organization and leadership of the strike, making no attempt to take over or lead the tenants' movement. Second, he mobilized broad-based community support for the strikers, to strengthen their hand in dealing with their adversaries. Third, he sought to draw third parties into the dispute by expanding its parameters beyond the limited resources of the tenants and the housing authority. Fourth, he devised creative tactics to educate and agitate the community around housing issues to help create a favorable climate for ending the strike.

It would have been understandable if Ivory Perry, an expert on housing issues, had attempted to take over direction and leadership of the rent strike. Nearly all the tenant leaders had less experience in social contestation and less expertise about housing than he did. Yet from the start, Perry valued the authenticity of the strike, the fact that tenants acted by and for themselves. "I thought the rent strikers did a very good job, that they had very good organization," he remembers. "In some of the projects like Pruitt-Igoe they had too little support, but at Webbe-Darst and Carr Square they had good organization and good leaders. All I could do was try to help. Besides, they were the ones living in public housing; they knew the problems better than anyone."[40] Perry recognized that no amount of abstract knowledge could surpass the positive benefits of indigenous tenant leadership waging and winning its own strike. He recognized and accepted his role as a supportive one.

In that supportive capacity, Perry worked to line up community backing for the rent strike. The coalition of black militant organizations that endorsed the strike in March, the demonstration in April at the airport protesting business leaders' efforts to circumvent the tenants, the demonstrations at the cathedral in June and July, protests at sessions of the housing court, and mobilization of the local MTO in support of the national NTO convention all combined to present the appearance of widespread and emphatic community support for the tenants. That appearance contributed to the legitimacy of the strike, but it also served as a warning to politicians and community leaders who might otherwise oppose the tenants. Politicians loyal to the local Democratic patronage apparatus that controlled the housing authority, and high-ranking officials in the Human Development Corporation did not give public support to the tenants, but they found it impossible to support the housing authority in the face of active and energetic community mobilization on their behalf.

Because tenants genuinely could not afford to pay higher rents, and because federal law mandated the housing authority to meet operating expenses out of current rents, neither side could win the rent strike without outside intervention. Yet that intervention might take many forms. If it came in the nature of sheriff's deputies evicting striking tenants or new federal regulations further limiting the role of tenants in housing management, the strikers would lose. Ivory Perry labored behind the scenes to bring about intervention on more favorable terms to the tenants. He directly confronted realtors and businessmen, and helped place indirect pressure on the mayor and on religious leaders. Most important, his work with the NTO and with Harold Gibbons led to eventual resolution of the dispute.

With businessmen nervous about the possibility of civil insurrection, with HUD anxious that the strike might spread to other cities, and with the mayor frightened that the public housing situation might drive a wedge between white and black Democrats and threaten popular support for redevelopment, Ivory Perry's agitation gave leaders of vested interest groups powerful motivation to settle the rent strike. He was hardly the only reason why business, labor, and government leaders intervened in the dispute, but he had a decided impact on their actions, especially after the NTO convention in September.

Ivory Perry neither instigated nor led the rent strike. But when it started he knew what to do and how to do it. Perry's knowledge of the history of housing issues and the interests at stake in them enabled him to select appropriate targets for direct action and appropriate tactics for securing their participation in the struggle on favorable terms. His years of activism helped prepare the terrain for contestation in many ways—in the lessons taught over the years by successful mobilizations and protests, in the network of organizers and activists nurtured within the movement, and in the apparatus of communication that generated, circulated, and legitimated the tenants' views on public housing in defiance of the accepted wisdom of housing administrators, politicians, editorial writers, and traditional intellectuals.

On October 28, 1969, Mayor Cervantes invited representatives from the housing authority, the City Wide Rent Strike Committee, and the Civic Alliance for Housing to his offices for the ceremonial signing of the agreement ending the rent strike. Millionaire businessmen born into social-register families stood next to impoverished black women raising their families on welfare. An idealistic young settlement-house minister whose parents had been sharecroppers shook hands with the mayor, a hard-nosed politician and flamboyant entrepreneur. The tough labor union leader whose initiative brought them all together posed for pictures with corporate executives and proudly announced the "peace agreement" to the press.[41]

The ceremonial ending to the rent strike reflected its ironies and contradictions. Rev. Buck Jones, a practitioner of nonviolence, secured victory because his opponents feared violence. Mayor Cervantes maintained his political stature by delegating authority over an important city agency to an ad hoc coalition of interest groups. Corporation presidents gained stability for multimillion-dollar redevelopment projects by allowing a labor leader to talk them into making concessions to welfare recipients. That labor leader gained his greatest political victory by "organizing" millionaire businessmen. Black public-housing tenants who could get no one to listen to their grievances in February, found themselves managing projects and serving on committees with business, labor, and civic leaders by October.

Ivory Perry was not among those invited to sign the agreement ending the rent strike, and there was no reason why he should have been. He had already made his contribution to the tenants' cause, and had moved on to other concerns. In his office at the Union-Sarah Gateway Center he had been receiving fifty to seventy-five calls a day from tenants with complaints about their landlords. These calls took him out into the community, where he encountered basements flooded with three feet of water, plaster falling from ceilings and walls, faulty wiring, and backed-up sewage pipes. Some landlords turned off the heat in their buildings when tenants fell behind in rent payments, even though that practice violated the municipal minimum standards code. He saw one building that was so cold children could see the steam from their own breath inside it.[42]

These conditions and his experiences with the rent strike propelled Ivory Perry into his next major campaign—a fight against lead poisoning caused by lead-based paint on the walls of slum dwellings. In that struggle he would have to take on the real estate industry, the city health department, private hospitals, and the local medical establishment to convince people that lead poisoning posed a serious threat to the health of poor children. But as he had done during the rent strike, Perry proved that determination and direct action can sometimes move the most resistant obstacles and win unexpected victories.

CHAPTER 7

Lead Poisoning: Peace and Pain
in the Struggle

In his capacity as housing coordinator for the Union-Sarah Gateway Center, Ivory Perry came face to face with the worst housing conditions in the ghetto. People generally turned to him for help when landlords refused to make needed repairs that endangered their health. So year in and year out, he visited apartments infested with vermin, houses with sewage backed up so badly that he could hardly stand the stench, and dwellings with collapsing stairs, leaking gas connections, and inadequate water and heat. Many of these buildings violated the municipal housing codes, but enforcement proved difficult. Layers of legal titles hid the true identities of slum property owners, and absentee landlords were hard to contact. Housing court judges hesitated to force landlords into repairing slum housing for fear they would simply abandon the buildings. Slumlords claimed their small profits could not justify extensive repairs, while people outside the ghetto rarely troubled themselves with questions about code violations in the slums. Only the slum dwellers themselves, and people like Ivory Perry, had to face up to the consequences of inadequate housing.

In the course of his home visits for HDC, Perry noticed one problem that seemed to defy explanation. In the oldest and poorest neighborhoods he found a disproportionate number of children suffering from skin problems, running eyes and noses, and constant recurring colds, even in the summertime. The quality of housing or housekeeping in these homes seemed to make little difference: in some parts of the city children just seemed unusually susceptible to these ailments. On one visit, Perry went to check on an apartment where the ceiling had collapsed. He noticed two baby cribs next to a bedroom wall that had a huge hunk of plaster dug out of it. As he watched the babies in their cribs, they picked at the plaster on the wall and put flakes of it in their mouths. When he asked their mother about this, she replied that they had been fed, but that they always seemed to be hungry.[1]

Perry decided to ask his friend Wilbur Thomas about the children eating plaster. Thomas worked as a research biologist at the Center for the Biology of Natural Systems (CBNS) at Washington University under the direction of the renowned scientist and environmental activist, Barry Commoner. CBNS pioneered research into the relationship between ecology and public health at a time when few scientific researchers displayed any interest in the social ramifications of technical decisions, and Perry thought Thomas might have some ideas as to why babies would want to put flakes of plaster in their mouths. The biologist suggested that the children might have been suffering from a condition called pica, the tendency to ingest nonfood substances. Thomas went on to explain that many young children, but especially those with nutrition deficiencies, craved plaster coated with lead-based paint because it tasted sweet to them. These children tended to absorb high levels of lead into their bloodstreams, which sometimes resulted in skin blemishes, running eyes and noses, and nasal congestion. Unchecked, lead in the bloodstream could do permanent brain damage and produce mental retardation.[2]

Most of the older buildings in St. Louis had been painted with lead-based paint, and the number of children that Ivory Perry noticed with symptoms of lead poisoning made him suspect that the disease had reached epidemic proportions. He learned that a sodium sulfide solution caused paint containing lead to turn black, so he began using it to test houses in the Union-Sarah neighborhood. "I tested about fifty houses and found out it was a waste of time, because they all had lead paint," he later told a reporter. Even though Missouri law banned interior lead paint after 1950, some of it remained on inside walls; outside windowsills and door frames contained lead-based paint legally. "Most poor people don't have air conditioning, and they raise the windows in the summertime, and most of the little kids put their mouths on the windowsills," Perry observed.[3]

Of all the housing problems Ivory Perry confronted, lead poisoning struck him as the most serious. It robbed children of their futures, deprived the community of the contributions those children might make, and operated so silently that no one even suspected its existence. Other housing conditions undermined health and morale, but their effects could be reversed; better housing could lead to better lives. But lead poisoning did permanent damage that could be arrested only by detoxifying both children and their environment, by removing lead from the children's bloodstreams and by scraping lead-based paint off ghetto walls. Those remedies cost time and money, and no resources existed to implement them because too few people recognized the hazards. No hospital or clinic in St. Louis had equipment or facilities for testing children for lead poisoning, and the city building commissioner refused to insist that landlords detoxify their property.[4]

Perry paid his own money to attend a seminar in Chicago about lead poisoning. There he learned that the disease was in older cities all across the nation, and that procedures existed for screening and testing children. He convinced the St. Louis board of education to let him use elementary schools as testing sites and he persuaded nurses and medical students to take blood samples. At the same time, he started political action designed to call attention to the problem, researching and publicizing the names of slumlords who owned buildings with lead-based paint, and calling on them to clean up their property and make it safe for their tenants.[5]

Late in 1969, Perry contacted Legal Aid attorney Henry "Hap" Freund about the lead poisoning problem. Freund researched the issue and presented his findings to Alderman Henry Stolar, who agreed to introduce legislation aimed at forcing landlords to detoxify leaded environments. On January 1, 1970, the *St. Louis Globe-Democrat* reported the start of a major community campaign against lead poisoning, "which causes untold damage in small children—from mental retardation and death to epileptic seizures, cerebral palsy, eye damage, and even to behavior problems." The newspaper story went on to note that the drive against the "silent epidemic" was about to commence, "thanks in large part to Ivory Perry, field housing specialist for the Human Development Corporation."[6]

Wilbur Thomas and Barry Commoner prevailed upon Washington University chancellor William Danforth to set up a series of meetings between Perry and members of the medical profession to discuss lead poisoning as a major public health problem in St. Louis. Social workers at the Yeatman Health Center (affiliated with the Human Development Corporation) began to inquire about the problem in their neighborhood, and medical students volunteered their services to screening programs at the center. In April 1970, Stolar's bill became law.[7]

However, this flurry of attention did little to solve the problems caused by lead poisoning in St. Louis. Perry felt that his meetings with doctors produced a lot of talk, but no tangible results. Hospitals and clinics still had no facilities for systematic screening and treatment. Alderman Stolar's ordinance had little impact when the municipal building commissioner and housing court judges displayed little enthusiasm for enforcing it. Along with other HDC employees, especially those at the Yeatman Health Center, Perry began to take direct action to address the problem by means of community mobilization.

Through the Metropolitan Tenants Organization, Ivory Perry organized a benefit dance to raise money for the city public health laboratory so that it could train technicians to operate lead poisoning testing equipment. He went door to door in slum neighborhoods on his days off, explaining the threat posed to children by lead in their bloodstreams and asking parents to let their sons and daughters undergo testing. He rented station wagons and vans for volunteers to drive children to screening centers at the Yeatman Health Center and at the Union-Sarah Gateway Center.[8] But he also took aggressive political action to place the problem before the public.

In August 1970, Perry led a dramatic confrontation between some community residents and city officials. The city budget director had requested $175 to send a technician to Chicago to learn how to operate equipment that tested for levels of lead in the bloodstream, but the board of aldermen had turned down that request. Angry parents and health workers challenged aldermanic representatives over that refusal. A. J. Henley, an administrator at Yeatman Health Center, complained:

> This is a problem that people have wanted to deny for a number of years simply because it calls for better housing. The load has been put on us to prove that lead poisoning exists when we already know that it does. The fact that children are dying should be ample evidence, but it is not.

Ivory Perry pleaded with the aldermen to provide money for testing, asking the city to allocate $1 per test. "One dollar can save a child's life," he told them, "but it costs the city $250,000 to care for a retarded person."[9] Yet the aldermen still refused to grant even the $175 needed to train a technician, much less thousands of dollars for testing and screening programs.

Some health care professionals seemed particularly hostile to the campaign against lead poisoning; they viewed other health issues as more important, and feared that community activists had chosen medical care as a political issue more out of a desire to embarrass landlords and change society in general than out of any responsible concern about public health. Dr. William C. Banton, the city health commissioner, worked energetically to secure funds for the treating and testing of lead poisoning, but he also struggled to educate other physicians about it. Banton recalled that his own medical school training included very little information about lead poisoning, and he speculated that the same was true for most of his professional colleagues. Physicians who did not treat large numbers of poor children might not notice how widespread the condition was, and those who were not specifically looking for lead poisoning might easily confuse its symptoms with milder conditions like head colds.[10]

Dr. Max Pepper, chairman of the Department of Community Medicine at St. Louis University, pointed to another dimension of the problem when he told a reporter that some public health professionals wrongly believed that hereditary genetic traits rather than environmental conditions caused children to suffer from lead poisoning. Perry remembers doctors telling him that lead poisoning did not exist to any significant degree. Even some black doctors refused to take the issue seriously, alleging that someone like Ivory Perry had no competence to advise them on medical issues. "A couple of black doctors told me they'd rather see their whole families dead and buried before they'd give up a dime to try to help on lead poisoning," he recalls.[11]

Health care professionals and city officials may have resisted Perry's call for action, but ordinary people in the community were eager to help. Maurice Williamson owned a tavern across the street from Perry's apartment, and he quickly agreed to put up signs in his establishment advertising the need for money and volunteers to help fight against the disease. "Everybody said he was crazy," Williamson remembers about the official response to Perry's activism on the issue, "but I knew he knew what he was talking about." Perry used the back room of Williamson's bar as the unofficial headquarters of the drive, and from that command post he sent high school and college student volunteers out to the screening centers and called everyone he could think of to ask for money, transportation, and volunteer work. That mobilization produced the first comprehensive lead poisoning screening program in St. Louis history, and the results proved astounding. Nearly 40 percent of the children tested had abnormally high levels of lead in their blood. No one could assert now that lead poisoning affected only a few individuals; clearly, it posed a major health hazard.[12]

Perry used every means at his disposal in the fight against lead poisoning, trying every chance he got to draw friends and acquaintances into his campaign. Sometimes he went too far. Pearlie Evans remembers the time when she, as vice president of the National Association of Social Workers, was scheduled to give the welcoming address for its national meeting in St. Louis. Before she started to speak, Ivory Perry banged on the doors of the auditorium, demanding the opportunity to speak to the delegates about lead poisoning. "I almost collapsed," Evans remembers. "I had to explain to the group that this was an individual who had given an incredible amount of time to the community, and that he only wanted to bring some issues to their attention. I gave him five minutes to speak, but when Ivory went on for fifteen minutes I finally had to cut him off."[13]

St. Louis commissioner of health William C. Banton announced early in 1971 that of 1,715 children screened since June 1970, 671 had abnormally high levels of lead in their blood, and 188 appeared to be actual victims of lead poisoning. In February 1971, prosecutors scored one of their first victories against violators of the lead control ordinance when a landlord pleaded guilty to failing to remove lead-based paint from one of his buildings. The landlord paid $157 of a $1,400 fine with the understanding that the remaining amount would go toward detoxifying his property. Judge Theodore McMillian remembers his reaction to Ivory Perry's efforts once the enormity of the lead poisoning situation became evident. "I had not really known the danger of this lead-based paint and the danger that it could pose to small children," McMillian recalls. "The politicians, landlords, and physicians were upset. They didn't like Ivory, they didn't feel that he had the expertise to make those charges. He's proven them to have been wrong."[14]

The St. Louis Urban League presented Ivory Perry with a special award in March 1971 for his service to the community in attacking the lead poisoning problem. A few days later, Mayor A. J. Cervantes wrote Perry a letter saying, "Your work with the detection and prevention of lead poisoning as well as your other outstanding work in the area of housing makes me very proud to know one as capable and committed as yourself." But honors and awards did not solve the problems posed by lead poisoning, and Perry immediately escalated his efforts to win a commitment of resources from the city, the medical profession, and the real estate business community. The day after he received his letter from Cervantes, Ivory Perry announced a drive to raise $40,000 for testing and screening centers throughout the city. Contending that health clinics currently engaged in screening did not reach people too poor to afford transportation to them, he proposed neighborhood testing and treatment centers. Perry repeated his contention that it cost the city $250,000 for the lifetime care of a mentally retarded person, and he contrasted that with the $59,000 that the city had spent the previous year on the prevention and cure of lead poisoning. He charged further that building inspectors had visited only 155 dwellings in the previous nine months to check for lead-based paint.[15]

The Metropolitan Tenants Organization, in conjunction with the newly formed People's Coalition Against Lead Poisoning, demanded enforcement of the city's lead-control ordinance, detoxification of dwellings, and establishment of testing and treatment centers for afflicted children. In April 1971, representatives of that coalition addressed the national convention of the American Academy of Pediatrics in St. Louis, and persuaded the delegates to pass a resolution "censuring" the city's political, business, and medical leadership for their failure to eradicate lead poisoning hazards. The Yeatman Health Center conducted a systematic screening program in its neighborhood and discovered that 95 percent of homes in the area had lead-based paint on the walls, and that more than half of 2,263 children tested had above-average levels of lead in their systems. Of these, 88 had enough lead to threaten brain damage.[16]

Late in April, an editorial in the *St. Louis Post-Dispatch* complained about the slow pace of lead-based paint removal in the city. It noted that screening since the previous June revealed elevated levels of lead in 1,121 out of 2,752 children but that building inspectors had examined only 213 dwelling units thus far. One month later, Barry Commoner told reporters that a proposed $230 million bond issue to build a convention center in St. Louis would bring far less public benefit than a similar expenditure for correcting conditions posed by lead-based paint. Dr. Ursula Rolfe, associate director of outpatient services at Cardinal Glennon Hospital, told reporters that as many as 30,000 St. Louis children lived under conditions that made them susceptible to lead poisoning.[17]

Even when the number of confirmed lead poisoning cases reached 1,500, St. Louis city officials and private charities did not commit themselves to an all-out assault on the disease. In September 1971, the Garfield

Community Action Program battled with the Red Cross for funds to address lead poisoning in its area. Program director Bill Preston expressed concern that powerful people did not want to permit his group to use funds for that end. "We tried to pressure City Hall and slum landlords to detoxify dangerous buildings and build better housing," he explained, but "our efforts met resistance all the way, even from hospital personnel who didn't want beds used by children whose parents couldn't pay." The Yeatman Health Center ran the only continuous testing program in the city, and none of the local hospitals established facilities for detoxification until 1972.[18]

Part of the problem was that city officials were reluctant to prosecute landlords. A KMOX-TV editorial in February 1972 alleged that after two years on the books, the anti-lead-poisoning law had resulted in only eighteen charges against landlords, with only eleven convictions. Those found guilty received fines averaging less than $100—far less than the cost of detoxifying a building. Public health officials estimated that detoxification cost $50 per room, but realtors argued that $250 per room would be a more accurate figure. All agreed that the cost of removing lead-based paint from slum environments would be extremely high, with some estimates as high as $100,000,000, and all agreed that those sums were not likely to be expended in the near future.[19]

In June 1972, the Department of Health, Education, and Welfare in Washington, D.C., announced a grant to the St. Louis city health department for lead poisoning prevention and treatment. But the grant included no funds for detoxification. So Ivory Perry and other activists renewed their efforts to pressure city officials into enforcing the lead-control ordinance. In October they staged a sit-in at the city counselor's office to demand systematic inspections of slum dwellings and vigorous prosecution of landlords violating the ordinance. Their press release explained:

> Over two years ago, Henry Stolar, Ivory Perry, Hap Freund, A. J. Henley and others had the good sense to recognize that lead poisoning was a major health problem in St. Louis and this influenced the passing of a good lead poisoning ordinance. Despite this limited success over 1,500 children have been lead poisoned and approximately 170 children seriously poisoned and hospitalized.

Their statement went on to note that only twenty-five violations of the ordinance had reached the courts, and the fines of those convicted averaged only $96. The demonstration ended when the city counselor met with the demonstrators and promised them vigorous enforcement of the law.[20]

That concession marked a turning point in the struggle over lead poisoning in St. Louis. From that point on, the city, the medical establishment, and even realtors conceded the seriousness of the problem and vowed to take steps to address it. Important differences still remained over how quickly action could be taken and who should pay for it, but nearly three years of education and agitation succeeded in placing the issue on the public agenda, mobilizing a coalition for change around it, and effecting policies and programs that saved lives.

OF ALL his accomplishments, the fight against lead poisoning brought Ivory Perry the most satisfaction and gratification. It confirmed his belief that determined collective action could overcome enormous obstacles and win permanent gains. His dedication brought about testing and treatment programs for poor children that saved them from physical and mental illness. His persistence generated increased recognition of the lead poisoning problem among health care professionals, teachers, and social workers who began to watch for symptoms of the disease among children under their care.[21] Perry's combination of self-help and direct-action protests pressured city building inspectors and housing court judges into vigorous enforcement of the law, and forced landlords to detoxify buildings. Most significant, the campaign exemplified his role as an organic intellectual: demonstrating his skill at analyzing and interpreting community needs, articulating and circulating oppositional positions, acting to mobilize effective coalitions for change, and finding ways of bringing to the surface submerged currents of criticism and protest.

Yet the fight against lead poisoning cost Ivory Perry time, money, effort, and energy, and it took a toll on his mind and spirit. It exposed him to the rapaciousness of landlords who endangered the lives of their tenants for the sake of a few dollars' profit. It subjected him to the hypocrisy of law enforcement officials who winked at widespread violations of city housing ordinances because the perpetrators had money and influence and their victims were "merely" impoverished children. On a more personal level, the campaign brought home to him the enormous costs of social activism for his private life, even when that activism produced real victories. During the battles over lead poisoning, Perry began to suffer once again from the nervous depression that had put him in the hospital after Dr. King's assassination. The urgency of the cause would not allow him time for rest, but fatigue led to periods of incapacitation that sent him back to the hospital for treatment. He began to see visions of what he took to be future events and to hear voices warning him about the dangers facing black people in America. His relationship with his family deteriorated. He saw his wife and children less and less, while the time that he did spend with them seemed more tense and pressured than ever before. Dispirited by the problems facing him, and despairing of ever being able to address them adequately, Ivory Perry called a press conference on December 3, 1973, to announce his "retirement" from the civil rights movement.

No one from the news media came to his press conference. Although he had given twenty years of his life to political activism and had made the front page of newspapers repeatedly in the previous decade, Ivory Perry's retirement from the movement drew no interest from the press. Reporters, editors, and station managers who had given him extensive coverage when he had participated in obstructive protests, saw no news value in his desire to make a statement about quitting the struggle. Perry headed no major organization, held no elective office, had no influential patrons, and had no obvious visible personal following. Consequently, his retirement went unnoticed in the local press, at least at first.[22]

One week after the scheduled press conference, Robert Joiner, a black reporter for the *St. Louis Post-Dispatch*, wrote a feature story about Ivory Perry. His opening paragraph read:

> When Ivory Perry called a press conference last week to announce his retirement from the civil rights movement, nobody showed up. But there must be hundreds of mothers on the North Side who are thankful to Perry for saving their children from brain damage through his drive to bring a lead poisoning screening program to St. Louis and to rid slum housing of chipping lead based paint which the children used to eat like candy.

The story went on to detail Perry's many contributions to the civil rights movement and to social justice in general. It concluded with a mention of rumors that psychiatric problems lay behind the activist's decision to drop out of the movement, followed by a poignant denial of that allegation by Perry, who produced a letter from a psychiatrist stating that he was competent to continue his employment at the Human Development Corporation.[23]

That story provoked a laudatory comment on Perry by *Post-Dispatch* columnist Jake McCarthy, formerly editor of the *Missouri Teamster* and a close associate of Teamster leader Harold Gibbons. Otis L. Bolden, assistant dean of instruction at Forest Park Community College, added his voice to the growing tributes to Ivory Perry in a letter to the *Post-Dispatch*.

> Ivory walked the hell zone of the decimated inner city to detoxify a building here, to place a family in substantial shelter there. He fought the good fight of commitment and involvement. Many black parents and more black children were touched in life sustaining ways by him.[24]

These belated yet sincere tributes called attention to Perry's years of social activism, but they also underscored the sadness of his predicament. One cannot discount the purely personal causes of Perry's bouts with depression: an unsettled childhood, psychosomatic reactions to combat stress in Korea, and physical and emotional pain in both his work and home lives. But it is also important to recognize the tragic irony of Ivory Perry's life—that the political activism that gave him a chance to be somebody special and to make extraordinary contributions also sapped his strength and energy by exposing him to unremitting pressures and tensions. A man who had done so much to help others found no help for himself when he needed it most. The courage and discipline that enabled him to fight so many battles failed to sustain him in his own battle with depression and fatigue. Like his nervous breakdown in the aftermath of the King assassination, Perry's retirement from the civil rights movement forced him to face the accumulated costs and agonies of his chosen path.

Robert Joiner, the newspaper reporter who first wrote about Ivory Perry's retirement, believes that Perry's emotional troubles stemmed from the difficult work he had chosen to do. "If Ivory has medical problems," Joiner maintains, "I'm not certain what the cause might be. But I think to some extent he has been very frustrated with the lack of change in the community, frustrated in the cutbacks of funds to bring about change, frustrated in just not having enough funds of his own to do some of the things he'd like to see done."[25]

Ivory Perry retired from social activism because it made his everyday life unbearable. Political engagement undermined his family life, exposed him to verbal abuse and physical dangers, demanded superhuman efforts and patience in the face of extreme provocations, and isolated him from the commonplace experiences and satisfactions of his community, even as he devoted himself to its well-being. By December 1973, he felt so pressured that retirement seemed to offer the only way out of his agonies. One especially painful contradiction came from the conflict between his public responsibilities and his private life. Time spent at the lead screening clinic or housing court meant time away from his wife and family (which now included another daughter—Jackie, born in 1969—and another son—Tony, born in 1971). Anna Cox had to work at her own job and raise their five children while Ivory participated in his civil rights activities, and she resented it. "Sometimes I would feel like, what the hell am I doing all this for?" she remembers thinking. "I'm having babies, and this man, he's got a job, but he's never home." Ivory's sister Kathen Wright also worried.

> It kind of upset me, you know, because when he got his family he was gone all the time. And every time when he got a job, if they found out he was demonstrating, they fired him. The family had to suffer. I didn't go along with that. It's all right for a single man, but he had a family.[26]

Activism not only pulled Perry away from his family, but it also led to unequal relations inside it. One time Anna Cox had an opportunity to go to Europe and perform with a gospel singing group from her church, but Ivory would not allow her to leave the children for that trip. "That really hurt me," Cox says, "because I thought, gosh, you can trust me when you're out of town and in jail, but I've got a life of my own to live." Even when they worked out equitable arrangements inside their household, other people treated them differently because of Ivory's notoriety. Cox remembers, "It was like I didn't have an identity. When we'd go somewhere it was always Mrs. Perry, never Anna. [I felt] I'm smothering here under the name of Ivory Perry."[27]

Cox's sense of subordination to her husband paralleled the experiences of many women from all strata of society in the 1960s and 1970s, experiences that eventually led to the formation of a feminist movement insisting on gender equality as an essential ingredient in a just and decent society. But before finding organized expression in feminism, resentments against sexism percolated in the lives of ordinary women and men faced with a problem that society did not seem to recognize. Tensions between men and women over the division of work within the home, and the opportunity for fulfillment outside it, affected people from all backgrounds. But they held particular relevance and import for people in the midst of a struggle for social change like Anna Cox and Ivory Perry.[28]

Sexism within the home undermined the struggle for equality outside it by inculcating exploitation and hierarchy into the patterns of everyday life so thoroughly that they appeared normal and inevitable. Such sexism suppressed the talents and abilities of women activists by relegating them to supportive roles at home and secondary positions outside it. Male power and male privilege in American society functioned as a reactionary force inhibiting social change at all levels, but especially in its separation between public and domestic life. Patriarchal norms resting on an idealized portrayal of domestic life as "a haven in a heartless world" legitimized the amorality of public life by channeling impulses and desires for happiness solely into the home. Suggesting that the public arena belonged to men and the domestic sphere to women, this ideal encouraged men to view their happiness as dependent upon the sacrifices of women, while suggesting to women that their desires for achievement and recognition should be filled vicariously through the accomplishments of their spouses. When the legitimate resentments of women clashed with the unrealistic demands of men, the "haven" turned into contested terrain, incapable of supplying either men or women with adequate affection or self-respect.[29]

The oppressions of race further complicated the problems of gender. The pathology of white racism includes an obsessive interest in black sexuality that has manifested itself in centuries of whites sexually abusing black males and females. Law, physical force, and custom historically denied to black men the rights and privileges extended to white males, while the dual oppressions of sexism and racism subjected black women to mistreatment because of their gender and their race. One consequence was that Afro-American females, unlike women in any other ethnic group, often rivaled men as breadwinners. High unemployment rates and low wages paid to black males, and the complicated sexual ideology fabricated to legitimize their class and racial oppression, tended to fragment the black nuclear family and produce a higher incidence of female-headed households.[30] To be sure, extended kinship networks, neighborhood support systems, and the determination of strong black

men and women created new and successful forms of family life in the
face of these realities; nonetheless, one recurrent effect of white racism
has been the extraordinary pressures and strains it has imposed upon
the black family.

Ivory Perry and Anna Cox had to grapple with the difficulties in their
relationship in the context of three structural and historical problems:
the changing nature of the family and male-female relations in the 1960s
and 1970s, the special demands placed on family life by social activism,
and the traditional pressures and strains imposed upon the black family
by white racism and its economic and social consequences.

Anna Cox endorsed all of Ivory Perry's civil rights activism, and she
encouraged the children to view their father's work with pride. Yet at the
same time, she could not ignore the extraordinary price that she and the
children paid for Perry's political work. When he got sent to jail or lost
his job because of civil rights activism, it fell to Anna Cox to keep the
family going. "I would say, 'Why can't you let someone else go? You're
always getting arrested, you're the one that always gets put in jail,'" but
Perry would go ahead and get arrested anyway. Ivory shared her regret
that his public life made life harder for them, but he did not regret it
enough to stop what he was doing. "My wife used to ask me, 'Why do
you care more about the peoples in the street than you do for me?'" he
recalls sadly. "But it's something that motivates me. It's hard for me to
explain. I can't put my finger on it, because I don't know."[31] He felt that
he had to sacrifice part of his personal life to do something positive for
the community as a whole, and he expected his family to understand
and support that decision.

Perhaps precisely because political activism exacted such a great price
on his personal life, Ivory Perry became increasingly committed to it.
Frustration, guilt, and pain that might have led him to give up his activities, instead generated an obsessive sense of mission, propelling him
into the forefront of every campaign that came along. It was as if the
sacrifices had to be justified by ever-escalating activities that proved the
significance of his mission. The consequences of that process often left
him overcommitted and fatigued, adding to his anguish and undercut-
ting his effectiveness.

One incident that reflected the dangers of overcommitment took place
in the spring of 1971. In the middle of the fight against lead poisoning,
Perry initiated support work in St. Louis for the Black United Front of

Cairo, Illinois. Racial strife had deeply divided that town of 6,000 people situated about 170 miles south of St. Louis, and the black activists there issued a call for outside help. Vigilante and police violence in Cairo put black activists under a constant state of siege, and a black boycott of white-owned downtown businesses brought tempers to the flash point. Along with other St. Louis activists, Perry made several trips to Cairo and worked with the Black United Front on the boycott and related educational activities.

In late April 1971, a black St. Louis police officer, Fred Grimes, accepted an appointment as a community relations specialist with the Cairo police department, an appointment opposed by the Black United Front, who feared that Grimes would take on a counterinsurgency role in the community. When Grimes was appointed, Ivory Perry had a vivid dream in which he witnessed Grimes's death in a fiery automobile crash. Believing that this represented an extrasensory perception, he called Grimes and told him about the dream. The next day, the newspapers reported that Ivory Perry had made a late-night death threat against Lieutenant Grimes to frighten him out of taking the position in Cairo.[32]

Perry read the newspaper stories reporting his "threat" to Grimes with horror. He immediately called a press conference to deny that he meant any harm to the officer. Ever since childhood, his dreams had shown him things that he took as premonitions of future events, and he felt that very often the things that he dreamed actually did take place. "Sometimes I can feel it," he explains, "like a ray of something on the top of my head. I don't question that. I can see things and I can hear things." Visions and premonitions constituted an ordinary part of his world. All his life he had known other people who had seen them. "My mother told me that when she was carrying me, she was walking through the woods and saw a black Arabian stallion, and that's why I'm so black," he relates. But other people had a more hostile attitude toward his vision about Officer Grimes, believing it a cover for a death threat or else evidence of Perry's mental instabilities. At the press conference he read a statement that explained:

At 12 a.m. on Wednesday April 28, 1971, I, Ivory Perry, called Lieutenant Fred Grimes because of extrasensory events that have happened to me. The vision was that I saw an uninterested party, a white man, intoxicated driving about fifty miles outside of Cairo, run into an automobile driven by Lieutenant Fred Grimes. Consequently since I believed in these extrasensory events I called Brother Grimes and revealed this to him.[33]

The phone call contributed to doubts about his rationality and reliability. People in the community still respected and trusted Ivory Perry, but they worried about the increasingly frenetic pace of his activism and the increasingly hysterical tone that seemed to accompany his actions.

Ivory Perry suffered another nervous breakdown on a cold winter night late in 1972. Anna Cox remembers him ranting incoherently and trying to wake the children. "He said that I was a false prophet and that someone told him to get rid of me so that the kids could be brought up in the right way."[34]

Cox could hardly believe what she heard. "I was afraid and furious at the same time," she says. "I thought, the nerve of you! There were times when he would leave town, and there would be no money, the rent was getting behind into the thousands of dollars." To hear him make accusations against her after all that was infuriating. According to Cox, Ivory woke up their children that night and told them that he had to take them back to Arkansas with him, so that they could get away from their mother and her "false prophecy." Once again she had to call the police to take her husband to the Veterans Administration hospital. Cox rode there with him, and she remembers that there was "snow on the ground and the streets were like glass, but in his mind it was beautiful—he said everything was just the way he wanted it."[35]

The incessant pressures and frustrations of activism certainly had something to do with Perry's mental condition. His certainty about the importance of his work drove him relentlessly into battles that offered little prospect for success. Housing-related issues proved especially nettling because change came about so slowly. "We have some cases against landlords that have been in the courts since 1965," Perry complained bitterly to a reporter in 1970. Legal maneuvers, judicial indifference, and the high costs of repairs combined to make landlords reluctant to adhere to the provisions of the city building code. "Our hands are tied even when we have a good case," Perry charged.[36]

In 1973, he asked the FBI to investigate the St. Louis housing court on the grounds that its favoritism to slumlords violated the civil rights of tenants. In a letter to the bureau's St. Louis office, Perry outlined his view of the problem:

I'm asking your department to investigate the judge in the night housing court and also the judge in the sanitation court in the Municipal Courts building, because the tenants' civil rights are being violated. They do not get the due process of law. When these slum lords go to court the judge fined them $500.00 for housing code violation and stays the $500.00 fine and they pay ten dollars and cost of court. Most of these tenants do not have any recourse of action to take against these slum lords and they are paying high rent with bad plumbing, bad wiring, and also lead poisoning paint on the wall. It is cheaper for these slum lords to go to court than to bring the building up to the minimum housing standard and at the end of the year they write the building off their income taxes as a lost. I allege that the judges and these slum lords are working together.

FBI agents questioned Perry about his letter, but they found nothing to warrant a detailed investigation, and they initiated no action on his complaints.[37]

Ivory Perry tried to get the attention of federal authorities in a more flamboyant way later that year over what he considered to be another violation of federal law—discrimination against black workers on federally funded construction projects. Unemployed black workers complained to Perry that contractors building the Arthur J. Kennedy Skills Center at Glasgow and North Market streets (in a black neighborhood) seemed to be hiring very few black workers on the $8.5 million federally funded project. Perry did some research and found that the project used no black subcontractors and had hired only eight black laborers working for white contractors. When complaints to the main contractor and the federal government brought no response, Perry decided on direct action.[38]

Minutes after workers entered the construction site at seven o'clock on July 23, 1973, Ivory Perry closed the gates behind them. With a chain draped around his body, he padlocked himself to the closed gates, making it impossible for anyone to enter or exit. The construction supervisor called the police, but Perry confused officers at the scene by taking his feet off the ground and hanging on to the fence. He claimed that since he was on federal property—the fence—city police had no jurisdiction there. The police officers called headquarters and asked for instructions. Their request filtered up through the entire chain of command until two-thirty, when St. Louis mayor John Poelker personally ordered the police to arrest Perry. By that time, a crowd of reporters and community residents had gathered around the construction site, and the police officers feared that arresting Perry might provoke a violent confrontation. The officers finally asked him to unchain himself at four in the afternoon so that the construction workers could go home, in return for a promise that they would not arrest him. Realizing that he had successfully dramatized his point, Perry accepted the deal and went home, but not before vowing to come back if the contractor did not change his hiring policies.[39]

Like many of his other direct-action protests, Ivory Perry's obstruction at the construction site helped publicize flagrant racial discrimination and a violation of federal law. But remedial action did not automatically follow exposure. Law enforcement officials moved slowly, if at all, on violations of federal fair hiring laws. "The law is not the law," observes Ivory's friend Maurice Williamson in detailing Perry's frustrations over the years. "The law is the law for people who have the money and the law is not the law for those who don't have it."[40]

The FBI had little evident interest in prosecuting slumlords and judges for violating the civil rights of tenants, or in investigating the hiring practices of builders with federal contracts, but it did devote enormous resources to its attempts to destroy community activists and civil rights groups all across the country. The bureau's notorious COINTELPRO (the acronym stands for counterintelligence program) attempted to harass individuals engaged in social protest, to disrupt their activities and deny them an effective following. In St. Louis, COINTELPRO fomented factional strife among activist groups by distributing forged leaflets attacking one group in the name of another. FBI agents sent anonymous letters to activists, falsely charging their spouses with marital infidelity, and they circulated letters and leaflets accusing prominent activists of misusing funds and engaging in sexual debauchery. ACTION provided a special target for COINTELPRO activities in St. Louis because FBI agents decided it was the most important black militant organization in the area. An agent in the St. Louis FBI office mailed a letter to the husband of a woman prominent in ACTION falsely charging that his wife had engaged in sexual relations with other men. Five months later, the St. Louis agent boasted to his superiors that his letter "certainly contributed very strongly" to the couple's impending divorce.[41]

Not all the COINTELPRO files have been opened to researchers, and the public will probably never know the full extent of FBI covert action against social protest movements. In response to his request under the Freedom of Information Act, the FBI acknowledged no specific actions directed against Ivory Perry personally. But clearly he operated in a climate poisoned by COINTELPRO activities. Perry often played a unifying role in the St. Louis movement, reconciling opposing factions, and in that capacity he had to deal with the destructive effects of COIN-TELPRO fabrications and tricks. In one instance, FBI operatives fanned a faction fight between two St. Louis black nationalist groups—the Black Liberators and the Zulu 1000s—at precisely the time that Perry was working to unite them in support of the public housing rent strike. In addition, during the COINTELPRO period, Perry and his family received countless threatening telephone calls at home, and on the streets Perry frequently noticed that he was being followed.[42]

COINTELPRO's campaign to harass organizers and foment factional disputes exacerbated the disunity and distrust already present within the black community. People had good reason to be suspicious of activists who counseled dangerous paths of resistance to racism; poor people might lose what little they had in pursuit of utopian goals that might never be realized. Conversely, activists often found themselves frustrated by the seeming apathy and defeatism that their community had absorbed from years of oppression. In times of mass mobilization, organizers transcended those problems, uniting with their communities in a voluntary and mutually beneficial alliance. But at other times, when pessimism and defeatism held sway, activists felt isolated from their constituency. Part of Ivory Perry's motivation for retiring from activism came from the frustrations of isolation, from the belief that no one else cared about the causes that commanded so much of his time and attention.

"I had gotten frustrated," Perry explains. "I could see like I was the only one out there fighting. Everyone else was being complacent. They weren't concerned about those kids being poisoned with lead paint." In truth, other people were concerned and were fighting. but not enough of them and not effectively enough. At a time when Ivory Perry's commitment to his community reached its peak, people around him seemed less committed than ever before. As early as March 1971, he had begun voicing complaints about people in the black community who spent money on "psychedelic shoes and zoot suits" but refused to contribute to the campaign against lead poisoning. He bemoaned what he perceived as the selfishness of their response to community needs. "Most blacks I talk to say 'My kids aren't lead poisoned so I'm not donating.' They may not be involved directly, but they are involved indirectly."[43]

Perry did not blame black people for the conditions they faced, but their response to white racism and institutionalized exploitation frustrated him. He often thought of himself as someone capable of communicating with both the upper and lower economic echelons of the black community, but now significant parts of both sectors seemed oblivious to his message. Among the poor he saw rage and frustration turned inward into a self-hatred manifested in random acts of violence and crime. "They are killing one another like it is open season on blacks, and breaking into one another's homes and stealing everything that isn't nailed down," he complained to a reporter from a black weekly newspaper. But the other side of the community frustrated him too. Middle-class blacks who profited from the advances made by the civil rights movement seemed to think of themselves as no longer connected to the problems of the ghetto. "They don't think that the same type of crime or institutionalized racism can happen to them," he charged.[44]

When he announced his retirement, it seemed to Ivory Perry that everyone else had abandoned the civil rights struggle. White people seemed as hostile to change as ever, even when their own interests would be advanced by reform. Sixty percent of the victims of lead poisoning in the city of St. Louis were white children, but the white community at large did little to press for the lead-control ordinance or for enforcement of the building code. Black people appeared to have given up on collective responses to common problems. The government had only a limited interest in enforcing civil rights laws, but it devoted extensive resources to persecuting and destroying oppositional movements. Tension and fatigue left Ivory Perry overcommitted and underequipped for the many battles he found himself in, and his political commitments left him estranged from his family. The movement that had done so much for him, that had given him a chance to be special, now seemed like little more than a source of unending and intolerable pain.

> I don't know if you ever been in love, but dedication to the struggle is just like being in love when you the only one in love. When you in love with someone and they're not in love with you, it hurts. You looking at your people and trying to educate them as to what's going on and they're not listening. You don't have no support. You out on Front Street by yourself, but they still call on you.[45]

The pressures that drove Ivory Perry into retirement from activism reflect structural tensions built into the process of social contestation. On one level, activism for social change constitutes a monumental act of arrogance. Activists perceive that society must be changed, and they attempt to win others to that view. They project utopian-sounding solutions to complex problems, and they ask others to risk safety and security by battling with more powerful opponents. Yet on another level, activism demands complete selflessness and submersion of individual ego desires into the general will of the community. Activists must respond to real people and their needs, not idealized abstractions. They are disciplined by objective realities, drawing a following only when they identify common problems and when they present solutions capable of mobilizing their constituency. They must face up to the failings and shortcomings of the people they are trying to reach, without losing confidence in their ultimate ability to change both themselves and the world.

A dynamic tension between human will and objective circumstances, between the possible and the practical, pervades the lives of social activists. They accept the limitations imposed on people by their experiences, but then struggle relentlessly against those limits. They envision a world transformed by collective political action, but realize that even the best visions must be tempered and modified by social practice. Activists seek to rebel against society without becoming so removed from it that they lose the ability to speak to individuals still under the sway of dominant values and beliefs. Too much emphasis on human will and what is possible alienates them from their natural constituency and renders them incapable of galvanizing others into action. Yet too much emphasis on objective reality and what is practical within the limits of existing power relations prevents activists from posing or implementing alternative futures. Finding a middle ground between pushing people into battles they do not wish to fight and accepting a status quo that perpetuates oppression requires an extraordinary combination of complex decisions and judgments.

By the end of 1973, the accumulated burdens of activism became intolerable for Ivory Perry. If he devoted all his time to the movement, it hurt his family. Yet if he pursued a conventional home life, he would not be able to mobilize the community for social change. If he turned his back on people in need, he ran the risk of becoming as callous as the system he wanted to change. But if he took up every cause that came along, his energy and effectiveness diminished. If he encouraged people to fight against the system, he asked them to risk making powerful enemies, but if he counseled them to work within a system that routinely violated their rights, he faced the danger of helping to reconcile them to oppressive conditions.

Perry did not face these dilemmas alone. As economic pressures and political realities combined to thwart the aspirations of social protest movements in the 1970s, activists confronted these same problems repeatedly. Some turned their energies toward electoral politics in the belief that the ballot box held the key to power. Others turned to revolutionary violence and armed struggle as the only course left. Ivory Perry understood both these responses to the problems of the 1970s, but he felt that neither one held viable prospects for success. The first ran the risk of absorption and co-optation, while the second seemed to offer sure defeat. He still believed in a "war of position" characterized by mass mobilizations and direct-action protests. But how could individuals find the resources to sustain such an extended struggle in a society so hostile to their goals and values?

Traditionally, oppositional groups nurture and sustain their struggle through a "movement culture." Ivory Perry felt that creating such a culture was one of his main tasks as a community organizer and activist. Again and again, he tried to provide ways for people to discover not only the possibility of activism, but the legitimacy of it. Along with Anna Cox he helped organize a "love and unity rally" in July 1970 on the steps of the old St. Louis courthouse, where slaves had been auctioned off before the Civil War. After some skits about black history, Lillian Mitchell of ACTION addressed the crowd, about fifty people, with a speech about how little love there seemed to be in the world. She asked her listeners to join hands for a moment of silent meditation and rededication to a more loving existence.[46]

On other occasions, Ivory Perry incorporated symbols of African life and culture into his movement activities in the hope that they would encourage a sense of black pride. He wore dashikis, used words from African languages, and displayed the black, red, and green flag of black nationalism and Pan-Africanism. For a time, he attended services at the Ahmadiyya Movement in Islam mosque because of his feeling that "most times, Christianity ain't black folks' religion; it's pushed down our throats by another race of people." But cultural activities like these never attained more than symbolic meaning for him. "I really love Islam," he relates, "but you can't live it in this country, you can't be a true Muslim in the Western world."[47]

Perry might employ symbols from African culture as an aid to bringing people to political consciousnesss, but he remained a political person committed to living in this society and addressing its problems. Even at the love and unity rally he couldn't resist showing a reporter a plaque on the courthouse wall that commemorated the Dred Scott case tried inside that building in 1846, commenting, "They had us in physical slavery back then. Now they've got us in economic slavery." Cultural symbols always brought him to direct political lessons; the love and unity rally reminded him of the fight against slavery, and African imagery more often than not got him started talking about his favorite African, the revolutionary anticolonialist leader Jomo Kenyatta.[48]

Without a viable culture of struggle, the burdens of social activism overwhelmed Ivory Perry and left him feeling isolated and abandoned. After two decades of dangerous engagement, he decided to retire from the struggle and devote the rest of his life to a quieter existence. He could not have known then that soon the pains of noninvolvement would make him decide to reenter the world of social contestation once again.

IVORY PERRY expected to find peace and quiet after his retirement from the civil rights movement, but he was mistaken. He was hospitalized again in 1974, and shortly after he was released, his marriage collapsed. Tired of the double standard that subordinated her life to her husband's, Anna Cox moved to California with their children: eleven-year-old Reggie, nine-year-old Angie, seven-year-old Chuckie, five-year-old Jackie, and three-year-old Tony. It was difficult to take her children halfway across the country and leave her husband, but Cox was certain that she was making the right decision. They had been through a lot together, by no means all bad. But Cox felt that divorce was necessary for her and the children to have a better life. For Ivory, the divorce brought mixed emotions. His family was important to him, but he knew that he had not been able to give them the time they needed. He hoped that he would remain a part of their lives, as he had with his son Roger and his daughter Corliss after his breakup with Earline Terry.

"You know, black families are close even when everybody is not together," Perry explains somewhat defensively. "My old man walked out when I was three." In fact, an extended-family network had been the family he had known growing up and he saw nothing wrong with it. Despite his absences from home, his preoccupation with politics, and his incidents of physical violence and threats against Earline Terry and Anna Cox, he never gave up hope that they would have a close family. "I hope that my children were educated by my role in the community and that as they get older, that we get closer."[49]

In some ways he has gotten his wish. His daughter Corliss says:

> I moved to New York in 1977, but I still always had contact with him. I'd call him up on the telephone or he'd call me. When I was growing up my father was always there. He'd come to see us and was always taking us out. Even though he didn't live with us, he lived about three or four blocks away and we always kept in touch.

Her mother Earline Terry has a more mixed view. "He really cares about his family, he's really devoted to them but they're alienated from him somewhat."[50]

Anna Cox and her five children suffered the most from whatever deficiencies Ivory Perry had as a parent and husband, but she expresses no bitterness about her relationship with him. "I don't feel like I was damaged," she says of her marriage. "Ivory taught me how to be strong. He taught me how to stand on my own two feet. And he also taught me not to depend on him so much."[51] For his part, Perry feels that he is on good terms with Cox and their children and that their relationship will continue to get better in the future.

Perry resumed his work as housing coordinator at HDC, and there he encountered a never-ending stream of housing problems that could not be remedied through conventional channels. He began to learn about "red-lining," the practice of denying loans to people in deteriorating neighborhoods, which accelerated the whittling away of the already inadequate supply of housing available to the poor. In addition, Perry read newspaper accounts revealing that city health officials continued to find alarming incidence of lead poisoning in children, some 20,000 cases in 1975 alone.[52]

For a time, Perry sat back and waited to see what the community would do without him. He often thought of ideas for direct-action protests, but he kept them to himself in the hope that others would fill the void left by his retirement. But watching demonstrations organized by others only reminded him of how much he wanted to get involved again. Maurice

Williamson, part of the network of sympathizers and activists sustaining Perry during his periods of intense activism, watched Perry very carefully during this period and he noticed his friend's eagerness to get back into the struggle. As they talked about the problems of the inner city, Williamson sensed that Perry would become active again. "You couldn't just sit and watch it and know better," Williamson explains. "It was like testing yourself about what's right and what's wrong."[53]

Ivory Perry decided that doing "what was right"—becoming active once again—would make him feel better than remaining on the sidelines. For all its problems, social activism enabled him to be the person he wanted to be. It gave him self-respect, purpose, and meaning. It enabled him to confront directly the real problems facing him and his neighbors. His brief retirement convinced Perry that the movement still needed him, and that he still needed the movement. He decided that whatever the personal costs may be, a life of peace and quiet could never be as satisfying as a life devoted to the struggle for justice.

CHAPTER 8

Politics in the Postindustrial City

After little more than a year in "retirement," Ivory Perry gradually resumed his activist role in the community. No single incident or event galvanized him into action, but the accumulated frustrations and grievances that he encountered at HDC made it impossible for him to remain on the sidelines. "Ivory has a need to help his people, because he can see the basic things that are hurting them," suggests Maurice Williamson in explaining Perry's return to activism.[1] Those basic things that had always commanded his attention—health care, shelter, and employment—continued to form the core concerns of Perry's renewed social activism. But in the context of the historical crisis facing older industrial cities like St. Louis in the late 1970s, those concerns took on new meaning.

From its beginnings after the Korean war up through his retirement in 1973, Ivory Perry's social activism took place in an expanding national economy. Economic growth in the 1950s and 1960s did not benefit all sectors of society equally, and activists like Ivory Perry took the lead in raising serious challenges to the ways the national prosperity failed to help, and in some cases actually hurt, poor and minority communities. But in an era of growth, they found it possible to campaign effectively for improved access to economic and political resources. Starting in 1973, the economy began to show signs of the structural tensions embedded in the previous decades of growth. Inflation, rising energy prices, shortages of resources and capital, and foreign competition all worked to cloud the nation's economic future. At the same time, the unraveling of the New Deal coalition produced political victories for conservative candidates after 1966, and made it possible for the federal government to shift spending priorities away from programs that benefited poor, working-class, and minority inner-city dwellers in favor of expenditures that worked to the advantage of large corporations, investors, and suburban property owners. As a result, activists like Ivory Perry confronted a fundamentally new situation. Instead of competing for a share of expanding resources, they found themselves in a defensive posture, trying to prevent the dismantling of the political and economic base that had made it possible for them to win gains in the past.

The change in national spending priorities became decisive in 1973, after Richard Nixon's reelection landslide the previous November. Before that, the momentum of the 1960s still enabled the poor to achieve some significant victories, like the 1.6 million new households that received federal housing assistance between 1969 and 1973—more than had been helped in the entire history of public housing between 1937 and 1969. But after his reelection, Nixon froze all public-housing subsidies for sixteen months and replaced them with federal revenue-sharing programs that directed federal funds toward local elites rather than the poor.[2]

In the first two years of revenue sharing, only 3 percent of funds went to poor people directly while more than half went to reduce city taxes, a move designed primarily for real estate interests and property owners. Law enforcement received most of the remaining monies, underscoring the philosophy behind revenue sharing: aid to the cities had to first protect the property and profit-making opportunities of the affluent, while aiding the poor only incidentally, if at all.[3] These policies reversed the meager progress that had been made by the War on Poverty, and they combined with other economic and political measures to exacerbate structural strains in the economy that soon exacted a price on all classes.

Inflationary pressures engendered by the Vietnam War, the unfavorable balance of payments created by huge military expenditures overseas, the rise of industrial competitors like Japan and West Germany, substantial increases in energy costs, and the instability of economies in the Third World, all contributed to the American economic crisis of the 1970s. The Nixon administration confronted the unprecedented combination of inflation and slow growth, while oil prices increased by 400 percent. Fiscal conservatives in government felt that only a recession could stop inflation, and their tight money policies brought about higher unemployment, which meant lowered tax revenues and a curtailment of government services that affected the poor most severely. Intense competition for scarce investment capital made manufacturers take a close look at the costs of environmental regulations, union contracts, and taxes within the continental United States and consider moving their operations overseas.[4]

The deep economic recession of 1973–1975 not only entailed a re-distribution of wealth from the poor upward, but it also facilitated a basic transformation in the American economy. A whole host of pro-grams created during times of growth to aid the poor and middle classes now seemed to block corporate access to capital. Bankers responsible for large loans to muncipalities responded by demanding austerity mea-sures like cuts in city services and employment as a precondition for renegotiating outstanding debts. Those policies freed capital for other investments, but sliced into the amenities and services won over the preceding decades by urban dwellers. Business leaders insisted that they needed a larger share of the nation's resources and more control over the direction of federal, state, and local government spending—needs that conflicted with the long-standing aspirations of ordinary workers and taxpayers. As a 1974 *Business Week* editorial explained:

> Some people will have to do with less—cities and states, the home mortgage market, small businesses and the consumer will all get less than they want. It will be a hard pill for many Americans to swal-low—the idea of doing with less so that big business can have more. Nothing that this nation or any other nation has done in modern history compares in difficulty with the selling job that must be done to make people accept the new reality.[5]

That "new reality" coalesced around two main thrusts of neoconser-vative federal policy in the 1970s and 1980s: the transformation of indus-trial cities into postindustrial service centers, and massive reductions in social service spending on the poor and middle classes in order to free large supplies of capital for big business.

Plant closings, stubborn resistance to union demands, and a firm re-fusal to invest in productive manufacturing facilities within the United States constituted one part of the big-business strategy—essentially a general strike by capital. The other part came through political mobiliza-tion: massive spending on political action committees, donations to con-servative candidates, and the funding of "think tanks" and lobbying centers designed to convince Americans that the social protest move-ments of the 1960s and 1970s were to blame for the nation's economic woes, and that only pro-business policies could salvage what had been lost. By 1978, business leaders realized that they had gained the upper hand. An article in *Fortune* boasted, "Suddenly business seems to pos-sess all the primary instruments of power—the leadership, the strategy, the supporting troops, the campaign money—and a new will to use them."[6]

The economic and political transformations of the 1970s created fundamentally new circumstances for social activists like Ivory Perry. The state sector of the economy played a particularly important role in providing employment opportunities and social services for minority and poor populations unable to influence the decision-making processes in the private sector. The attack on the state sector in the 1970s worked special hardships on these people and their institutions. In St. Louis, that process made itself felt most vividly in the struggle over the closing of Homer G. Phillips Hospital, one of the first battles to engage Ivory Perry's attentions after his return to social activism, and one that would prefigure much of his future organizing activities.

The city of St. Louis had built Homer G. Phillips Hospital in the 1930s as a full-care health facility for the black community. For years, Homer G. Phillips Hospital served the health needs of black St. Louisans and functioned as one of the few training centers for black physicians nationwide. When the federal courts compelled the city to desegregate its hospitals, white politicians began to campaign to close Phillips Hospital as an economy measure. Located in the heart of the black ghetto, far from convenient highways and isolated from the bulk of the region's increasingly suburban population, Phillips seemed like a needless expense to many white St. Louisans. Yet to the black community, the hospital had real importance, not only as a source of comprehensive medical care but as one of the few viable institutions still providing employment within the North Side ghetto. It also retained symbolic significance as the tangible evidence of the black community's long struggle for concessions from a frequently insensitive and unresponsive city government.[7] In 1978, St. Louis mayor James Conway announced that the fiscal crisis confronting the city had reached such extraordinary proportions that it was necessary to shut down Homer G. Phillips Hospital.

Conway's plan to close the hospital provoked immediate and vehement protests from the black community. Ivory Perry organized a mass march and demonstration to challenge the decision, bringing former St. Louisan Dick Gregory to town to help focus public attention on the crisis. Perry also participated in direct-action protests at the hospital that forced the city government to reconsider the decision.

In the 1981 Democratic primary, Alderman Vincent Schoemehl defeated incumbent Mayor Conway largely because he attracted an overwhelming proportion of the black vote on the basis of his promise to keep the hospital open. Yet after pursuing a variety of schemes to fund the facility, Schoemehl reversed his earlier stand and announced that it was fiscally impossible for the city to maintain a full-care health facility on the North Side.[8]

The closing of Homer G. Phillips represented only the most public facet of the crisis facing inner-city residents in St. Louis as a result of the economic changes of the 1970s. At HDC, Ivory Perry directly confronted the results of political and economic retrenchment as he encountered an increasing number of people unable to secure the basic necessities of life. Inflation and rising energy costs worked extreme hardships on senior citizens and welfare recipients struggling to make ends meet on small fixed incomes. If they fell behind in their bills, they faced the hazards of terminated services. In addition, blacks complained repeatedly to Perry that they seemed to pay larger deposits and receive estimated bills more frequently than white customers did.

On March 9, 1978, Ivory Perry brought two busloads of senior citizens and poor people to the Missouri Public Service Commission hearings in St. Louis to protest proposed utility rate hikes. Perry then led the group to the Laclede Gas Company building, where they staged a demonstration against that firm's practices in dealing with its customers from poverty-stricken neighborhoods. Acting as spokesperson for the demonstrators, Perry complained to reporters about high utility rates, estimated bills, and high deposit charges. Shortly after that demonstration, he filed a formal complaint with the Missouri Human Rights Commission contending that the gas company discriminated against black workers in its hiring and promotion policies, and that the company had no blacks in policy-making positions.[9] The commission dismissed his charges and found in favor of the utility.

On August 23, 1978, an entire wall of a deteriorating building caved in on Mrs. Beatrice Dunn and her seven children as they slept. Ivory Perry summoned reporters to the building the next day, telling them that the incident demonstrated the dangers faced by tenants with negligent landlords. "They don't live in the city," he said of the building's owners: "they press for rent, and then they don't put any money back into the building."[10]

Two months later, a group of tenants in rent-subsidized apartments faced eviction when their landlord sold the building. An official from the Department of Housing and Urban Development told the tenants they had to leave, but he offered them no places to relocate. When HUD turned off the electricity and water in an effort to force them out, the tenants turned to Ivory Perry for help. He told them that they hadn't gotten mad enough yet, that their polite requests had given HUD no incentive for negotiating with them. The next day, they started a sit-in demonstration to protest the agency's threat to evict them. "They're going to sit in until HUD tells them where they can go to live," Perry explained to reporters. The resulting media coverage and public pressure convinced the agency's staff to find relocation apartments for the evicted tenants.[11]

In the midst of his renewed activism at HDC, Ivory Perry met Anita Reed. She came to the Union-Sarah Gateway Center one day to inquire about available housing in the neighborhood, and soon they established a relationship. Reed felt that Perry was different from other men she had met.

> He just doesn't reach out and grab anything. You know it's like when you have dinner, and everything is all laid out and people are supposed to come up and get what they want. You know how some people are, they're just all over it—grab, grab, grab, trying to get the most out of everything and keep it over there for themselves. He's not like that.[12]

Perry helped Reed find an apartment and a grant to attend college. His generosity toward her and his commitment to the community struck her as two sides of the same coin, and Reed respected and admired the man behind them. "Ivory Perry has been as good as gold to me," Reed asserts. But Reed objected strongly to Perry's possessiveness and jealousy. Sometimes their disagreements ended in arguments where he hit her.

> He's jumped on me a few times. He felt that I was cheating on him, and we really got into it. Sometimes I felt that he had everything all bottled up inside, and he would find some kind of reason, and it would trigger him off, and he would take out all of his frustrations on me. Sometimes i'd say, "Hey, why don't you go out and jump on one of those people out in the street that's always doing something to you? Why do you want to do this to me?"[13]

For his part, Perry regrets his episodes of domestic violence and feels they cannot be justified. "I don't like no jumping on women and I don't

like violence," he insists. But he also feels that the pressures on him as a
black male contributed to the anger and frustration that resulted in
sometimes hitting or threatening people he loved. As he explains it:

> It's harder on black men than on white men, because a lot of black
> women will be looking at TV and see how the white woman's hus-
> bands treat them. But it's different for black males, because they
> don't make that kind of money, they can't afford to buy this or buy
> that. You have a lot of pressure. You have to rob Peter to pay Paul.
> Like your utility bill is due one week and your rent is due the next
> week, and you just don't have the kind of money to be able to pay
> all your bills on time. So there'd be a lot of pressure back and forth.
> You know, the utility be on your back, the landlord will be on your
> back, and then you had to go through hell on the job for the little
> pay that you get. You had to do things that you really wouldn't
> ordinarily do. But you have to try and survive, so you have to kiss
> booty in order to hold that little job, which you really don't want
> to do.[14]

Although the pressures Perry describes are real enough, a convincing
body of contemporary social science research indicates that domestic violence against women transcends issues of economics, affecting families
in all classes. The same research also reveals domestic violence to be part
of a social rather than an individual pattern, a part of a larger social
sanction both for violent behavior and for the subordination of women.
As Wini Breines and Linda Gordon point out, individual acts of wife
abuse may have rational or irrational motivations, but taken as a totality
they function as a means of intimidating and controlling all women.[15]

So much of Perry's political activism has involved working with wom-
en and addressing the particular problems they face, that it is especially
sad to realize that at times his behavior has made him the enemy of the
women closest to him. His sensitivity to hierarchies of race and class has
put him on the side of the oppressed in battle after battle, yet within his
own home his inattention to gender as a category of domination has
placed him in the role of oppressor. One of the appeals of politics for
Ivory Perry lay precisely in the opportunity to channel his rage and frustration toward their real causes, rather than taking them out on those
closest to him. It was not as if politics simply took him away from domestic bliss. On the contrary, politics enabled him to find a constructive

outlet for frustrations that might be expressed destructively at home. He could feel better about himself, and more in control of his own life, when he vented those frustrations through social activism.

Perry continued his activism, sometimes flamboyantly, sometimes quietly. Dramatic moments of crisis—like a demonstration before the Public Service Commission, a wall caving in on a sleeping family, or a tenant sit-in to secure relocation housing—called attention to the symptoms of urban decay, but they produced no program addressing its root causes. Perry believed that inner-city health and housing problems stemmed from conscious decisions by leaders of both the public and private sectors. From the excess destruction of urban renewal to the underfunding of public housing, each policy decision helped force poor and black people into marginal areas with inferior dwellings. Financial institutions followed policies that discouraged loans to homeowners building or renovating houses in black neighborhoods, but those same institutions generously financed downtown redevelopment, housing in white suburbs, or "gentrification" of older deteriorating neighborhoods by middle- and upper-income professionals interested in renovating older homes. Perry saw the accumulated effect of these policies over three decades leaving blacks with precious few housing opportunities in St. Louis. As he complained to a reporter in 1979:

> The county [made up largely of white suburbs] doesn't want subsidized housing and in effect doesn't want the poor blacks who would live in it. The West End [a gentrified inner-city neighborhood] is becoming too expensive for them to afford and they find it hard to get loans to repair their homes in north St. Louis where most of them live.[16]

In the past, Perry attempted to address such problems by mobilizing popular pressure to get elected officials to respond. But in the late 1970s, the local government most susceptible to that kind of pressure lacked the resources to solve the problems, while the federal government supported the very forces responsible for the problems in the first place. In fact, federal policies often invoked the rhetoric of social activists in order to put in place policies inimical to their interests, as evidenced by the "desegregation" rhetoric accompanying the Department of Housing and Urban Development's Regional Housing Mobility Plan. Ostensibly designed to aid black migration out of the central city into the suburbs, the plan seemed in Perry's view to instead disperse blacks to isolated inferior housing on the periphery of the metropolitan area in order to open up housing opportunities for white professionals in areas close to downtown.

At one time, Perry might have favored a plan to open up the suburbs to black settlement—back in the 1950s when restrictive covenants and discriminatory loan policies enriched the white suburbs at the expense of the black inner city. But in the late 1970s, suburban commuters faced rising energy costs that made it more difficult for them to travel to downtown offices and cultural attractions. Renovated older housing near the central business district attracted the attention of young professionals with high disposable incomes. Perry believed that black families had more to gain by remaining inside the central city where new jobs were likely to be created and where they could enjoy the political advantages of concentrated population. He feared that dispersal to suburban hinterlands would leave them cut off from vital services and fragment their political strength. Having witnessed the effects of urban renewal on the black community in the 1950s and 1960s, he could not imagine that the Regional Housing Mobility Plan would amount to anything more than what he termed "black removal with white approval."[17]

Defenders of the plan argued that relocation to the suburbs would help blacks desegregate previously all-white areas and enable them to share in the advantages of suburban life with its open spaces and single-family dwellings. Some housing experts who had generally sided with Perry in the past felt that he was exaggerating the dangers of this program, which they viewed as an extremely modest and essentially harmless effort. But Perry insisted that the plan amounted to a South African–style solution to the race problem in America: sequestering blacks in residential enclaves on the periphery and allowing them to enter the central city only as poorly paid laborers.[18]

He began to speak out against the plan before a variety of community groups, and convinced a group of black law students to take the lead in opposing the plan. In a letter to one of the city's black weekly newspapers, Mrs. Fern Buchanan, a resident of the Union-Sarah neighborhood, wrote:

Mr. Perry is monitoring this situation very closely for us! We've got to stick with him because no one in the city is going to help us like he does. Don't just sit around watching TV and let yourself be railroaded out of St. Louis. This happened before. That's how we lost

Homer G. Phillips Hospital. If we don't take an active interest in our own housing and community problems who will? We're lucky to have Mr. Perry, we better make the best of him.[19]

Protests against the plan attracted national attention, especially from activist groups in other cities concerned about similar proposals. Through the National Tenants Organization and informal contacts he had built up over the years, Perry contacted a national network of opponents. He traveled to meetings and conferences called to formulate a concerted national tenants' response to the plan. At one of these conferences in Cleveland in March 1980, Perry outlined to a reporter the scenario that he believed lay behind the plan.

There's a gas crunch, many of the professional jobs are in the city and all of the major cities are looking for ways to get more money into their operating funds through taxes. . . . The only way to get money and whites back into the city is to move the poor people out, clear the land and rebuild.[20]

To prevent that, Perry reiterated his counsel that blacks remain in the central cities, consolidate their political and economic power there, and position themselves to share in the benefits of any future urban revitalization. For those reasons, he opposed another federal initiative in 1980 that under other circumstances he might have supported. Federal court judge William Hungate found that St. Louis city and county had illegally conspired to segregate public education and he ordered a desegregation plan that bused students between city and county schools. Ivory Perry agreed that the schools had been desegregated illegally and he opposed discriminatory policies that undermined the resources available for educating black children. But he opposed this desegregation plan, because he thought it proceeded at the expense of the black community and its institutions. Just as "desegregation" of the city's hospitals meant closing Homer G. Phillips and "integration" into a facility less responsive, Perry felt that the school desegregation plan outlined by Hungate would scatter inner-city black students to far-flung regions of the county while creating a few "model" predominantly white schools in central city neighborhoods targeted for gentrification.

In the wake of the Regional Housing Mobility Plan, Perry perceived this particular structure of desegregation as part of an overall plan to bring whites back into the central city and to disperse blacks out to the county. He joined black parents in mounting protest demonstrations against the terms of the desegregation plan, and organized one protest outside the public relations firm representing Civic Progress, an organization made up of the chief executive officers of St. Louis's largest corporations. Arguing that HUD, the federal courts, and the local boards of education were just pawns, Perry explained to reporters that the parents had brought their grievances before Civic Progress because "Civic Progress is what really runs the city." When asked if the opposition to Judge Hungate's plan represented a change in his attitude toward integration, Perry replied, "Integration is not important; I'm looking at economic development and survival."[21]

Community protests contributed to modifications of the desegregation plan and rejection of the Regional Housing Mobility Plan, but the long-range imperatives that Ivory Perry detected behind them remained in place. In the next five years, a variety of scholars and government officials, using the tools and techniques of traditional intellectuals, would echo Perry's critique of federal urban policy.

In 1983, political scientist John Mollenkopf published *The Contested City*, which argued that federal urban policy reflects a struggle for resources conducted in the context of electoral politics. Under the political maxim of rewarding friends and punishing enemies, Democrats tend to funnel money and resources to the voters in older industrial cities who make up a key component of their electoral coalition, while Republicans support policies designed to advance the interests of suburban residents and the inhabitants of the service-industry-oriented cities of the South and West. Thus the public housing programs of the Truman years and the antipoverty initiatives of the Kennedy-Johnson era represented the use of federal resources to support an urban formation that bolstered the electoral base of the Democratic party. Similarly, the federal home loan, highway, and defense policies of the Eisenhower administration and the revenue-sharing plans of the Nixon and Ford presidencies accelerated the growth of those parts of metropolitan regions more likely to support Republicans.

Politicians not only reward their friends under these procedures, but they undermine the social base of their opponents. The success of the Nixon administration's counteroffensive against the programs of the 1960s, shifts in population and resources engendered by Eisenhower-era initiatives, and the fiscal crisis of the state in the 1970s combined to make even the Democratic administration headed by President Carter favor essentially neoconservative urban policies. These involved the very kinds of curtailment of services to the inner city and subsidies for gentrification and redevelopment that Perry perceived to be behind the closing of Homer G. Phillips Hospital and the Regional Housing Mobility Plan.[22]

Historian Robert Fisher detailed the impact of the economic crisis of the 1970s on community activists in his 1984 publication, *Let the People Decide*. Fisher contends that both the conservative consensus of the 1950s and the welfare state liberalism of the 1960s rested on assumptions of an ever-expanding economy. Those assumptions made it possible for oppositional groups to advance affirmative agendas that demanded revolutionary social changes and concrete improvements in the standard of living available to the poor.

But the economic retrenchment of the 1970s produced a new kind of business-government urban policy that necessitated different responses. The neoconservative policy toward the cities in the 1970s expressed what Fisher terms "planned shrinkage" or "triage" of inner-city neighborhoods. Bankers used the fiscal crisis of cities as a pretext for demanding dismantling of "expensive" social programs that sustained the poor, and urban planners favored curtailment of city services as a means of forcing the poor to leave the industrial cities of the Northeast, presumably to migrate to the booming cities of the Sunbelt.

Fisher cites the counsel of New York City housing and development administrator Roger Starr in 1976 that closing public schools, firehouses, and police stations in slum areas constituted an efficient means of bringing about a desired decline in the population of the city's poor.[23] Those policies forced activists everywhere to take on a more defensive posture. Ivory Perry's resistance to the "planned shrinkage" implicit in the Regional Housing Mobility Plan manifested precisely the kind of strategy that Fisher found characteristic of activists throughout the country.

Even some administrators involved in implementing the new urban policies came to see the problems that activists like Ivory Perry identified as early as 1979. Floyd Lapp served as the director of housing and community development for the Tri-State Regional Planning Commission of Metropolitan New York in the late 1970s and early 1980s. In June 1985 he wrote a letter to the *New York Times* recounting his experiences with the Regional Housing Mobility Plan. "It was not a popular program with low-income, moderate-income and minority households. Although the goal was to promote choice, it was perceived as an effort to reduce the

coalition of political strength that had finally been established over decades in urban centers." Lapp went on to say that the Brookings Institute,
which initially articulated policies like the Regional Housing Mobility
Plan, favored the abandonment of federal policies designed to help the
cities, and that the acceptance of their view by business and political
leaders left "those with the greatest need with far less hope."[24]

Many intellectuals disagreed with the perceptions voiced by Mollenkopf, Fisher, and Lapp himself. Neoconservative urban and social
policy experts like Anthony Downs, George Sternlieb, and Charles Murray blamed the fiscal crisis of the cities on wasteful and unproductive
subsidies to the poor that impinged on the legitimate capital needs of
productive investors. As Sternlieb expressed it, "You can't support the
poor without the rich, and every time someone rich stays in Manhattan
it's a triumph for the poor."[25] Intellectuals lined up on different sides of
the issue because of the centrality of conflict to public policy making and
because of their identification with the various social groups contesting
for the right to define the "general interest" of society. In both the articulation of those ideas and their implementation in practice, organic intellectuals like Ivory Perry played an important role.

The revolutionary changes in urban policies inaugurated by the neoconservative agenda of the 1970s compelled Ivory Perry to champion a
new kind of activism. Instead of proposing new programs and expanded commitments to serve deprived populations, he had to struggle
against the dismantling of existing community resources and institutions. St. Louis newspaperman Robert Joiner notes both the peril and
the promise of activism under these changed conditions. He observes
that Ivory "still has the illusion that if he should get nailed to the cross,
that people are going to come and take him off. But times have changed
so much that the kind of backing that ordinarily would be around for
that kind of confrontation is just not here." But on the other hand, Joiner
still sees great relevance in Perry's goals and tactics.

Some people look at Ivory as still fighting the old civil rights struggles whereas times and tactics have changed. And to them, he just
didn't grow. On the other hand, and I kind of sympathize with him,
in saying that those people who would make that comment really
happen to be people who are in the positions, who got the jobs,
primarily or partly because of people like himself. But in terms of
just working-class people, they probably have more identification

with Ivory Perry than they would with their alderman, for the simple reason that Ivory's zeroing in, day after day, on the issues that are closest to them.[26]

The historical memory of the community played an important role in shaping its perceptions. Black St. Louisans felt that they had a right to a complete health care facility in their community, and that superficial desegregation of suburban subdivisions and classrooms would not offset the political losses incurred by fragmentation of concentrated black population centers. Traditional standards and expectations nurtured through the struggles of the past offered a basis for challenging the legitimacy of declining city services and "black removal by white approval" in the present. The surface and sedimented community networks and associations built up over the years created an infrastructure capable of carrying on that right, but it required the active intervention of organic intellectuals to galvanize that infrastructure into action.

The fate of the postindustrial city took on more than abstract political significance for Ivory Perry in 1981 when the full impact of the neoconservative urban agenda hit him personally. Drastic reductions in federal expenditures on urban social programs necessitated cutbacks at the St. Louis Human Development Corporation, and that agency had to eliminate the position of housing coordinator and terminate Ivory Perry's employment. In the middle of the worst economic recession in forty years, he found himself looking for work. He was a fifty-one-year-old semi-skilled black worker with a history of social activism, nervous breakdowns, and repeated sentences in the city jail. The survival issues that had occupied his attention for the previous sixteen years at HDC now took on a distinctly personal character as he searched for a way to continue earning a living and to continue his existence as an organic intellectual and activist.

Sixteen years as housing coordinator at the Union-Sarah Gateway Center left Ivory Perry with no savings and no property. "My job was really just something to survive on while I was organizing," he explains. "Financially, I was doing worse than most people out on the streets. I wasn't making no big salary. With the little money that they was paying me, by the time I paid my rent, my light bill, my gas bill, and got my clothes out of the cleaners, I was broke again."[27] Getting fired meant losing even that subsistence income, and it severed Perry from the institution that had been his base of operations for most of his career as a community activist. He worried about his ability to secure another job, but even more feared losing the opportunity to do meaningful work.

While collecting his unemployment benefits, Perry volunteered his services to the Jeff-Vander-Lou Corporation, a community self-help group in the North Side ghetto. On Saturday mornings, the organization showed free movies to neighborhood children, and Ivory Perry volunteered to be the projectionist. Seeing the nearly 200 children between the ages of seven and twelve that attended the films every week, Perry began to think of ways to occupy their time more productively. Many adults in the neighborhood had complained about the litter in vacant lots and alleys that the city seemed unwilling or unable to pick up, so along with others at the Jeff-Vander-Lou Corporation, Perry mobilized the children for a clean-up campaign on Saturday afternoons. They gave out free hot dogs as a reward, and soon had more volunteers than they could handle. When the children complained to Perry that it was difficult to clear the vacant lots because the weeds in them were so high, he took pictures of the weeds and led a delegation of youths to City Hall. They presented the mayor's representatives with the pictures and demanded that the city take appropriate action.[28]

Shortly after his visit to the mayor's office, Perry received a telephone call from Jack Kane, aide to newly elected Mayor Vincent Schoemehl. Kane had seen the pictures and asked Perry if he wanted to work on Operation Brightside, a municipal program offering summer jobs to young people by hiring them to pick up litter from streets and alleys. The mayor viewed the project as a showcase for his administration's efforts to revive local pride, and he jumped at the opportunity to hire Perry with his many contacts within the black community. Yet the city's financial problems made Operation Brightside a short-lived venture, and when the project ended after a year, so did Perry's job.[29]

Another stint as a volunteer led to Perry's next job. Throughout his tenure at HDC, he had worked with many individuals connected with the eighteenth ward Democratic party organization. When his job with Operation Brightside ended, Perry began to volunteer his services to the ward organization, helping them with voter registration drives, and serving as liaison between the party regulars in the community and the ward committeeman. The ward organization provided another context for doing the kinds of neighborhood work he had done at HDC, and he threw himself into its activities with enthusiasm. When a job opened up in the city treasurer's office parking meters division, the ward committeeman recommended Perry for the post. Starting in 1982 he began work there, putting the coins collected from city parking meters into counting machines. The job made little use of the many things he had learned from his years of social commitment, but it enabled him to make a living and continue his community activities with the Metropolitan Tenants Organization and with the ward organization as well.

During the winter of 1982–1983, Ivory Perry involved himself in the voter registration projects organized by the ward organization. A similar drive in Chicago in those same months helped make Congressman Harold Washington that city's first black mayor, a victory that sparked hopes for similar gains in St. Louis, where blacks constituted nearly half of the electorate. The fiscal policies of the federal government were the most important problem facing the black community, and voter registration seemed the only logical way to mount a political counterattack. Ivory Perry had long favored voter registration drives, having worked on them back in his CORE days in the early 1960s. He did not believe that electoral action by itself could solve most of the problems facing poor and black people, but he did feel that heavy voter turnouts gave activists important leverage with city officials and helped create favorable circumstances for social change.[30]

Voter registration drives in black St. Louis drew sharp criticism from the St. Louis election board chairman, Republican Jerry Wamser, as well as from Circuit Attorney George Peach, a conservative Democrat. Wamser and Peach claimed that efforts to register voters included attempts by machine politicians to manipulate absentee ballots. The *St. Louis Globe-Democrat* ran a series of articles alleging abuses of absentee ballot procedures late in 1982, and called on the proper authorities to investigate. On March 10, 1983, that appeal bore fruit. The *Globe-Democrat* announced in a front-page story that Circuit Attorney Peach had filed charges against Ivory Perry of attempted absentee-vote fraud, charges that could bring four years in prison and a $4,000 fine.[31]

Perry denied any wrongdoing and insisted that he had engaged in no fraud. The charges against him stemmed from twenty-three requests for absentee ballots from the eighteenth ward. All were first-time voters, and the circuit attorney claimed that none of them knew that they were requesting absentee ballots. In response, Perry acknowledged that he had helped all twenty-three voters to register—"I put 186 people on the books myself, in one month," he proclaimed—but he denied that he knew anything about attempts to confuse anyone about the nature of absentee ballots. City treasurer (and eighteenth-ward politician) Larry Williams stood behind his employee. "We're talking about a man who has been involved in the civil rights movement in St. Louis for over 30 years. . . . He's never had the kind of reputation as a manipulator. . . . It looks like a political move and I don't think there is any substance to it."[32]

After several procedural delays, the case came to trial in late November 1983. Monsignor John Shocklee, now human rights director of the archdiocese of St. Louis, appeared as a character witness on Perry's behalf. Shocklee knew nothing about the particulars of the voter-fraud charge, but he wanted to tell the court that he had known the defendant for over twenty years and that he had the highest regard for Ivory Perry's character and for his career of "sensitizing people to more of a feeling for justice." But as it turned out, the defense did not need the monsignor's testimony. After hearing the state's case, Judge Michael Calvin directed the acquittal of the defendant on all charges. The judge noted that although the indictment accused Perry of defrauding people of their votes, the circuit attorney's case alleged no such thing—he had only alleged fraudulent efforts to obtain absentee ballots, a distinctly different offense. Perry thanked his court-appointed attorney and left the courtroom a free man.[33]

If Perry had been the only black activist charged with voter registration fraud, the implications of political corruption in the charges brought against him might hold more weight. But in the context of Justice Department persecutions of black activists in Alabama for registering large numbers of voters while it ignored complaints about intimidation employed to keep blacks from registering, it raises the possibility of self-serving political manipulation. Both the circuit attorney and the election board chairman in St. Louis belonged to political factions that would have been harmed by a large turnout of black voters. The newspaper that trumpeted the charges of voter registration irregularities had a long-standing antipathy to the civil rights movement that bordered on fanaticism: it opposed every major civil rights campaign, printed false information planted by the FBI defaming Martin Luther King, Jr., and in one editorial referred to Rochester, the feisty servant on the Jack Benny radio and television shows, as "the most liberated black man who ever lived."[34] While the directed verdict of acquittal may seem to rest on a

technicality, the prosecutor had nine months after the indictment to develop a case, and the opportunity to reintroduce charges after the acquittal. He did neither.

Less than a year later. Perry found himself once again facing legal
charges, this time emanating from his efforts to help build support for
laundry workers on strike at the Morgan Systems Company. Thirty black
workers, most of them women, called a strike against that firm on July
30, 1984, after working without a contract for six months. They complained about demeaning treatment from supervisors (including having
to raise their hands and ask permission to use the bathroom), and they
resented the compulsory overtime that often kept them on the hot floor
of the laundry from seven in the morning until eight at night.

Company officials claimed that they no longer required workers to
raise their hands to ask permission to use the bathroom and that the
business needed to keep employees on hand past regular working hours
to deal with unexpected rush orders. After three weeks of the strike,
Morgan Systems management withdrew bargaining recognition from
the laundry workers' union and began hiring "permanent replacements"
for those on strike. Technicalities in federal labor law prevented the firm
from firing strikers, but hiring permanent replacements threatened to
accomplish the same end within the letter of the law. The company
spokesmen made it clear that striking workers would get their jobs back
only if new positions opened up in the future, and even then, only those
with "exemplary conduct" on the picket lines would be considered.[35]

Fifteen years earlier, employees at the Morgan Systems Company had
gone on strike over low wages. They read about Ivory Perry in the paper
and telephoned him to ask for help with their strike. Perry talked to
Percy Green of ACTION, who launched a boycott of linen companies
that helped the strikers win union recognition and a raise in pay. Many
of those same employees remained with the company in 1984, and when
the company began hiring replacement workers they once again contacted Ivory Perry for help. He arranged meeting space for the strikers at
Maurice Williamson's tavern (Maurice's Gold Coast Lounge) and helped
buy dinner and drinks for them. He explains that strategy:

> In order to get people organized, sometimes you have to spend
> money, like on lunches or something, to keep them together while
> you're trying to talk with them. Most of the time they're angry,
> they're frustrated, they're upset, so we had a couple of dinners for

them. We bought them beer or whatever they wanted to drink out of our own pockets. . . . People are not going to take time to sit and listen if they're not seeing what they're going to get out of it.[36]

At those meetings, Perry talked to the strikers about their problems, and together they worked out a strategy for a militant response to the company's hard-line position.

On August 22, Ivory Perry led an enthusiastic picket line in front of Morgan Systems Company. The picket line—more than sixty demonstrators—presented an impressive picture of broad-based community backing. It included state representatives Quincey Troupe (a former bus driver and civil rights activist) and Louis Ford (who had participated in the 1964 CORE demonstrations at the New York World's Fair) and two announced black candidates for mayor: Alderman Freeman Bosley, Sr., and former housing authority official Alphonso Jackson. Showing broad community support for the laundry workers, the picket line threatened to make the dispute the focal point of renewed civil rights activity in St. Louis.[37]

Morgan Systems officials responded by taking pictures of those on the picket line, implying retaliatory action against the strikers. When management personnel tried to take Perry's picture, he turned away, but one of the Morgan employees grabbed his arm to turn him toward the camera. According to Perry, the man then spat in his face. Perry picked up a rock and threw it at him and charged him. "He tried to spit on me," Perry recalls; "that's when I just blew up. You know, I've been on many demonstrations and I'm always nonviolent, but that just took something out of me when he tried to spit on me. Like when I was down in Bogalusa, I was hit with rocks, soda bottles, rotten eggs and so forth, and I didn't blow up. But that belittled my manhood when somebody spit on me. So I just reached out and picked up a rock and threw it at him."[38]

The police ran over to the picket line and arrested Perry on the spot. At the downtown central jail, he waited seven hours before his friends could post bond. When the case came to trial months later, the judge found Perry guilty of two counts of disturbing the peace, and fined him $50 for each one. The strikers from Morgan Systems helped him pay the fines, and they assured Perry that their work stoppages and demonstration had been responsible for small improvements in their situation at work. But the entire experience left a bitter taste in Ivory Perry's mouth.

"I think I was frustrated because after ten, twelve years, the conditions there at Morgan Linen were worse than when I first went in there and helped them organize in 1969."[39] It was one thing to go to jail as part of a campaign to win new jobs, better housing, and political power, but yet another to be fighting the same battles year after year with no assurances of real progress.

In that picket line incident, Ivory Perry lashed out violently for the first time in more than thirty years of social activism. In the voter registration case, he faced a stiffer fine and longer jail sentence than for anything he had ever done before. In both cases, Perry found himself embroiled in local controversies that reflected significant national trends. The neoconservative economic and political agenda of the 1970s and 1980s attempted to trim the power of organized labor and reduce the role of government in solving the problems of disadvantaged populations.

On a national level, those policies manifested themselves in diverse ways. On the economic plane, they entailed Congressional resistance to the AFL-CIO's common sites picketing bill in 1978, President Reagan's firing of striking air traffic controllers in 1981, and labor-management contracts throughout the country that used the crisis of the industrial sector as justification for union concessions that bargained away previous gains for workers. On the political plane, they included state redistricting and registration plans that diluted minority voting strength. The Justice Department displayed great reluctance to pursue black complaints about violations of the 1965 Voting Rights Act, but eagerly prosecuted black activists involved in voter registration drives in Marion and Greene counties in Alabama.[40] At the Morgan Systems strike, and in the charges brought against him for fraudulent voter registration, Ivory Perry confronted the local manifestations of those national policies. He also suffered from the shortcomings of the two main institutions targeted by those policies: the trade unions and the Democratic party.

Ivory Perry's strike support and voter registration efforts were aimed at preserving the historic gains won by black workers and voters in St. Louis, gains made within the context of trade unions and the Democratic party. Certainly both had engaged in extensive racist resistance to black aspirations many times in the past, but when black workers made economic gains, and when black voters increased their political power, the institutional resources of trade unions and the Democratic party helped consolidate and preserve those advances. But when under attack by neoconservative forces, both the unions and the party tended to make concessions designed to preserve their institutional privileges rather than risk everything in a battle on behalf of their traditional constituencies. Consequently, unions preferred to make concessions to management that preserved the institutional identity (and secure flow of dues and benefits) of the trade union rather than battling against the decline in wages, conditions, and future opportunities augured by the neoconservative deindustrialization of America. Similarly, the Democratic party worked to consolidate its control over existing institutions like city governments and trade unions, rather than mounting a challenge to policies that effectively undermined the social formations that produced its traditional electoral base. On a national level, these responses left the neoconservative agenda virtually unchallenged, while in localities like St. Louis, it left activists like Ivory Perry vulnerable to the shortcomings and weaknesses of allies in the labor movement and the political establishment.

Ivory Perry had no complaint against the workers at Morgan Systems: he understood why they might be unable to wage a sustained struggle against their employer, but he had less sympathy for their union. "I'm for unions," he insists, "but this union wasn't doing anything to help the dues payers. They paid something like $13 a month with no representation. We got the union back involved in it."[41] That involvement led to a settlement of the strike, but it was not one that seemed worth the effort to Perry. The workers won a small increase in wages, but the conditions that precipitated their strike seemed unresolved to him, and he felt that it was just a matter of time before the company broke their power altogether.

Connections to the Democratic party also embroiled Ivory Perry in the internal contradictions of local politics. For most of his tenure at HDC, he had remained independent of ward leaders and organizations. He had supported candidates from time to time, and had always assisted in voter registration drives, but his constituency in the streets and neighborhoods always had command of his first loyalties. But with the demise of the antipoverty program, the only institutional base strong enough to support his activities came from one of the ward organizations. Since he worked for the city treasurer, and conducted his registration activities through the auspices of the treasurer's home ward organization, it was easy for the circuit attorney to plant the suspicion that Perry violated the law in order to keep his job. Perry expressly denies that charge, insisting that the ward organization has never asked him to do anything he considered illegal, unethical, or not in the best interests of the community.[42]

One can only work with the structures to which one has access, and it is not surprising that Ivory Perry could easily participate in Democratic organizing activities that corresponded to his own goals, like registering voters or publicizing neighborhood complaints about problems with city services. But his work in the Democratic party differed sharply from what he had been able to do in the past in the antipoverty effort and the civil rights movement. Previously, he had always been able to work within institutions without becoming too wedded to their bureaucratic practices or needs for institutional survival. His contacts with the community enabled him to provide CORE or HDC with the credibility they needed to advance their own goals. In spite of numerous schisms and faction fights, both the civil rights movement and the antipoverty program stood for a clear set of economic and social interests. As an electoral coalition made up of more antagonistic parts, the Democratic party in the 1980s could not take on such an unambiguous identity, and its institutional needs differed from Ivory Perry's goals more frequently.

One example was the 1984 Presidential primary election. Ivory Perry worked for Walter Mondale rather than Jesse Jackson. "I had to go along with my committeeman," Perry relates, "because he's the one who got me my job." Even when working for candidates whose views mirrored his own, Perry found that politics drew him into some unfamiliar circumstances. During the 1986 primary election, a bitter power struggle between St. Louis's black Congressman, William Clay (whom Perry had known since their days together as young civil rights activists in the 1950s), and its white mayor, Vincent Schoemehl, created bitter divisions within the Democratic party. In the election Perry worked on behalf of legislative candidate William Clay, Jr., the Congressman's son. A candidate opposed to Clay swore out a complaint against Perry, charging him with tearing down campaign signs. Perry considered the charge merely an attempt to get him off the streets on election day to prevent him from getting voters to the polls. He told a reporter that he had indeed been removing the signs, but only because they had been placed on the property of Clay supporters without their permission; he claimed that neighborhood residents told him they wanted this "trash" removed. The police did arrest Perry and hold him for several hours, but ultimately those complaining about his behavior dropped their charges. William Clay, Jr., won the election with the aid of Perry's enthusiastic organizing, but the incident did little to enhance Perry's reputation in some circles or allay doubts about his independence.[43]

Perry brushes off any suggestions that working for the Democratic party compromises his integrity or freedom of action. "I know how to maneuver," he asserts. "I know what it takes to put them in office and I know what it takes to get them out of office, so I kind of still have the upper hand there. I know what they want and what they need. I know how to give it to them and how to take it away." He has always prided himself on being both an idealist *and* a realist; experience has taught him to look for any possible lever to bring about needed changes. "You got to compromise," he insists. "You just can't go in to someone and say, 'I want twenty jobs in this department.' He might give you twenty jobs, but you have to give up something too."[44]

Yet many of Perry's old friends wonder if he really feels as comfortable with his new role as he claims. Pearlie Evans notes, "At HDC he was free to do things for people. He had a base of operations and important contacts. He could lead and people would follow. It was important to his self-esteem. But once he lost that job, he's been greatly disappointed. He has to do some things to earn a living that he really doesn't want to do." Similarly, Robert Joiner observes, "I think he's had to compromise a lot because I wouldn't be surprised if a part of his job wasn't that he had to work at the polls. He has to promote things, and I think that takes away from issues he's most concerned about. He's had to stretch himself a little bit."[45]

But political action of any kind depends on the available opportunities as well as on the beliefs and preferences of activists. The incident at the Morgan Systems Company picket line and Perry's brushes with the law in the course of his electoral politicking take place within the context of economic and social contestation in the 1980s. As Perry struggles for the retention of past gains, he encounters new arenas of conflict and new forms of resistance and repression.

The shifts in American society from an industrial economy to a postindustrial service society, and from welfare-state liberalism to supply-side capitalism, have produced an entirely new context for social contestation. That context entails the loss of high-paying blue-collar jobs, the flight of capital and jobs to the Third World, a loss of consumer purchasing power, cutbacks in social services, and a decline in the political power of inner-city urban dwellers. The emerging "high tech" and service economy threatens to polarize workers into two groups—highly skilled and educated technical workers on one side, and unskilled service workers on the other. In addition, tax cuts, heavy defense spending, and huge federal deficits advance the neoconservative agenda by making the state incapable of funding the needs of the poor and middle classes. Despite their antigovernment rhetoric, the neoconservatives have actually increased the size of government markedly, but they have channeled its benefits to capital rather than to consumers, the middle class, workers, or the poor.

In Ivory Perry's world those economic transformations have had a devastating effect. "What's here today is a city that died because they let it die," observes Maurice Williamson as he surveys the squalor of the inner-city ghetto.[46] At a time when the number of poor people had surpassed 15.2 percent of the entire population, when nearly one out of every four children lived below the poverty line, the social services designed to make their lives bearable and to bring hope for the future disappeared for lack of funding. Meager gains in opportunity and income among poor and black people in the 1960s and early 1970s evaporated in the wake of policies widening the income gaps between rich and poor and between whites and blacks. Between 1981 and 1983 alone, close to 800,000 families fell into poverty. When adjusted to take inflation into account, the value of Aid to Dependent Children in the United States fell by one-third between 1969 and 1985. The Reagan administration's 1981 "Deficit Reduction Act" deprived the poor of a dollar's worth of benefits for every dollar earned.[47] A federal treasury that rushed funds to aid mismanaged corporations like Chrysler and Continental Illinois claimed to have insufficient resources to lessen the suffering of the victims of the neoconservative agenda.

Every aspect of Ivory Perry's accomplishments was undermined by these changes. In the 1950s when Perry first became interested in housing issues, two-thirds of American heads of households could afford to buy a single-family home. By 1984 that ratio fell to one in ten. In addition, the gap between renters and homeowners grew larger. In 1970, the median household income of tenants was 64.9 percent of the income of homeowners; by 1980 it had fallen to only 53.5 percent. In 1981, *Business Week* admitted that the nation "has backed away from its longtime commitment to housing as a top national priority. For the next decade at least, the U.S. is in danger of splitting into a nation of housing haves and have-nots. At best Americans are going to be paying more for smaller and smaller lower quality dwellings."[48] The housing crisis emanating from those conditions affected many Americans, but none more so than the poor people that Perry had concerned himself with for so many years. The neoconservative policies of the 1970s and 1980s all but wiped out the gains in housing secured by Ivory Perry's tenant organizing, rent strikes, and demands for building code enforcement during his years at HDC.

The fiscal crisis of the state engineered by tax cuts and increases in defense spending also undermined the traditional resources available to inner-city residents. The closing of Homer G. Phillips Hospital and inadequate funding for clinics undermined many of the gains made in black St. Louis in the 1960s in the area of health care. For example, screening for lead poisoning had to be all but abandoned for lack of funds. Social service professionals and physicians reported widespread hunger in the St. Louis ghettos, while the few private charities dispensing food reported inadequate supplies and excessive demand. Yet federal policy remained oriented toward ever-increasing cutbacks in services to the destitute.

On a national level, neoconservative policies led to retrenchment on the two major gains made by the social protest movements of the 1960s: economic opportunity and political empowerment. Scholars reported a widening gap between white and black incomes after the early 1970s, and argued that even under the most optimistic predictions of economic growth, blacks and whites would not enjoy equal opportunity for at least a century.[49]

In politics, tactics ranging from gerrymandering districts to election formats inimical to the interests of minority voters worked effectively to dilute black political power. One study of seven southern states found that black people, although 25.8 percent of the population, constituted only 5.6 percent of elected officials. If whites were to experience similarly disproportionate underrepresentation in those states, the percentage of white elected officials would drop from 94.4 percent to about 15 percent. In northern states. gerrymandering and residency requirements contributed to the dilution of the black vote and deindustrialization undercut the social base and population areas most influenced by black voters.[50]

Yet even in the face of the extraordinary social changes of the 1970s and 1980s, Ivory Perry did not abandon his commitment to social activism. He continued to see himself as having an important role to play, even if the goals of his activism became more modest and if the victories came less frequently. "I have to help people, whether it makes the front page of the newspaper or not," he explains. "I can't help what happens in the rest of the society. I know that some things are never going to change. You know a leopard don't change its spots. Racism's been around a long time before I was here and it'll continue to be around a long time after I'm gone. All I can do is to help people survive in this society the way it is."[51]

Pearlie Evans understands the pressures on antipoverty activists like Perry in the postindustrial city.

> People don't really care about the poor. There are individuals who care and who form groups that function as centers of concern. And there are institutions that are supposed to care about the poor, but they always suffer from too little money and too few staff people. It takes somebody like Ivory to care about the people caught in the cracks, the people who are outsiders in their own village.[52]

Yet Perry persists, even in the face of overwhelming odds. Jacquelyn Butler Barnes remembers meeting Perry at her first CORE meeting, as a high school student in 1965. Sixteen years later her daughter got her first summer job from Operation Brightside and found Ivory Perry there waiting to sign her up. "Ivory just never stops helping black people," Barnes points out; "he's *been* there, and he's *still* there." Anita Reed expresses a similar view. "He's like a brick wall; you can't break him. Some people, they go to work and do their jobs, and then, hey that's it. But his work is like twenty-four hours a day. If somebody needs help at three o'clock in the morning, he'll get up and go."[53]

Ivory Perry's continued dedication to activism at times has been something of a mixed blessing for his friends. They admire his single-minded devotion to social change, but sometimes marvel at his unrestrained willingness to make demands on them. Robert Joiner of the *St. Louis Post-Dispatch* recalls affectionately:

> During some of the coldest winters in St. Louis he has bugged me to death, about throwing some light not on himself, but on the fact that people are living in places that have no heat, where ice is forming around the windows, that have no food—these were the concerns. He'll call me at the worst times and assume I have nothing else to do but worry about what he's pushing, about what's happening to some poor people any time of the night, any time of the day. He doesn't

believe in doing things in an orderly fashion. Whatever needs to be taken care of, he just assumes the world works this way and everybody's supposed to take note of his problems.[54]

But even when they get frustrated with Perry's methods, the network of people around him still respect his intentions and accomplishments. Dorie Ladner observes:

Perry is a persuader, a manipulator. He's able to get people to do things—that's an organizer. . . . I would describe him as being a "doer," kind of like a Fannie Lou Hamer type. Mrs. Hamer was similar to Ivory in that she had little formal education, but she was a very strong and determined person. . . . A lot of people who have dealt with certain issues have felt comfortable leaving the struggle alone, but Perry was here last year with a tenants group, and the fervor was just as real as it was in 1966.[55]

As an organic intellectual, Ivory Perry recognizes the constraints imposed upon an activist agenda by the grim realities of postindustrial urban life, but he also understands the enduring needs of his community that can be articulated and addressed only by some kind of activist response.

CHAPTER 9

Collective Memory and Social Learning: Deep Like the Rivers

Ivory Perry's life of social activisim has value and meaning because of the people he has helped and because of the injustices he has helped to correct. His story offers lessons about the difficult choices facing ordinary citizens and it illuminates the moral and material tensions confronting us all. But at the same time, Ivory Perry's life history also has value and meaning for what it can teach scholars about the historical and sociological significance of social protest.

How can we assess the "historical" significance of an individual like Ivory Perry? He has lived most of his life distant from the centers of economic, political, and military power that usually form the core of historical narratives, yet he has played an important role in movements for social change. He never sought elective office, but he has pressured politicians into serving their constituents. He never earned a high school diploma, but he has educated an entire city about complex social problems. He never accumulated any great sum of money from his years of hard work, but his activism has secured the necessities of life for many needy families.

How can we evaluate and understand the sustained social commitment at the core of Ivory Perry's identity? By some standards, Perry might appear to be a failure and a malcontent, venting his frustrations against society through antagonistic political activism. While other people have pursued wealth, position, and security, Perry has moved from crisis to crisis, his accomplishments recorded more thoroughly in his police record than anywhere else. Yet from another perspective, he might emerge as a hero, someone who cleverly marshaled limited resources in an effort to make America's social practice live up to the grandeur of its social promise.

To answer these questions, we need to go beyond Ivory Perry as an individual and understand how he represents a social type—the organic intellectual. First and foremost, he has been a manipulator of signs and symbols, an educator and an agitator rationally translating the needs and aspirations of his community into effective remedial action. His life has meaning not so much because he "rose above" other people through exemplary accomplishments, but rather because all his accomplishments have been so rooted in social networks and associations that have kept him connected to others. In order to succeed, organic intellectuals rely on collective memory—shared experiences and perceptions about the past that legitimate action in the present—and on social learning—experiences with contestation in the present that transform values and goals for the future. Properly understood, Ivory Perry's identity as an organic intellectual expands the parameters of historical and sociological knowledge and raises important challenges to prevailing scholarly interpretations of social protest, race relations, and American political culture.

"I know what the community wants, because they *tell* me what they want," Perry explains. "By me being black, I'm around them. I hear them in their conversation. I hear them in the ghetto. I hear them wherever I go, discussing in the lounges, in the schoolyards, in the meetings. Anywhere I go, I hear blacks talking about what they're dissatisfied with."[1] Yet while Perry's attentiveness to what he hears in the ghetto does account for much of his success as an organizer, he also succeeds by understanding the context in which his ideas will be received and the means of struggle most likely to give them maximum impact. Whenever he raises an issue, Perry knows that he is speaking to a community with a history of struggle and an in-built understanding that protest is often legitimate and necessary. He also knows that once people start participating in acts of social contestation, the process of struggle itself can educate them about what to do next. He can succeed as an organic intellectual only by tapping into collective memory and social learning.

THE FIRST and most important strain of collective memory influencing Ivory Perry comes from his identity as a black American. Langston Hughes captures the power of the Afro-American past in a 1926 poem, "The Negro Speaks of Rivers," where he connects the achievements of the Harlem Renaissance of the 1920s to the traditions of the past. Blending individual and collective themes into a unified totality, Hughes tells us:

I've known rivers:
I've known rivers ancient as the world and older than the
    flow of human blood in human veins.
My soul has grown deep like the rivers.
I bathed in the Euphrates when dawns were young.
I built my hut near the Congo and it lulled me to sleep.
I looked upon the Nile and raised pyramids above it.
I heard the singing on the Mississippi when Abe Lincoln
    went down to New Orleans, and I've seen its muddy
    bosom turn all golden in the sunset.
I've known rivers:
Ancient, dusky rivers.
My soul has grown deep like the rivers.[2]

Ivory Perry has known rivers too. He grew up working in the rich
bottom lands irrigated by the Arkansas River and its tributaries. He
fought in a war on the frozen waters of the Yalu River in Korea. Many
times he risked arrest and injury during demonstrations near the banks
of the Pearl River in Bogalusa and the Mississippi River in St. Louis. But
like Langston Hughes, the rivers that deepened his soul were rivers of
mind and spirit, submerged currents of tradition and history that tied
him to the past.

Perry's childhood community resonated with the histories of Africa, of
slavery, of Reconstruction, and of twentieth-century racism. In his for-
mative years in Pine Bluff, long-suppressed currents of resistance manifested themselves in the community boycott of the Henry Marx department store to support Leo Branton and in the Committee of Negro
Organizations' campaign for access to public accommodations. Within
Perry's family he learned about the virtues of hard work and self-respect, and saw individuals like his cousin Robert Pierce refuse to accept
as legitimate anything less than historically sanctioned standards of decent and just behavior.

At every stage of his life, Perry found himself connected to under-
ground streams of resistance from the past. In the army and in the black
ghetto of a declining industrial city, in the civil rights movement and the
antipoverty program, in voter registration drives and strike support,
Perry drew upon individual and collective perceptions of the recent and
distant past. He may have been a rebel by society's standards, but his

conduct reflected absolute fidelity to the traditional values of his family and community. Political activism necessitated no traumatic break with the past for Ivory Perry, no cathartic transformation from accommodation to resistance. Instead, the moral imperatives and character traits instilled in him as a youth shaped the public actions that defined his life as an adult.

Of course the black experience is not uniform and the black community is not monolithic. To say that a current of historical resistance permeates black life does not mean that all blacks approve of all protests at all times. Frequently Ivory Perry found that his actions antagonized blacks as much as they bothered whites, or more. "I irritate a lot of blacks," he concedes. "I do. I have to do that. You have to take the bitter with the sweet. It can't all be roses. Some people I irritate, some I don't. Some like what I do, some hate me."[3] But whatever divisions about him existed in the black community, Perry always knew that a sizable part of his community saw social protest as sanctioned by historical experience and necessary for change.

While race and racism established the basic historical parameters of Ivory Perry's experiences, social class also played an important role. The man who started working in the cotton fields when he was two years old, who shined shoes and carried bags in a hotel as a teenager, who spent his days as a young adult in difficult and dirty factory jobs, found his entire experience bounded by the constraints of alienated labor. He saw that sharecroppers, bellhops, and factory workers performed the hard work that no one else wanted to do, but that the rewards from their labor went mostly to their employers. In his many different work situations, Perry found a collective memory and shared social consciousness that had been passed on from the past. Like race, class encouraged a sense of collectivity. People exploited as a group logically seek group solutions to their common problems.

The entire history of workplace organization, trade unionism, and working class political action testifies to the powerful and recurrent appeal of collective categories for working-class people. The Industrial Workers of the World recruited almost one million members in the early part of the twentieth century under the slogan "An Injury to One Is an Injury to All," a slogan that embodied a massive rejection of the creed of rugged individualism. The great American Socialist and trade unionist Eugene Victor Debs voiced the essence of that view in one famous statement: "While there is a lower class I am of it, while there is a criminal class I am of it, while there is a soul in prison I am not free."[4]

Race and class have never constituted totally separate spheres of existence for Perry; rather they have overlapped in ways that make him view racial problems from a class perspective and infuse his understanding of class issues with racial insights. In Bogalusa, Perry felt comfortable with the Civic and Voters League leadership partly because they were mill workers and cab drivers whose connection between racial and class concerns appealed to him. In St. Louis, while he kept open channels of communication with several civil rights groups, he had a special affinity for ACTION, with its working-class leadership. In housing campaigns, he felt closest to the political views articulated by Jesse Gray of the National Tenants Organization, like Perry a southern-born worker who migrated to a northern industrial city in the 1950s.

The extraordinary stability of American politics and the dearth of European-style Socialist opposition parties has led many scholars to conclude that social contestation exists only on the margins of the American experience, and even there only temporarily. But Ivory Perry and the networks of opposition that have nurtured and sustained him testify to another possibility—that opposition and contestation are deeply rooted in American history and political culture. Race and class provide two specific contexts of collective memory available to Ivory Perry, but they do not exhaust the possibilities for his work as an organic intellectual. Resistance to hierarchy and oppression provides a central theme in the history of blacks and workers, but it is a theme with an honorable tradition among other groups as well. As historians Sara Evans and Harry Boyte point out, the struggle for "free spaces" defines much of the American experience and provides rich streams of collective memory among women, farmers, immigrants, intellectuals, and other groups responsible for important democratic changes in the American past.[5]

Historians commenting on social protest from a variety of perspectives have tended to believe that the "hegemony" (which they define as a near-complete internalization of materialism, individualism, and privatism) of the dominant ideology in America has rendered radical challengers insignificant and irrelevant. For example, Aileen Kraditor, a conservative, argues that radicalism flourished only in the fantasies of "deracinated" individuals during the late nineteenth and early twentieth centuries because they could not adjust to the "shake-up" period of industrial expansion. Kraditor goes on to charge that radicals failed because they did not understand how the rewards of family and community offset the temporary inequities of the world of work. John Patrick Diggins, a liberal, finds no significant radical challenge to materialism, individualism, and privatism in America since the Civil War, claiming that ostensibly "radical" movements simply sought access to the material and personal rewards offered by the system, not a fundamental change in it. T. J. Jackson Lears, a radical critic of capitalism, places the demise of oppositional thought and action at the turn of the century, when, in his view, the rise of modernism and consumer capitalism left conservative antimodernists as the only true American radicals.

Despite many major disagreements and differences, Kraditor, Diggins, and Lears tend to see hegemony as static rather than dynamic, resting more on the voluntary consent of subordinated groups than on grudging concessions made to them. Yet dominant groups in America have often been forced to make important political and ideological changes in response to even unsuccessful protest movements. The role of historical blocs, the temporary and unstable nature of hegemony, and the key role played by organic intellectuals in framing an active counterhegemony play only a small role in these historians' scenarios about how power is established and maintained.

Consequently, the three historians demolish a straw man when they emphasize the absence of radicalism from American political culture. Because they tend to study ideology as it influences political theorists, authors, artists, and other "traditional" intellectuals, they have little opportunity to study ideology as it influences the organic intellectuals in American history. For Kraditor, Diggins, and Lears, radicalism must come from outside the main currents of social and intellectual life, and it must demand changes that cannot be made by the existing power structure. Otherwise radicalism amounts to mere reform calculated to make the existing system work better.

But Gramsci's careful distinction between a "war of maneuver" whereby radicals fight to seize state power and a "war of position" whereby they try to establish a prefigurative counterhegemony within the existing society, reveals another side to ostensibly "reformist" efforts. Gramsci assumes that under conditions of bourgeois hegemony, acts of contestation can be reformist in their goals but radical in their processes if they call into question the legitimacy of bourgeois hegemony and stimulate the creation of a new historical bloc.

In this "war of position," radicals do not storm the barricades, but try to engage in practical activity that undermines the legitimacy of existing power and builds a taste for something better. When grounded in the real structural tensions and antagonisms of social life, these acts of contestation can lay the groundwork for profound changes. Even if they fail eventually to unite oppositional groups into a historical bloc powerful enough to impose a counterhegemony on society, they nonetheless win concessions and transform the terms of political debate within the hegemony that exists.

Thus the "discovery" of bourgeois hegemony in American political culture by Kraditor, Diggins, and Lears rests on false premises. In her study of the Socialist movement in late nineteenth and early twentieth-century America, Kraditor finds no real challenge to capitalism, not even in the mass radical activity among American workers between 1890 and 1917, because their actions lead to melioristic reforms rather than revolution. In his elegantly argued examinations of American political culture since the Civil War, Diggins sees primarily self-interest and a desire for upward mobility among the workers who formed the Knights of Labor and other collective movements of the late nineteenth century, because at no point did their struggles articulate a true "class" consciousness. In an otherwise persuasive and moving study of antimodernist thought, Lears dismisses the democratic thrusts of twentieth-century labor, black, and feminist movements as "therapeutic" delusions that only strengthened the modernist order they presumed to criticize. But this standard of "radicalism" allows no middle ground between capitulation and mass insurrection.

In fact, even mass insurrections do not meet the standards of radical opposition demanded by Kraditor, Diggins, and Lears. Kraditor argues that unlike allegiance to family or ethnicity, radical ideologies are not "natural." She portrays radical mass actions as artificial, symbolic, and misplaced solutions to what were essentially personal and psychological needs. Diggins contends that American political culture revolves around individualism and private property. Yet when confronted by the example of John Brown, a white man who became a national hero by taking up arms against his own government in order to deny the legitimacy of property held in the form of slaves, Diggins can only dismiss Brown as a madman.[6]

Lears presents the triumph of modernism at the turn of the twentieth century as so thorough and complete that even subsequent oppositional movements have been unable to challenge its fundamental principles. Thus he hails the "agrarian communards of the 1960s" as remnants of nineteenth-century radicalism because of their antimodernism, while at the same time he neglects the challenges to dominate ideology nurtured under modern conditions during that very decade by the followers of Malcolm X and Martin Luther King, by urban riots and student rebellions, and by feminist mobilizations and working class insurgencies.[7]

By deeming all oppositional practice either reformist or deracinated, these historians leave bourgeois hegemony as the only possible description of American political culture. Certainly much of what they say is indeed true about the dominant values in American society, especially as those values are explained and interpreted among traditional intellectuals. But their analysis does too little to explore the oppositional practices and ideas that remain alive in the activisim of organic intellectuals like Ivory Perry.

In the sense that they respond to a legitimacy that reflects the power of the elite, and in the sense that they do not completely break away from the imperatives and traditions of bourgeois society, organic intellectuals are not "radical" as Kraditor, Diggins, and Lears want to define the term. But a radicalism so far removed from the political practice and legitimizing instruments of American society would be inaccessible to the American people, and would separate the "radicals" from the very people they wish to persuade and motivate. A "pure" radicalism uncontaminated by bourgeois ideology and at war with the basic premises and assumptions of American society might provide the basis for a coup d'état, but it could never bring about the changes in values and social practices sought by organic intellectuals.

By experience and ideology, organic intellectuals emerge from the concrete conditions and alienations of American life. They seek to identify and nurture the oppositional impulses already present within dominant ideological formulations in order to bring about social changes. Theirs is not a "war of maneuver" by which radical groups contest for power with the elite, but rather a "war of position" that seeks to build a counterhegemony from the repressed aspirations and suppressed desires already existing within this society.

Perry and organic intellectuals like him recognize that they have been shaped by the past; they draw on its moral lessons to fashion their critiques of the present. But they also recognize new possibilities and opportunities in the contradictions and conflicts of the present. They draw upon sedimented collective resources that reveal the past as more radical than the historians acknowledge, and they struggle to build historical blocs in a present that is more unstable and unresolved than the historians assume it to be.

One difficulty in applying Gramsci's categories to the United States stems from the complicated realities of race as a social category. Clearly a working class divided by race is different from one that sees no fundamental racial divisions, and opposition to the double burden of race and class manifests itself differently from reactions to direct class oppression. Yet precisely *because* race constitutes such a fundamental category in American society, all class issues are in part racial, and all questions about race have relevance to other hierarchies. Black Americans have been the most persistent critics of exploitation and hierarchy in American history because their status forced them to confront the worst consequences of the society's shortcomings.

But their criticisms amounted to more than a protest against black exclusion and a desire to join the ranks of the exploiters; from Richard Allen to Frederick Douglass to A. Philip Randolph, representatives of black America have addressed not just the racially biased implementation of the American dream, but the deficiencies of the dream itself. As a result, black voices have been crucial to the dialogue that has produced American culture. As jazz critic and author Albert Murray points out:

Identity is best defined in terms of culture, and the culture of the nation over which the white Anglo-Saxon power elite exercises such exclusive political, economic, and social control is not all-white by any measurement ever devised. American culture, even in its most rigidly segregated precincts, is patently and irrevocably composite. It is, regardless of all the hysterical protestations of those who would have it otherwise, incontestably mulatto.[8]

The composite that Murray describes is what makes the formation of historical blocs possible. The necessity of recognizing the composite nature of American culture makes black Americans particularly suited to participating in constructing alliances to fashion a counterhegemony against individualism, privatism, and materialism. Because their "river of resistance" ties them to the concrete historical contradictions of the American past, black organic intellectuals like Ivory Perry represent interests and beliefs that are at one and the same time particular to the Afro-American experience and generalizable to all of American society.

IN ADDITION to the broad currents of race and class history behind Ivory Perry's activism, the specific chronology of his life gave determinate shape to his actions as an organic intellectual. As an individual and as part of a social movement, Perry learned from his experiences and continuously reshaped and reformulated his ideology on the basis of new evidence and understanding. The alienations and indignities of sharecropping shaped much of Perry's perceptions of life in Pine Bluff, while his experiences in that city shaped his view of conditions in the army. The horrors of war and the hypocrisies of racism attendant to it prepared Ivory Perry for activism once he returned to St. Louis, and life in the urban ghetto led to attitudes and beliefs conducive to civil rights activism. The civil rights movement taught Perry lessons that became the basis for his outlook during his tenure with the War on Poverty, and his community organizing in that role made him sensitive to the costs of the neoconservatism of the 1970s and 1980s.

What held true for Perry as an individual in this regard also held true for the movement as a collective entity. By adapting and changing under the pressure of events, the movement renewed and reshaped the culture of opposition in which Ivory Perry operated. There was never a single oppositional ideology or consciousness; rather consciousness and ideology evolved organically through actions and dialogue. At any given moment activists may have appeared to act "spontaneously" but that "spontaneity" only made visible individual and collective grievances long suppressed. As Gramsci argues, "Spontaneity is the history of the subaltern classes."[9]

Just as Ivory Perry's role as an organic intellectual sheds new light on historical interpretations of American political culture, his capacity for social learning holds important implications for sociological analyses of social protest and Afro-American life. Unlike many historians, most social scientists concerned with grass-roots protest movements readily concede that social protest contains important lessons about society at large. Yet the presuppositions and methods of inquiry common to most sociological studies neglect the important historical continuities and connections that produce an organic intellectual like Ivory Perry.

Consistent with the theoretical purposes of their discipline, sociologists tend to emphasize macro-social forces as the key to individual acts of contestation. They have generally focused on determining the necessary circumstances under which protest movements originate, flourish, or decline, and they have also been concerned with delineating the relationships between social protest and forces like individual psychological needs, historical opportunities, social strain, indigenous community resources, changing self-esteem, and actions by opponents. The mass society model employed by William Kornhauser contends that social movements grow out of social isolation, that individuals on the margins of society reduce their alienation and anxiety by joining movements that provide opportunities for extremist behavior. Collective behavior theory as articulated by Neil Smelser asserts that systemic strain leads individuals to be confused about their values, but that joining social movements allows them to articulate and codify new standards. The status inconsistency approach typified by James Geschwender stresses the tensions generated by disparities between self-esteem and social treatment.[10]

Although each of these interpretations touches on real aspects of Ivory Perry's life, collectively they fail to account adequately for his oppositional activity. Their stress on activisim as a function of personal discomfort underestimates and trivializes the specific goals Perry has pursued and fails to locate his actions in their proper collective historical and social contexts. For black people like Ivory Perry, alienation, normative ambiguity, and status inconsistency constitute permanent and enduring consequences of white racism, but they do not always lead to social activism. Activists often find peace of mind and legitimacy through their participation in social movements, but activism also involves excruciatingly painful costs not usually incurred by "therapeutic" efforts to resolve personal conflicts. Periods of structural strain may increase the psychological tensions confronting oppressed populations, but they also generate political opportunities for the realization of long-suppressed desires.

Like other organic intellectuals, Perry drew upon deep reservoirs of self-affirmation in his social activism. He responded as much to the collective memory of his childhood community and to the relevance of its values to solving current problems as he did to personal anxieties and ambiguities. Had his actions not been grounded in commonly recognized grievances or had they seemed unlikely to solve real problems, he could not have mobilized oppositional activity, no matter how much his community suffered from structural strain, marginality, or status inconsistency.

Social scientists critical of mass society, collective behavior, and status inconsistency theories offer different explanations for activism like Ivory Perry's. The resource mobilization model identifies the manipulation of resources and institutions under favorable opportunity conditions as the key to successful social protest. The organizational approach advanced by William Gamson and Charles Tilley identifies organizations and communications networks within oppressed communities as the organic nuclei of social movements. In their view, community leaders guide their followers in rational, planned, and deliberate efforts to maximize the granting of concessions by those in power. The third-party approach exemplified by Michael Lipsky and Anthony Oberschall contends that groups lacking sufficient organizational resources on their own resort to disruptive measures to force powerful elites to intervene on their behalf.[11]

Like mass society, collective behavior, and status inconsistency theorists, resource mobilization advocates acknowledge the importance of structural strain, but they emphasize its effect on structures that provide opportunities to intervene in the workings of powerful institutions. National emergencies, disputes beteeen rival factions of the power structure, or historically created power vacuums stimulate social movements by giving oppressed populations access to resources previously outside their reach. When those opportunities arise, resource mobilization theorists believe that the quality of organization and solidarity within the aggrieved population determines its capacity to transform grievances into effective action.

No one familiar with the history of social protest can discount the importance of internal organization and the significance of alliances with elite groups in providing a favorable climate for protest. But as Doug McAdam correctly observes, the existence of resources does not guarantee their constructive use.[12] Organizations have bureaucratic tendencies that often place the institutional survival of the group ahead of the pursuit of social change. Unless goaded into action by a constituency ready to struggle for agreed-upon goals, organizations can as easily serve conservative ends as they can become forces for social change. The very powerlessness of aggrieved populations can encourage sectarian infighting among competing groups that have few opportunities to confront their real enemies.

In his years of social contestation, Ivory Perry has displayed little enthusiasm for bureaucratic or institutional power, but he always worked with formal organizations and in fact relied upon their institutional resources. Perry formed the Metropolitan Tenants Organization in St. Louis largely because he believed that a formal organization could do some things that an informal network of activists could not. MTO could involve powerful people in the community in housing issues by inviting them to serve on its board of directors; by affiliating with the National Tenants Organization the group could share experiences and perceptions with housing activists from other cities.

Perry's direct-action protests also often relied on the legal, financial, and political resources of community groups and institutions; at the very least their existence made it easier for him to act. But he also tried to work through informal networks of cadres whose very lack of formal organization mandated collective discussion and democratic decision making.[13] For example, his rent strikes and his mobilization of volunteers for lead poisoning tests relied on word of mouth and improvised strategy more than on any institutional resources.

Perry trusts collective mobilization as a force in itself, rather than as a means of building membership organizations. "Ninety-nine out of a hundred times, big organizations become social clubs devoted to making speeches," he contends.[14] Perry claims that he directs his efforts at "the people on the lower levels" because their willingness to disrupt the status quo is a weapon in itself as well as a means of enlightening and pressuring those above them with access to significant institutional resources.

Always open to alliances with third parties and opportunities for involving powerful elites in the struggles of the oppressed (as he demonstrated in his dealings with Harold Gibbons and the Teamsters Union during the 1969 public housing rent strike), he nonetheless expresses fears about becoming too reliant on outside help. "In the final analysis, black people and poor people have to solve their own problems," he contends. "I figure if you got a problem and you're black, if you got a problem and you're poor, if I'm black and poor that I got a problem too." Institutions like the black church, which might seem indispensable to community mobilization to most observers, hold a more ambiguous identity for Perry. Despite his belief in the centrality of religion to Afro-American life, he also feels:

> The black churches is also really a hindrance to the black community. They're not really telling the truth. They're up there talking about Christianity and religion; they're not giving the public the real issue of what's happening in today's society. . . . A lot of people in this

town are using it, they use religion to line the inside of their coat pockets, and keep their iceboxes and refrigerators, and wear $300 suits and drive $20,000 Cadillacs.[15]

Sociologists committed to mass insurgency and political process models share some of Perry's discomfort with an overemphasis on community institutions. While conceding the importance of community networks and institutions for political mobilization, these scholars stress the ways in which the indigenous resources of aggrieved peoples can bring change not just by spurring more powerful groups to action but by themselves. Frances Fox Piven and Richard Cloward identify the mass disruptions staged by ad hoc community organizations as key instruments by which aggrieved populations wrest concessions from the powerful. They locate the origins of the civil rights movement in the demise of the rural plantation system and the attendant loosening of the control structure of the rural South. Forced off the land and denied adequate living conditions in the cities, blacks responded with disruptive protests waged by informal "cadre organizations." In the context of divisions within the national and local Democratic party organizations around the country, these disruptions posed concrete threats to the material interests of elites, according to Piven and Cloward. Those real threats compelled passage of civil rights laws and made possible the War on Poverty.

According to this view, the flamboyant kinds of protest favored by Ivory Perry amounted to more than symbolic representation of social ills, actually bringing into play one real resource of aggrieved populations—the capacity to disrupt business as usual. As Piven and Cloward explain:

> The effectiveness of these tactics does not depend only on dramatic presentations. They are intended to command attention and win concessions by the actual trouble they cause in the ongoing operations of major institutions by interfering with the daily business of city agencies or with the movement of traffic or the profits of businessmen. Such disruptions cause commotion among bureaucrats, excitement in the media, disarray among influential segments of the community, and strain for political leaders.[16]

For all its insights, the mass insurgency model articulated by Piven and Cloward leaves unanswered some important questions about the origins and nature of social protest. Its emphasis on external factors—from historical crises to elite responses—can make social activists and oppressed populations seem so weak that their periodic insurgencies stem from forces beyond their control. The mass insurgency model does not explain how aggrieved communities maintain the potential for rebellion during quiescent periods. Critics of the mass insurgency approach ask, What happens in between eruptions of mass protest? How do communities and individuals store up the oppositional consciousness and resources required for direct action? How do communities and individuals determine long-range goals or consolidate their holds on past victories?

Aldon D. Morris shows how the mass insurgency model underestimates the indigenous resources available to oppressed groups. His extraordinary study of the southern civil rights movement shows how community organizations and institutions nurture resources necessary for wresting concessions from the dominant power structure. To Morris, disruptive mass protest serves as an effective means of contestation only when backed up by legal, financial, and political resources capable of confronting the power structure on its own terms. Doug McAdam also stresses community resources in his study of civil rights protest between 1930 and 1970. He contends that social protest takes place when aggrieved populations enjoy sufficient organizational resources to challenge dominant power, when political alignments within the larger society provide opportunities for third-party involvement, and when the oppositional group embraces common goals and shared expectations for victory.[17]

Thus social movement theory tends to bifurcate along two distinct lines. One group stresses the recruitment of individual activists to movements, considering it largely as an internal psychological process unrelated to the goals and accomplishments of the movements themselves. The other group details the important issues, accomplishments, and structural determinants necessary for movement success without adequately acknowledging the importance of individual subjectivity and consciousness. In addition, by stressing resources and their mobilization in the present, social scientists tend to obscure both the important relationship between ideas and actions and the significant dialogue between the past and present necessary for social contestation.

Power in the modern world is not just a matter of the allocation of resources, it is also a matter of legitimation. Organic intellectuals challenge the material interests of dominant groups, but they also under-mine the legitimacy of elite rule—and it is that challenge to legitimacy that holds the key to the mobilization of allies into a historical bloc. Even when oppositional groups confront an unfavorable outside opportunity structure, or when their own institutions are bureaucratic, sectarian, or weak, they still retain the capacity to fashion a counterhegemonic strug-gle by drawing on the collective memory of the past as a critique of the present. McAdam recognizes a part of this when he stresses the impor-tance of common goals and shared expectations for victory among ag-grieved populations, but his focus on historical moments of mass ac-tivism obscures the long-term historical processes behind it. The social science emphasis on abstract social forces reveals much about social pro-test, but it underestimates the importance of subjectivity and ideology and their links to the collective history of activists.

Most historians of Afro-American social protest have been aware of the deep historical strains informing direct action. Theodore Rosengar-ten's *All God's Dangers* sets the stage for its protagonist's confrontation with the law in a dispute over sharecropper organizing by delineating the ways an entire lifetime of experiences led him to make that stand. Nell Irvin Painter's *Narrative of Hosea Hudson* recognizes the similarities between Hudson's activities in the Communist party and life patterns encouraged within the Afro-American Baptist church. Clayborne Car-son, August Meier and Elliott Rudwick, and William Chafe connect the struggles of significant civil rights groups to the historical experiences and beliefs of key activists. Yet where Rosengarten and Painter focus so much on the personal stories of individuals that they have little time to account for broader historical forces, Carson, Rudwick and Meier, and Chafe concentrate so fully on organizations at peak moments of activism that they can do little to convey the sense of historical necessity that drives individuals to action.[18] Ivory Perry's life story demonstrates that the convergence of individual and collective history provides a crucial element for the existence and endurance of grass roots activism.

Sociological interpretations of social protest provide important in-sights into structural determinants, but neglect the subjective con-sciousness necessary to turn opportunities into action. On the other hand, historical studies of protest often delineate the consciousness and ideology of activists quite fully, without adequately exploring the struc-tural contexts in which activism takes place. George Rawick, trained as both a historian and a sociologist, identifies the importance of structural forces, historical continuity, and collective subjectivity in his seminal work on the American slave community. Rawick argues that Afro-Americans came to this continent with one very important resource—their culture. Memories of Africa provided a basis for challenging the legitimacy of American slavery and racism, and the cumulative struggle engendered by that challenge developed collective resources capable of being tapped during moments of crisis.

Overt and covert acts of resistance kept alive this oppositional consciousness, black abolitionists worked to build a historical bloc opposed to slavery, and during the crisis of the Civil War emancipation became possible. During Reconstruction and other periods of crisis, the culture of Afro-Americans challenged dominant values and participated in the building of coalitions that changed all of society. While never reaching the point of forging a hegemony of its own, the persistent traditions of counterhegemonic practice within the black community nurtured the river of resistance that informed the activism of Ivory Perry and organic intellectuals like him.[19]

Gramsci used the term *praxis* to describe the activity of organic intellectuals. He meant that a combination of theory and action made practical social contestation a matter of both power and legitimation. Through praxis, organic intellectuals learn about the world and pass their learning along to others. But praxis also reflects the cumulative experiences of oppositional groups, the social learning that emerges from struggle. Through praxis, history, necessity, and desire shape the consciousness and activity of an oppositional culture. Movements for social change develop out of praxis because activists come to see oppositional activity as historically sanctioned, politically necessary, and ideologically legitimate and desirable.

Ivory Perry's story is in part a story of mass society, collective behavior, status inconsistency, resource mobilization, mass insurgency, indigenous resources, and political process models of activism. But it is primarily a story of praxis, an example of the ways collective memory and social learning challenge the legitimacy of bourgeois ideology by mobilizing an oppositional historical bloc around counterhegemonic principles.

Emphasizing the historical continuity behind Ivory Perry's activity does not deny the impact of dislocation and disruption on his life. Perry acted in response to immediate needs as well as out of historical commitments. Social and economic changes left him facing conditions that necessitated some response. He witnessed the collapse of southern tenant farming and the evisceration of the rural economy and culture built up around it. He migrated to an industrial city at the precise moment when investment decisions about the inner city and the suburbs signaled an end to traditional patterns of urban life. Historical changes that could be ignored or evaded by more privileged individuals confronted Ivory Perry in direct and inescapable ways. He saw the impact of these changes on the bottom rung of the social ladder, but they also taught him something about those at the top. He saw the world he had always known being destroyed by new technologies and economic patterns, but he had keen insights as well into the world they created.

The mass migration to industrial cities by displaced rural workers in the 1940s and 1950s masked a severe structural urban crisis. The poverty facing them in the inner city reflected the declining economic infrastructure of manufacturing and the forms of upward mobility it allowed. Rural migrants paid more for inferior housing, they received lower wages and endured worse working conditions than their predecessors in the urban working class, and they lacked their predecessors' political power as well. As a readily exploitable group, these migrants created short-term opportunities for profit for an urban elite unaware that short-term gains were creating long-range problems. The subsequent transition from industrial to postindustrial cities had enormous consequences for all urban dwellers, but it hit people like Ivory Perry and his community first.

Like others who felt the effects of social change firsthand, Ivory Perry saw the shortcomings of the new urban society. His experience with historical changes in the plantation economy made him sensitive to the ways that technological change might affect the quality of individual lives. He believed that the problems of the inner city stemmed from systemic failings and from the structural roles assigned to the poor, not from their individual personalities and character structures. He thought that the extreme contrasts between rich and poor that characterized America amounted to more than a paradox: to him they reflected a causal relationship in which concentrations of wealth at the top necessitated the existence of many poor people at the bottom. Recognizing that state power and government decisions often played the key role in diverting public resources for the benefit of the powerful, Perry reasoned that public pressure and protest constituted a logical and necessary tactic for the poor.

Ivory Perry did not learn about the problems facing industrial cities through formal study or even through personal reflection and contemplation. His own life experiences pointed him toward direct action. The city proved to be a good teacher; in it Perry found out about the respective interests of rich and poor people. Social protest threatened the self-image, material interests, and legitimacy of the elite, while it also changed the self-image of the oppressed, educating them about their own conditions and involving them in a process of bringing about change. Activists like Ivory Perry could not create social protest capriciously; they had to work within the context of real grievances and the parameters of their individual and collective histories.

In his elegant exegesis and commentary on Gramsci's writings, Jerome Karabel argues that modern society contains no institutional base adequate to form the oppositional culture necessary for the creation of organic intellectuals. Certainly a proletariat, in the sense that orthodox Marxists define it, has not emerged as the agency of social revolution anywhere in the world. But if we take E. P. Thompson's definition of class ("a social and cultural formation arising from the processes which can only be studied as they work themselves out over a considerable period") and combine it with Gramsci's notion of the "historical bloc" (a coalition waging a war of position in its struggle for hegemony), then the institutional base for organic intellectuals becomes evident.[20]

Ivory Perry's activity as an organic intellectual gave voice to the alienations of both class and race, and it waged a war of position by making alliances with other alienated groups. The working class and Afro-American communities that sustained Ivory Perry's activism may not have had the institutional power to replace the hegemony of capitalism and racism with an egalitarian nonexploitative counterhegemony. But they could generate and sustain oppositional ideas and practices, which in alliance with the aspirations of other groups could keep open the possibility for radical change.

Throughout the campaign against lead poisoning in St. Louis, Ivory Perry personified the traits that Gramsci ascribed to the organic intellectual, engaging in practical action to serve as "constructor, organiser, and permanent persuader." Strategic political activity intertwined with the generation and circulation of knowledge. Perry's practical activity as a community organizer led him to realize the severity of the housing situation in the city and to the discovery of the misery caused by lead-based paint. Circulation of his findings about the disease among sympathetic scientists, health care professionals, and community members led to the screening and testing at the Yeatman Health Center that proved that the disease had reached epidemic proportions.

Perry's "war of position" proceeded in incremental steps to simultaneously build knowledge about the disease and to promote public willingness to do something about it. His own testing for the presence of lead in slum dwellings led to his request that the board of education set up testing and screening centers. Those centers produced evidence that made it possible for him to organize fund-raising and volunteer campaigns that in turned helped build a constituency for confrontive direct-action protests. The campaign involved a fight for hegemony with city officials and the medical establishment over who got to define the public interest.

Perry's ability to win publicity about the dangers posed by lead-based paint through confrontations with representatives of the board of aldermen and the city counselor provided powerful incentives for city officials to defend their own reputations by addressing the problem rather than by evading it. What Gramsci termed "active participation in practical life" enabled Perry to build a coalition that enlisted the expertise and enthusiasm of scientists, lawyers, and medical students on behalf of the interests of the poor. By mobilizing the community through fund-raising and volunteer activities, Ivory Perry laid the groundwork for a political coalition that united students, tenants, black business owners, politicians, social workers, and pediatricians.[21]

The same historical experiences that deprived Ivory Perry of the benefits of the American dream also enabled him to discover the unglamorous realities behind that dream. It promised wealth and happiness to everyone who competed successfully, but the illusion of individual competition obscured the reality of monopoly power. Large corporations and powerful real estate interests used their influence to foster urban renewal and urban redevelopment policies that enhanced their own profits while destroying the housing stock, tax base, and cultural infrastructure of the central city. People like Ivory Perry confronted the dire consequences of these policies, not just for the poor but for the city as a whole. Responding initially to the problems in his own community, Perry came to see that everyone suffered from the blight of inadequate housing, crime, unemployment, and dangers to the public health. His success at mobilizing alliances to change conditions stemmed in part from his ability to demonstrate that his vision of the city would help others, not just his own community.

In his activism, Perry focused on survival issues—income, employment, health, and housing. For his constituents, grandiose visions of the future took a back seat to more immediate and pressing needs. In the streets of St. Louis, Ivory Perry decided that a good society would be one that housed its homeless people, fed the hungry, and protected people from exploitation. His vision appeared foolishly idealistic and utopian to many, but to Perry it constituted a practical and realistic response to the suffering he saw every day. Conversely, the operative principles of urban economics and politics with their trickle-down mentality seemed dangerously unrealistic to Perry. His social activism did not counter unglamorous realism with an unrealistic utopianism; rather he addressed practical problems in a way that presented a different vision of necessity.

Ivory Perry's life of social protest demonstrates the existence of organic intellectuals and their importance to movements of social contestation. Their resistance to dominant values challenges the legitimacy of those in power and forces concessions to aggrieved populations. Even when defeated on immediate goals, organic intellectuals change power realities in the present and keep open the possibility for greater changes in the future. Their activism is both personal and social, a product of analysis and understanding honed through collective memory and social learning.

Epilogue: A Drum Major for Justice

Ivory Perry's struggle against the domination of materialism, individualism, and privatism in American society connects him to another historical actor whose life led him to a similar task. Dr. Martin Luther King, Jr., who was both a traditional and an organic intellectual, devoted his life to instigating revolutionary changes in American society. King initially viewed racism as an aberration in the American character that could be purged through education and reform. But as he confronted the magnitude of the racial problem, King began to feel that a much greater revolution in values would have to take place than he had originally anticipated.

Dr. King recognized that deep-seated ideological beliefs prevented most Americans from seeing the flaws in their own country. American exceptionalism—the belief that divine providence or historical accidents spared America from the problems that plague other nations—and American individualism—the belief that people fulfill their highest destinies when they accumulate individual wealth free from the demands of others—worked inexorably to prevent collective social solutions to the racism and exploitation that King viewed as dominant in American society. Dr. King attempted to recast American exceptionalism and American individualism in a way that would discard their destructive trappings but retain their positive core. He did so by talking about "the drum major instinct"—the desire to be important and significant, to stand out from others by marching in front of the parade like a drum major. King contended that the abuse of that instinct led to racism, war, and exploitation because it convinced people that they could elevate themselves only by surpassing others.

Yet Dr. King did not condemn the drum major instinct itself, only its misguided applications. He argued that used correctly, the instinct could be a wonderful force for good, because it could motivate people to seek distinction in socially constructive ways by serving others. Used properly, the drum major instinct could be positive; everyone could succeed because everyone could serve. Redefining the American dream by making collective and inclusive what had previously been individual and exclusive, Dr. King drew direct political conclusions from this philosophy: our country and its citizens misused the drum major instinct by resorting to racism as a means of feeling superior to others, by indulging in the false pride of uncritical nationalism, and by pursuing wealth through exploiting others. Instead, he offered a vision of the good life in which individuals sated their desires for greatness by engaging in the great work of serving others—building a country that would be first in peace, first in social justice, and first in moral excellence.

Dr. King's most forceful articulation of the drum major instinct came in a sermon delivered on February 4, 1968. He told his congregation that sometimes he thought about his own death (he would be murdered two months later) and that he wanted them to know the words that he would like to have said at his funeral. In a moving expression of his own values and a powerful challenge to his followers, King stated:

> I want you to be able to say on that day that I did try to feed the hungry. I want you to be able to say on that day that I did try in my life to clothe those that were naked. I want you to say on that day that I did try to visit those that were in prison. I want you to say that I tried to love and serve humanity. Yes, if you want to say that I was a drum major, say that I was a drum major for justice. Say that I was a drum major for peace. And all of the shallow things will not matter. I won't have any money to leave behind. I won't have any of the fine and luxurious things of life to leave behind. But I just want to leave a committed life behind.[1]

Following a different path through life than Dr. King, Ivory Perry came to the same conclusions—not because he heard King speak about the drum major instinct directly, but because his own intellect and experiences caused him to identify the nature of America's problems and the potential for solving them in a similar manner. Perry's history of commitment affirms King's faith in his followers, and demonstrates the social nature of his formulation. Operating as an organic intellectual, Perry used sedimented traditions of resistance to mobilize coalitions capable of addressing current problems. In the process, he changed not only society but himself as well, internalizing desired social relations into his everyday behavior. Like Dr. King, he passed up opportunities for personal recognition and reward out of a commitment to seeking fulfillment as a drum major for justice.

Ivory Perry's history of social activism offers a demonstration of the connections between famous leaders like Dr. King and their mass following. It testifies to the indigenous resources within the black community that nurture and sustain social protest, but it also illuminates the intellectual and political processes required to transform those resources into effective acts of contestation. It concedes the hegemony of materialism, individualism, and privatism in American culture without losing sight of the oppositional traditions that generate and circulate competing values and beliefs. It expands our knowledge of social protest and its place in American political culture by examining the crucial role played by organic intellectuals.

The continuity of Ivory Perry's commitment, his persistence despite setbacks and defeats, and his resourcefulness in adapting to changed circumstances have enabled Perry to understand the vision articulated by Dr. King. Everybody likes to be significant and important, everyone likes recognition and respect, but the only way for everyone to succeed is to build a society in which service to others supersedes self-aggrandizement. Individuals like Ivory Perry thrive and survive because their efforts keep that vision alive.

Dr. King presented his sermon about the drum major instinct as a solution to America's serious social problems, but he also intended it as personal advice to his followers about how to live their lives. In his own life he had made many sacrifices for the causes in which he believed. But the significant point of his sermon was not about sacrifice, about the things that had to be surrendered in the name of a higher goal. Rather, King presented becoming a drum major for justice as a way to be happy, as a way of loving oneself by loving others. He recognized that the obsessive desire to hold dominion over others never brought safisfaction because it could never be sated. The need to belong to the dominant class, or the dominant race, or the dominant country could never bring happiness because it automatically turned other people into enemies and oneself into an instrument of selfish aggrandizement. If life became reduced to a battle for supremacy over others, most people would have to lose and even the "winners" could never rest easy. But if life became a process of serving and helping others, then everyone could succeed, because everyone could serve.

Ivory Perry discusses his own activisim in similar terms. "I'm always compensated within because I know when it's right and when it's wrong," he explains. "I'm not really hooked up on material things; I'm more hooked up on humanitarian things." More important, he believes that his activism can have a ripple effect, changing others and then changing all of society. Perry explains:

> I love people. In order to love myself, I got to love others. So I love other people, then I love myself. If I help just one person out of one thousand, I'm satisfied. If I give one slice of bread to one kid in a thousand at least I tried to help somebody, so I'm happy. And maybe that one person will help somebody else, and that person will help two other people. So it just goes in a circle like that. A lot of times I help people and they say "I'm gonna take care of you later." I say "No, just take care of another brother in need, so maybe he can help somebody else too.[2]

Yet it is very difficult to live with values like that in this society. Perry also paid a terrible price for his commitments. He has never made much money and has very few possessions now. His many arrests, his failed marriages, and his bouts with depression hardly seem like an advertisement for the activist's life. Yet Perry points out that people who are not activists have problems too. The pursuit of wealth, position, and security has its casualties too, and it is impossible to know whether he would have been any happier taking another path. He signs all his letters "peace in the struggle," because for all its pain, social protest has enabled him to learn, to grow, and to make his mark by helping others.

Still, the doubts remain. From time to time Perry has visions about the end of the world, about how hatred and war and pollution have all gone too far gone to be corrected. Anita Reed relates:

> A lot of times he'll hear spirits knocking and making different weird sounds, but it doesn't bother him. He knows they're not going to hurt him. Sometimes he might feel like somebody's touching him. Or a cold breeze would go by and then go away. But it was always when he was alone, or writing a proposal or something like that where he had to be by himself. He might hear voices or hear noises.[3]

Perry knows that people find his visions strange. "A lot of the time people say there's something wrong with you," he admits, but he feels comfortable with the visions himself. "One time I was up in my office on

Delmar and I was doing some research [on the origins of the political crises in the Middle East], and books and stuff started opening all by themselves. Late at night, opening and slamming together. I could hear voices and noises, and breathing around me, real loud. But I didn't get afraid."[4]

Some of the people who have known him best wonder if Perry is not bitter about his lack of reward for all he has done. "I truly feel that Ivory has a great feeling of disappointment that he wasn't appreciated enough," suggests Pearlie Evans. Maurice Williamson observes that "Ivory was one of the people who for some reason was always looked over when the good jobs came down, but he was the guy that was always there that was making people aware of what was up against us as a people." Donald Rankins, the police officer who monitored so many of Perry's demonstrations for the St. Louis police department's intelligence squad, sees Perry as a victim of his own sincerity. "He still does what he did and continues on with the neighborhood activities," Rankins notes admiringly. "The others that were out there are nowhere around. Ivory got the raw end of all of it. He took the lumps and never really got anything out of it."[5]

Judge Clyde Cahill sees Perry's fidelity to 1960s tactics in the 1980s as an exercise in futility. "It's a dream," Cahill says sadly of Perry's effort to mobilize the community for social change. In the context of the political and economic realities of the 1980s the judge sees Perry's efforts as unrealistic. "He's a modern-day Don Quixote, tilting at windmills," Cahill suggests, and then adds quietly, "We all are." Robert Joiner feels that the changes that have taken place in society since the 1960s have undercut Perry's ability to function as an activist. "The old anchors that really held up that kind of movement are no longer there," Joiner points out.[6]

But Perry does not see his life as a tragedy: quite the contrary. He feels proud that he has played a role in preserving the values of the past and keeping alive hopes for the future. Whether he finds his name on the front page of the newspapers or not, he has so thoroughly internalized the principles of direct-action protest that they are second nature to him now. He assembles photo exhibits for Black History Month every year. He organizes car washes in his neighborhood so that the children can earn money to visit a local amusement park. He even staged a Black History Easter Egg Hunt, where the children in his neighborhood searched a football field for seventy-five dozen eggs that Ivory and some of his friends had dyed and hidden the day before. When they brought the eggs back, the children passed by an exhibit of photographs and newspaper clippings about the civil rights movement.

Perry holds no unrealistic illusions about the likelihood of radical social change; he harbors no expectation of living to see a day when there will be no more racism or exploitation. But he has an extraordinarily secure sense that he is doing the right things, and that knowledge helps him remain happy. Even though society at large seems to be regressing, embracing materialism, individualism, and privatism more than ever before, Perry feels comfortable sticking to values that he sees as historically sanctioned and ideologically compelling. As Percy Green explains about his own decision to remain an activist:

> The question is, "Do I want to integrate into a society that's responsible for the situation we find ourselves in?" No. My answer is no. That's what makes me a revolutionary, because my values are 180 degrees out of phase with what exists. . . . Monetary and material values by white American standards takes precedence over anything that is human. And we operate just the opposite. Our values is that human values should take precedence over anything that is monetary and material.[7]

Inevitably, the hegemony of individualism, materialism, and privatism will lead many people to view Perry's path as quite foolish. Others with real doubts about the legitimacy and morality of current society will still shy away from Perry's example for fear of the consequences of a life given over to serving others. Some who admire his choices and values will conclude that they cannot emulate him because they do not share his specific experiences and problems. But some people—black and white, male and female, young and old—will find a compelling quality in his life. They will sense that they can do important work by helping to house the homeless, by feeding the hungry, and by challenging the injustices of society. They will be the ones who realize that everyone wants to be special and that everyone wants to be important. Everyone would like to be a drum major out in front of the parade. But the only way for everyone to be first, is for everyone to serve, and for everyone to be part of a country that is itself first in love, first in justice, and first in moral excellence.

Anna Cox was married to Ivory Perry during some of his best years, and some of his worst. When asked what people should know about

him, she answers without hesitation in words that eloquently sum up
the meaning of his life:

> People kind of look for the Martin Luther Kings and the Malcolm Xs.
> And a lot of youngsters nowadays, they don't think about somebody
> right there in an old common neighborhood who's just an ordinary
> person, that is doing and has done all these things. They're geared
> and they're programmed to look for the big guys. But an ordinary
> person, who suffered all the human things, who did some things
> that were extraordinary, and got away with it, and helped people in
> the process! I think it would mean a lot to the generation coming to
> know that you can start out right here in your own neighborhood,
> start getting on folks' backs about old people's gas being turned off,
> start making sure that the slumlords fix up their places and don't rip
> people off. Do what you can, right on your own street.[8]

On January 20, 1986, Americans celebrated the first official national
holiday honoring the memory of Dr. Martin Luther King, Jr. In St. Louis,
more than 2,000 marchers paraded in the downtown streets to demonstrate their commitment to the principles that King exemplified and their
devotion to the dream he articulated. In past years, marchers had commemorated Dr. King's birthday in St. Louis by marching through downtown's most crowded shopping areas east of Tucker Boulevard. But complaints from downtown business owners and concerns about possible
traffic tie-ups led city officials to restrict the 1986 King Day parade permit
to the streets west of Tucker Boulevard.

When the parade reached Tucker Boulevard, Ivory Perry and a small
group of activists led the marchers east, into the crowded downtown
streets and past Dillard's department store, once the target of an NAACP
boycott for alleged discriminatory hiring practices. When a police officer
handed him a summons for violating the parade permit, Perry lay down
on his back in the middle of Thirteenth Street. Pointing out that they had
been marching east of Tucker Boulevard on King's birthday for seventeen
years, Perry predicted, "Next year, we won't be able to go east of Jefferson. And the next thing you know we won't be able to come downtown
and will have to march in the suburbs." Perry stayed on the street until he
was sure that all the photographers had taken his picture. Later he explained to a reporter:

> I went downtown for three reasons. One, because we've been going
> that way for seventeen years; two, because Dillard's discriminates

against blacks and minorities. We wanted to let them know that we're still watching them; and thirdly, because I believe that Dr. King's blood was my blood, his life is my life, and my life is his life. I'm committed.[9]

Beyond that specific message lay a more general point. Ivory Perry wanted to signal to his friends and foes alike that no matter how much society had changed, some things would always remain the same for him. He wanted to let them know that he was still around, that he was ready for whatever challenges the future might bring. He wanted to tell them that for all his pain, Ivory Perry had found peace in the struggle.

Notes

Introduction

1. "Social Protest in St. Louis," Missouri Committee for the Humanities Program, March 21, 1982.
2. Antonio Gramsci, *Selections from the Prison Notebooks*, ed. Quintin Hoare and Geoffrey Nowell Smith (New York: International Publishers, 1971), 9, 10.
3. See Jerome Karabel, "Revolutionary Contradictions: Antonio Gramsci and the Problem of the Intellectuals," *Politics and Society* 6 (1976): 123–72.
4. Gramsci, *Selections from the Prison Notebooks* 108–10.
5. George Lipsitz, *Class and Culture in Cold War America: A Rainbow at Midnight* (South Hadley, Mass.: Bergin and Garvey, 1982).
6. Gramsci's discussions of the historical bloc, in *Selections from the Prison Notebooks*.
7. Obviously both rupture and continuity are important in any moment of mass activism. My work on the 1940s acknowledged sedimented layers of opposition within the experiences of work, but it focused on a moment in history when new possibilities joined with suppressed hopes to spark mass insurgency.
8. See Nick Salvatore, *Eugene Victor Debs: Citizen and Socialist* (Champaign: University of Illinois Press, 1984) and Aileen Kraditor, *The Radical Persuasion* (Baton Rouge: Louisiana State University Press, 1981).
9. Michael Bristol, *Carnival and Theater* (New York: Methuen, 1985). Bristol presents an extraordinary demonstration of the application of Mikhail Bakhtin's "dialogic" literary criticism to the production of theater texts; this sense of dialogue has broader applications to politics, which I outline here and in Chapter 9.
10. I am indebted to Michael Schwartz for his careful reading and helpful comments on an earlier draft of this manuscript, especially in his letter of February 27, 1987, that directed me toward clearer articulation of these principles.

Chapter 1

1. Interview with Ivory Perry, October 3, 1982, St. Louis.
2. Interviews with Maggie Lewis, June 11, 1983, Little Rock, Arkansas; with

Kathen Wright, September 16, 1984, St. Louis; and with Ivory Perry, June 10, 1983, Pine Bluff, Arkansas.

3. Interviews with Kathen Wright, September 16, 1984, St. Louis; with Ivory Perry, Katherine Jiner, and Doris Caldwell, June 10, 1983, Pine Bluff, Arkansas; and with Maggie Lewis, June 11, 1983, Little Rock, Arkansas.

4. Interview with Ivory Perry, October 3, 1982, St. Louis. William Lyle Dobbins, "Southern Tenant Farmers Union in Jefferson County, Arkansas," *Jefferson County Historical Quarterly*, vol. 4 (1973), no. 4.

5. Interview with Ivory Perry, October 3, 1982, St. Louis.

6. Interviews with Kathen Wright, September 16, 1984, and with Ivory Perry, October 3, 1982, St. Louis.

7. Interview with Kathen Wright, September 16, 1984, St. Louis.

8. Interview with Ivory Perry, October 3, 1982, St. Louis.

9. Ibid.

10. See Frances Fox Piven and Richard Cloward, *Poor People's Movements* (New York: Pantheon Books, 1977), 186.

11. Fredric Jameson, *The Political Unconscious* (Ithaca, N.Y.: Cornell University Press, 1981), 102.

12. George P. Rawick, *The American Slave* (Westport, Conn.: Greenwood Press, 1972), vol. 8, pt. 2, p. 111.

13. Ibid., pt. 1, pp. 154, 295; vol. 10, pts. 5 and 6, p. 305.

14. Alex Yard, "Arkansas Farm Workers and the Southern Tenant Farmers Union: Modernization and Independence, Change and Resistance" (unpublished paper, St. Louis, n.d., p. 3).

15. Ibid., 10–11.

16. Lawrence Levine, *Black Culture, Black Consciousness* (New York: Oxford University Press, 1978), 315.

17. Arthur I. Waskow, *From Race Riot to Sit-In, 1919 and the 1960s.* (Garden City, N.Y.: Anchor Books, Doubleday, 1967), 124–25. Langston Hughes, *Fight for Freedom: The Story of the NAACP* (New York: Norton, 1962), 60–61. Ralph Desmarais, "Military Intelligence Reports on Arkansas Riots: 1919–1920," *Arkansas Historical Quarterly* 33 (Summer 1974): 177–89.

18. Press release, January 14, 1925, National Association for the Advancement of Colored People Collection, Library of Congress, Washington, D.C. branch files, group 1, series D, box 44. For an opposing view, see J. W. Butts and Dorothy James, "The Underlying Causes of the Elaine Riot of 1919," *Arkansas Historical Quarterly* 1 (Spring 1961): 95.

19. Charles Johnson, *Growing Up in the Black Belt* (Washington, D.C.: American Council on Education, 1941), viii. William Lyle Dobbins, "Southern Tenant Farmers Union in Jefferson County, Arkansas," *Jefferson County Historical Quarterly* (1973): 34–35.

20. Yard, "Arkansas Farm Workers," 10–11. Piven and Cloward, *Poor People's Movements*, 190.

21. Lowell Dyson, *Red Harvest* (Lincoln: University of Nebraska Press, 1982), 150. Yard, "Arkansas Farm Workers," 2.

22. Dyson, *Red Harvest*; Piven and Cloward, *Poor People's Movements*, chap. 1; Yard, "Arkansas Farm Workers."

23. William Simmons, *Men of Mark* (New York: Arno Press, *New York Times*, 1911), 280.

24. James Leslie, "Ferd Havis: Jefferson County's Black Republican Leader," *Arkansas Historical Quarterly* 37 (Autumn 1978): 240–51. See also Carl Moneyhon, "Black Politicians in Arkansas During the Gilded Age, 1876–1900," *Arkansas Historical Quarterly* 44 (Autumn 1985): 222–45. J. Morgan Kousser, "A Black Protest in the 'Era of Accommodation': Documents," *Arkansas Historical Quarterly* 34 (Summer 1975): 152.

25. Simmons, *Men of Mark*, 830. See Doug McAdam, *Political Process and the Development of Black Insurgency* (Chicago: University of Chicago Press, 1982), 100–103.

26. Dobbins, "Southern Tenant Farmers Union in Jefferson County, Arkansas," 34–35. Piven and Cloward, *Poor People's Movements*, 197. Interviews with Ivory Perry, Doris Caldwell, Robert Pierce and Harold Terrell, June 10, 1983, Pine Bluff, Arkansas; with Maggie Lewis, June 11, 1983, Little Rock, Arkansas; and with Kathen Wright, September 16, 1984, St. Louis.

27. Jacquelyn Jones, *Labor of Love, Labor of Sorrow* (New York: Basic Books, 1985), 84, 110.

28. Interviews with Ivory Perry, June 10, 1983, Pine Bluff, Arkansas, and with Kathen Wright, September 16, 1984, St. Louis.

29. Interviews with Ivory Perry, June 10, 1983, Pine Bluff, Arkansas; October 3 and July 13, 1982, St. Louis.

30. Interview with Robert Pierce, June 10, 1983, Pine Bluff, Arkansas.

31. Ibid.

32. Ibid.

33. Ibid.

34. Interview with Doris Caldwell, June 10, 1983, Pine Bluff, Arkansas. On March 25, 1960, the Pine Bluff NAACP chapter announced a boycott of local stores that did not serve blacks at lunch counters. The stores included Newberry's (*Arkansas Gazette*, March 25, 1960).

35. Interview with Myrtle Jones, June 10, 1983, Pine Bluff, Arkansas.

36. Ibid.

37. Ibid.

38. Interviews with Ivory Perry, June 10, 1983, Pine Bluff, Arkansas, and April 9, 1985, St. Louis; with Robert Pierce, June 10, 1983, Pine Bluff, Arkansas.

39. Interviews with Doris Caldwell, Katherine Jiner, and Robert Pierce, June 10, 1983, Pine Bluff, Arkansas; with Maggie Lewis, June 11, 1983, Little Rock, Arkansas; and with Kathen Wright, September 16, 1984, St. Louis.

40. Interview with Ivory Perry, October 3, 1982, St. Louis.

41. Ibid.
42. Ibid.; interview with Kathen Wright, September 16, 1984, St. Louis. For an alternative reading of "Amos 'n Andy," see Julius Lester, *All Is Well* (New York: Morrow, 1976), 14.
43. Interviews with Ivory Perry, October 3, 1982, and April 17, 1983, St. Louis.
44. Interviews with Jewel Gonder and Ivory Perry, June 10, 1983, Pine Bluff, Arkansas. Donald "Red" Barry was known as "the James Cagney of the plains." Born Donald Barry de Acosta in Houston, Texas, on January 11, 1912, Barry was one of Hollywood's top western stars between 1942 and 1945. Barry costarred with Lash Larue in several films between 1945 and 1948.
45. Interviews with Jewel Gonder and Ivory Perry, June 10, 1983, Pine Bluff, Arkansas. For a useful analysis of "joning," see John W. Roberts, "Joning: An Afro-American Verbal Form in St. Louis," *Journal of the Folklore Institute* 19 (April 1982): 61–70.
46. Letter from W. B. Cloman to Roy Wilkins, June 11, 1937, National Association for the Advancement of Colored People Collection, group 1, series G, box 13.
47. Interviews with Leo Branton, January 9, 1984, Los Angeles; with Wiley Branton, November 30, 1983, Washington, D.C.; with Robert Pierce and Doris Caldwell, June 10, 1983, Pine Bluff, Arkansas.
48. Interviews with Leo Branton, January 9, 1984, Los Angeles, and Wiley Branton, November 30, 1983, Washington, D.C.
49. Interview with Leo Branton, January 9, 1984, Los Angeles.
50. Ibid.
51. Interviews with Wiley Branton, November 30, 1983, Washington, D.C.; with Leo Branton, January 9, 1984, Los Angeles; and with Robert Pierce, June 10, 1983, Pine Bluff, Arkansas.
52. Interview with Leo Branton, January 9, 1984, Los Angeles.
53. Ibid. Interview with Wiley Branton, November 30, 1983, Washington, D.C.
54. Interview with Wiley Branton, November 30, 1983, Washington, D.C.
55. Richard Dorson, *Negro Tales from Pine Bluff, Arkansas and Calvin, Michigan* (Bloomington: University of Indiana Press, 1958), 119.
56. Jervis Anderson, *A. Philip Randolph* (New York: Harcourt Brace Jovanovich, 1972), 241–73. George Lipsitz, *Class and Culture in Cold War America: A Rainbow at Midnight* (South Hadley, Mass.: Bergin and Garvey, 1982), chap. 1.
57. *Arkansas State Press*, August 8, 1941, p. 1; May 3, 1942, p. 5; July 7, 1942, p. 3.
58. C. Calvin Smith, "Diluting an Institution: The Social Impact of WWII on the Arkansas Family," *Arkansas Historical Quarterly* 39 (Spring 1980): 21–34. Karen Tucker Anderson, *Wartime Women* (Westport, Conn.: Greenwood Press, 1982).
59. Interview with Kathen Wright, September 16, 1984, St. Louis.
60. Interviews with Ivory Perry, July 13, 1982, St. Louis; and June 10, 1983, Pine

Bluff, Arkansas. U.S. Army, "Report of Separation from the Armed Forces of the United States," November 2, 1951, Ivory Perry RA18 333 463; obtained by request from the Veterans Administration, Personnel Records Center, St. Louis, Missouri.

Chapter 2

1. Interviews with Ivory Perry, April 17, 1983, St. Louis; and June 10, 1983, Pine Bluff, Arkansas.
2. Ibid.
3. Richard Dalfiume, *Desegregation of the U.S. Armed Forces* (Columbia: University of Missouri Press, 1969), Gerald Patton, *The Black Officer* (Westport, Conn.: Greenwood Press, 1982).
4. Interview with Ivory Perry, April 17, 1983, St. Louis.
5. Ibid.
6. See Edwin P. Hoyt, *The Pusan Perimeter* (Briarcliff Manor, N.Y.: Stein and Day, 1984), 33. Stephen Ambrose, *Rise to Globalism* (New York: Penguin Books, 1974), chap. 5. Roy F. Appleman, *U.S. Army in the Korean War—South to the Naktong, North to the Yalu* (Washington, D.C.: Office of the Chief of Military History. Department of the Army, 1961).
7. Interviews with Harold Terrell, June 10, 1983, Pine Bluff, Arkansas; and with Ivory Perry, April 17, 1983, St. Louis.
8. Interview with Harold Terrell, June 10, 1983, Pine Bluff, Arkansas.
9. Appleman, *U.S. Army in the Korean War*, 195.
10. *New York Times*, October 15, 1950, p. 9.
11. Interviews with Ivory Perry and Harold Terrell, June 10, 1983, Pine Bluff, Arkansas. Appleman, *U.S. Army in the Korean War*.
12. Interviews with Harold Terrell and Ivory Perry, June 10, 1983, Pine Bluff, Arkansas.
13. Holding by the Board of Review, Officers of the Judge Advocate General's Corps, *United States* v. *First Lieutenant Leon A. Gilbert*, October 9, 1950, HQAA JAAJ CC NASSIF Building, Bailey Crossroads, Virginia, p. 17.
14. Opinion of the Judicial Council, Officers of the Judge Advocate General's Corps, *United States* v. *First Lieutenant Leon A. Gilbert*, November 16, 1950, HQAA JAAJ CC NASSIF Building, Bailey Crossroads, Virginia, pp. 3–5. General Court-Martial Orders 88, Department of the Army, Washington, D.C., December 1, 1950, corrected copy, HQAA JAAJ CC NASSIF Building, Bailey Crossroads, Virginia.
15. Opinion of the Judicial Council, *United States* v. *Gilbert*, p. 18.
16. William K. Krause, certificate of medical testimony, Holding by the Board of Review, *United States* v. *Gilbert*, p. 4.
17. *Ebony*, December 1955, p. 100.

18. Harry S. Truman, commutation of sentence, November 27, 1950, Washington, D.C. Record of Trial of First Lieutenant Leon A. Gilbert, October 4, 1950, HQAA JAAJ CC NASSIF Building, Bailey Crossroads, Virginia.

19. Report to General MacArthur from Thurgood Marshall, February 15, 1951, ibid., pp. 1, 2.

20. Ibid., pp. 3–4.

21. *Pittsburgh Courier*, March 3, 1951, p. 5. Thurgood Marshall, "Summary Justice—the Negro GI in Korea," *Crisis*, May 1951, p. 303.

22. Appleman, *U.S. Army in the Korean War*, 194.

23. Richard Stillman, *Integration of the U.S. Armed Forces* (New York: Praeger, 1968), 51.

24. Appleman, *U.S. Army in the Korean War*, 486.

25. *Saturday Evening Post*, June 16, 1951, p. 30.

26. Frances Fox Piven and Richard Cloward, *Poor People's Movements* (New York: Pantheon Books, 1977), 267. Hoyt, *The Pusan Perimeter*, 288.

27. Leo Bogart, ed., *Social Research and the Desegregation of the U.S. Army: Two Original Field Reports* (New York: Markham Publishing, 1969), 53–54, 59–60.

28. Ibid., 96. *Pittsburgh Courier*, September 9, 1950, p. 1.

29. Bogart, *Social Research and the Desegregation of the U.S. Army*, 97.

30. *Pittsburgh Courier*, September 9, 1950, p. 1, and September 2, 1950, p. 5.

31. *Los Angeles Times*, January 5, 1984, pt. 4, p. 10.

32. A representative critic is Appleman, a defender is Marshall, and Stillman and Bogart represent the middle position.

33. Hoyt, *The Pusan Perimeter* 130, 153, 268, 288.

34. Ibid., 154. He refers to Marshall as a lawyer for the NAACP and White as a publicist for the group, with no other acknowledgment of their long and distinguished careers. Nor does Hoyt admit the long history within the military of denigrating the accomplishments of black soldiers.

35. L. Albert Scipio, *Last of the Black Regulars: A History of the 24th Infantry Regiment* (Silver Spring, Md.: Roman Publications, 1983). Also see *Los Angeles Times*, January 5, 1984, pt. 4, p. 10.

36. Samuel L. Banks, "The Korean Conflict," *Negro History Bulletin* 36 (1973): 131–32. See also David Carlisle's very important review of Bernald C. Nalty's *Strength for the Fight* (New York: Free Press, 1986) in the *Los Angeles Times* Book Review Section, June 15, 1986, p. 5.

37. Stanley Davis, "Stress in Combat," *Scientific American* 194 (March 1956): 34. See also Bogart, *Social Research and the Desegregation of the U.S. Army*, 96, 97.

38. Interview with Harold Terrell, June 10, 1983, Pine Bluff, Arkansas. Hoyt, *The Pusan Perimeter*, 39.

39. Ambrose, *Rise to Globalism*.

40. Amiri Baraka (LeRoi Jones), *Blues People* (New York: Random House, 1963).

41. For example Harvard Sitkoff, *The Struggle for Black Equality* (New York: Hill

and Wang, 1981) and Aldon D. Morris, *The Origins of the Civil Rights Movement* (New York: Free Press, 1984).

42. Dalfiume, *Desegregation of the U.S. Armed Forces.*
43. Interview with Ivory Perry, April 17, 1983, St. Louis, Missouri.
44. Interview with Ivory Perry, June 10, 1983, Pine Bluff, Arkansas.
45. Ibid. *25th Infantry Division Secret Command Report,* Washington National Records Center, Archives Branch, NCWN, Suitland, Maryland, records group 407, box 3841.
46. Ivory Perry, Abbreviated Clinical Record, 128th Station Hospital, APO, February 27, 1951–March 19, 1951; obtained from Veterans Administration, St. Louis, Missouri by request. 24th Infantry Regiment Records, Washington National Records Center, Archives Branch, NCWN, Suitland, Maryland, December 1951, records group 407, box 3770. Ivory Perry, Physical Condition Report, 361st Station Hospital, APO 1055, April 24, 1951; obtained from Veterans Administration, St. Louis, Missouri, by request.
47. Ivory Perry, Intake History, Neuropsychiatric Service, 361st Station Hospital, APO 1055, April 17, 1951, obtained from Veterans Administration, St. Louis, Missouri, by request.
48. Interview with Ivory Perry, June 10, 1983, Pine Bluff, Arkansas.
49. Ibid. Samuel Fuller uses a similar line in his 1951 film *Steel Helmet* when he has an American soldier say, "He's a South Korean if he's running with you and a North Korean if he is running at you."
50. Interview with Ivory Perry, April 17, 1983, St. Louis.
51. Interview with Ivory Perry, June 10, 1983, Pine Bluff, Arkansas.
52. Interviews with Ivory Perry, April 17, 1983, and April 18, 1987, St. Louis.
53. Interviews with Ivory Perry, April 17, 1983, St. Louis; and with Harold Terrell, June 10, 1983, Pine Bluff, Arkansas.
54. Interviews with Ivory Perry, October 3, 1982, St. Louis; and with Harold Terrell, June 10, 1983, Pine Bluff, Arkansas.
55. Interview with Ivory Perry, October 3, 1982, St. Louis.
56. Interviews with Ivory Perry, October 3, 1982, and September 13, 1983, St. Louis. Report of Separation from the Armed Forces of the United States, Ivory Perry, November 2, 1951; obtained from Veterans Administration, St. Louis, Missouri, by request. Verbatim Record of Trial, Ivory Perry, Office of the Judge Advocate General, HQAA JAAJ CC NASSIF Building, Bailey Crossroads, Virginia, p. 48.
57. Verbatim Record of Trial, Ivory Perry, p. 4, 13–14, 15–16, 50.
58. Ibid., pp. 18, 48.
59. Ibid., pp. 31, 35–36.
60. Ibid., pp. 5–7, 8–11, 25–26.
61. Ibid., pp. 40–41.
62. Ibid., p. 23.

63. Report of Separation from the Armed Forces of the United States, Ivory Perry, November 2, 1951. Verbatim Record of Trial, Ivory Perry, pp. 41, 45.
64. Verbatim Record of Trial, Ivory Perry, p. 48.
65. Verbatim Record of Trial, Ivory Perry, pp. 48–49.
66. Verbatim Report of Trial Summary, Lt. Colonel Edward Duvall, Office of the Judge Advocate General, HQAA JAAJ CC NASSIF Building, Bailey Crossroads, Virginia, pp. 6–7. Verbatim Record of Trial, Ivory Perry, p. 50.
67. Interviews with Ivory Perry, July 13, 1982, and September 13, 1983, St. Louis.
68. Report of Separation from the Armed Forces of the United States, Ivory Perry, March 3, 1954, National Personnel Records Center, St. Louis, Missouri; obtained by request.
69. Interviews with Harold Terrell, June 10, 1983, Pine Bluff, Arkansas; and with Ivory Perry, April 17, 1983, St. Louis, and June 10, 1983, Pine Bluff, Arkansas.
70. Interview with Harold Terrell, June 10, 1983, Pine Bluff, Arkansas.
71. Interview with Ivory Perry, April 18, 1987, St. Louis.

Chapter 3

1. Interview with Ivory Perry, October 3, 1982, St. Louis.
2. Interviews with Ivory Perry, June 10, 1983, Pine Bluff, Arkansas, July 13, 1982, and April 9, 1985, St. Louis. John T. Clark files, Urban League Collection, Washington University Libraries, St. Louis, Missouri, boxes 6 and 7. National Urban League Papers, Library of Congress, Washington, D.C., series 3, box 61. *St. Louis Post-Dispatch,* December 15, 1949, p. 8c. Leo Bohannon files, Urban League Collection, box T. John T. Clark files, Urban League Collection, box 6.
3. William E. Douthit files, Urban League Collection, box 2. Frances Fox Piven and Richard Cloward, *Poor People's Movements* (New York: Pantheon Books, 1977), 188.
4. James Neal Primm, *The Lion of the Valley* (Boulder, Colo.: Pruett Publishing, 1981), 61–65.
5. *American History School Project,* National Endowment for the Humanities, Missouri Historical Society, I LP 12, III.
6. Selwyn K. Troen, *The Public and the Schools* (Columbia: University of Missouri Press, 1975), 36–37.
7. John T. Clark files, Urban League Collection, series 1, box 2. Primm, *Lion of the Valley,* 435–38.
8. Primm, *Lion of the Valley,* 333–34, 448. Troen, *The Public and the Schools* 36–37.
9. Rudi Blesh, *They All Played Ragtime* (New York: Grove Press, 1959), 35. Lynn Haney, *Naked at the Feast* (New York: Dodd, Mead, 1981). George Lipsitz, "Biddle Street, Biddle Street," *St. Louis Magazine,* April 1983, 32–34.

10. Aldon D. Morris, *The Origins of the Civil Rights Movement* (New York: Free Press, 1984), 42–44. 78–80.

11. Interviews with Ivory Perry, July 13, 1982, and September 13, 1983, St. Louis. According to R. L. Polk's *City Directory* (St. Louis, 1955), the address was 5157 Cabanne. On restrictive covenants, see Clement Vose, *Caucasians Only* (New York: Free Press, 1960), 35–50.

12. John T. Clark files, Urban League Collection, series 1, box 2. Interviews with Ivory Perry, July 13, 1982, and September 13, 1983, St. Louis.

13. Interview with Kathen Wright, September 16, 1984, St. Louis.

14. Telephone interview with Earline Terry Whitfield, February 2, 1986.

15. Ibid.

16. Interviews with Ivory Perry, July 13, 1982, and September 13, 1983, St. Louis.

17. Federal Bureau of Investigation Files, Ivory Perry, SL-173-28, pp. 40–41.

18. Metropolitan Police Department, City of St. Louis, Offense Report, Complaint Number 4390, January 7, 1960.

19. *St. Louis Post-Dispatch*, September 19, 1960, p. 3; September 22, 1960, p. 9A; September 24, 1960, p. 3A. *St. Louis Argus*, September 30, 1960, p. 1.

20. *St. Louis Post-Dispatch*, September 26, 1960, p. 1.

21. Interview with Ivory Perry, September 13, 1983, St. Louis.

22. Congress of Racial Equality Papers, State Historical Society, Madison, Wisconsin, series 3, box 10, folders 9 and 10. This pressure against black children evoked memories of the Fairgrounds Park incident in 1949 in which white thugs, egged on by neo-Nazis, attacked black children attempting to use a previously all-white swimming pool. Robert Curtis, one of those children, later became a CORE leader and a prominent figure during the Jefferson Bank dispute. See "Survey, January 1950," John T. Clark files, Urban League Collection, box 6.

23. *New York Times*, September 2, 18, 23, 24, November 10, and December 7, 1955. Harvard Sitkoff, *The Struggle for Black Equality* (New York: Hill and Wang, 1981), 49. David Lewis, *King: A Critical Biography* (New York: Penguin Books, 1970), chap. 3. Morris, *The Origins of the Civil Rights Movement*, pp. 51–63 on Montgomery and pp. 17–25 on Baton Rouge.

24. Telephone interview with Earline Terry Whitfield, February 2, 1986.

25. See August Meier and Elliott Rudwick, *CORE* (New York: Oxford University Press, 1973), and Morris, *The Origins of the Civil Rights Movement*, 128–38.

26. Interviews with Charles Oldham, March 16, 1984; and Ivory Perry, July 13, 1982, St. Louis. Congress of Racial Equality Papers, series 1, box 1, and series 1, box 8.

27. Interviews with Marian Oldham, March 16, 1984; and Father John Shocklee, March 16, 1984, St. Louis.

28. Telephone interview with Earline Terry Whitfield, February 2, 1986. St. Louis Police Department, Supplementary Report, Complaint Number 235341, Oc-

tober 18, 1959, Supplementary Report 234803, October 27, 1959; Supplementary Report, Complaint Number 230606, October 21, 1959; Supplementary Report, Complaint Number 230437, October 21, 1959: Supplementary Report, Complaint Number 230021, October 18, 1959.

29. Interview with Anna Cox, December 27, 1983, Sacramento.
30. Ibid.
31. Ibid. Interview with Ivory Perry, October 3, 1982, St. Louis.
32. Civil Rights Collection, University Research Library, University of California, Los Angeles, box 7, folder 12B. *Core-lator* 103, November 1963. Meier and Rudwick, *CORE*, 237.
33. *St. Louis Post-Dispatch*, September 1, 1963, p. 1, September 2, 1963, p. 1. Meier and Rudwick, *CORE*, Robert Curtis, March 8, 1967, speech outside City Hall. Telephone interview with Ivory Perry, July 3, 1985.
34. *Core-lator* 103, November 1963.
35. Interview with Percy Green, September 18, 1984, St. Louis.
36. *Freedom Now* (CORE newsletter), March 1964, St. Louis.
37. Telephone interview with Gene Tournour, July 28, 1987.
38. Ibid.
39. *St. Louis Post-Dispatch*, November 22, 1963, pp. 1, 7; December 5, 1963, p. 1; December 17, 1963, p. 12. Interview with Ivory Perry, July 13 and October 3, 1982, St. Louis, and January 20, 1984 (telephone). Federal Bureau of Investigation Files, Ivory Perry, pp. 40–41.
40. *St. Louis Post-Dispatch*, February 14, 1964, p. 1, and February 15, 1964, p. 1.
41. Interview with Percy Green, September 18, 1984, St. Louis.
42. Interview with Monsignor John Shocklee, March 16, 1984, St. Louis.
43. Interview with Ivory Perry, October 3, 1982, and April 18, 1987, St. Louis.
44. Interview with Ivory Perry, July 13, 1982, St. Louis, and January 20, 1984 (telephone). For a related story see *St. Louis Post-Dispatch*, December 23, 1963, p. 1.
45. *Core-lator* 106, April 1964. Meier and Rudwick, *CORE*, 237.
46. Interview with Percy Green, September 18, 1984, St. Louis.
47. Civil Rights Collection, University of California Los Angeles, box 7, folder 12C. *Core-lator* 106, April 1964.
48. Interviews with Ivory Perry, April 17, 1983, St. Louis, and January 20, 1984 (telephone). *New York Times*, April 17, 1964, p. 1, and April 22, 1964, pp. 1, 5.
49. Memo from Martin Luther King, Jr., to Wiley Branton, James Farmer, John Lewis, A. Philip Randolph, Roy Wilkins, Whitney Young, Miss Dorothy Height, April 1964, Martin Luther King Papers, the Martin Luther King, Jr., Center for Nonviolent Change, Inc., Atlanta, Georgia, pp. 2, 3.
50. Congress of Racial Equality Papers, series B, box 22, folder 5. Telephone interviews with Ivory Perry, January 20, 1984, and with Jacquelyn Butler Barnes, October 27, 1984.

51. *New York Times*, April 23, 1964, p. 28. Congress of Racial Equality Papers, series 5, box 22, folder 5. Telephone interviews with Ivory Perry, January 20, 1984, and with Jacquelyn Butler Barnes, October 27, 1984.

52. Interview with Charles Oldham, March 16, 1984, St. Louis.

53. Interviews with Percy Green, September 18, 1984, and Ivory Perry, October 3, 1982, St. Louis. Meier and Rudwick, *CORE*, 31, 312.

54. Telephone interview with Ivory Perry, July 3, 1985.

55. *Core-lator* 108, September–October 1964.

56. *St. Louis Post-Dispatch*, July 14, 1964, p. 1. *Core-lator* 108, September–October 1964. Interview with Percy Green, September 18, 1984, St. Louis.

57. *St. Louis Post-Dispatch*, July 14, 1964, p. 1. Interview with Ivory Perry, October 3, 1982, St. Louis. *Affirmative Action to Open the Doors of Job Opportunity*, Citizen's Commission on Civil Rights, Washington, D.C., June 19, 1984, p. 42.

58. Ivory Perry, Chrysler Corporation employment record, St. Louis assembly plant; furnished at the author's request by Chrysler Corporation. Interviews with Ivory Perry, October 3, 1982, and September 13, 1983, St. Louis.

59. Interviews with Ivory Perry, July 13 and October 3, 1982, and September 16, 1984, St. Louis. Metropolitan Police Department, City of St. Louis, Supplementary Arrest Report, Complaint Number 65-77327, March 15, 1965.

60. Thomas F. Parker, ed., *Violence in the U.S.*, vol. 1, *1956–67* (New York: Facts on File, 1974), 100. David Garrow, *Protest at Selma* (New Haven, Conn.: Yale University Press, 1978), 61–67, 78–82, 91–92. Stephen B. Oates, *Let the Trumpet Sound* (New York: Harper & Row, 1982), 346–49, 353–54. Lewis, *King: A Critical Biography*, 274–76, 282–83. Jimmie Lee Jackson's shooting took place in Marion, Alabama, not Selma, but the demonstration where the shooting took place was led by the Reverend C. T. Vivian as part of the Southern Christian Leadership Project's voter registration effort.

61. Interviews with Ivory Perry, October 3, 1982, April 17, 1983, and September 16, 1984, St. Louis.

62. Interview with Ivory Perry, September 16, 1984, St. Louis. *St. Louis Globe-Democrat*, March 16, 1965, pp. 1, 6A. *St. Louis Post-Dispatch*, March 16, 1965, p. 1.

63. Interview with Ivory Perry, September 16, 1984, St. Louis. *St. Louis Globe-Democrat*, March 16, 1965, p. 6A. Perry recalls that the two youths had been playing on the other side of a nearby fence and climbed the fence when they saw people gathered around the truck.

64. *St. Louis Post-Dispatch*, March 16, 1965, p. 1. Metropolitan Police Department, Supplementary Arrest Report. Complaint Number 65-77327, March 15, 1965. Interview with Ivory Perry, October 3, 1982, St. Louis.

65. Interview with Ivory Perry, October 3, 1982, St. Louis. *New York Times*, July 18, 1965, p. 26. Lewis, *King: A Critical Biography*, 291–92. Oates, *Let the*

Trumpet Sound, 346–54. C. T. Vivian's estimate in the *Times* does not include St. Louisans who traveled to Selma by private cars.

66. NAACP press release, April 15, 1958, NAACP Papers, Library of Congress, Washington, D.C., group 3, series A, box 75. Interviews with Ivory Perry, April 17, 1983; and with Percy Green, September 18, 1984, St. Louis. *St. Louis Post-Dispatch*, May 13, 1965, p. 1.

67. *St. Louis Post-Dispatch*, May 13, 1965, pp. 1, 3. Metropolitan Police Department, City of St. Louis, Peace Disturbance and Common Assaults, Complaint Number 146299, May 12, 1965.

68. *St. Louis Post-Dispatch*, May 13, 1965, p. 1, and September 17, 1965, p. 3A. Metropolitan Police Department, City of St. Louis, Peace Disturbance and Common Assaults, Complaint Number 146299, May 12, 1965. Interview with Ivory Perry, October 3, 1982, St. Louis, and January 20, 1984 (telephone). *St. Louis Globe-Democrat*, June 15, 1965, p. 4A.

69. Telephone interview with Donald Rankins, August 6, 1985.

70. Interview with Ivory Perry, September 13, 1983, St. Louis.

Chapter 4

1. *Ebony*, September 1965, p. 25. Thomas Parker, ed., *Violence in the U.S.*, vol. 1, *1956–1967* (New York: Facts on File, 1974), 115–17. Interview with Ivory Perry, July 13, 1982, St. Louis.

2. CORE Report on Bogalusa, Civil Rights Collection, University Research Library, University of California, Los Angeles, box 2, folder 7B. Interview with Ivory Perry, September 13, 1983, St. Louis.

3. Interview with Ivory Perry, September 13, 1983, St. Louis.

4. Ibid.

5. Howell Raines, *My Soul Is Rested* (New York: Penguin Books, 1977), 417.

6. Ibid., 420. This interview took place under what seem like less than ideal conditions of trust between interviewer and interviewee, and there seems to be a large performance element in Mr. Sims's responses. Yet even if his descriptions are not totally accurate, Sims's philosophy and sentiments reflect at least the narrative conventions and political culture of one part of the movement.

7. Interview with Ivory Perry, September 13, 1983, St. Louis.

8. *Baton Rouge State Times*, July 19, 1965, p. 1, Bogalusa Clippings File, Louisiana Room, Troy Middleton Library, Louisiana State University, Baton Rouge.

9. Telephone interview with Richard Haley, January 30, 1984.

10. *Baton Rouge State Times*, July 19, 1965, p. 1.

11. "The CORE of It," *Amsterdam News*, July 7, 1965; the Papers of the Congress

of Racial Equality, 1941–1967, microfilm on loan from the State Historical Society, Madison, Wisconsin, supplement Reel 1.

12. Telephone Interview with Ivory Perry, July 3, 1985.

13. Vera Runy, "Bogalusa, the Economics of Tragedy," in Jeremy Larner and Irving Howe, eds., *Poverty, Views from the Left* (New York: Morrow, 1968), 280, 283. See also Frances Fox Piven and Richard Cloward, *Poor People's Movements* (New York: Pantheon Books, 1977), especially chap. 4.

14. Runy, "Bogalusa, The Economics of Tragedy," 282. CORE Report on Bogalusa.

15. "The Bogalusa Story;" letter of Bogalusa Committee for Concern asking distribution of "The Bogalusa Story," April 22, 1965; telegram from James Farmer to P. T. Sinclair, president, Crown Zellerbach, February 19, 1965; CORE Fact Sheet on Bogalusa, Louisiana; the Papers of the Congress of Racial Equality, 1941–1967, Microfilming Corporation of America, Sanford, North Carolina; copies obtained from Amistad Research Center, New Orleans.

16. Runy, "Bogalusa, The Economics of Tragedy," 283.

17. For descriptions of typical patterns see Doug McAdam, *Political Process and the Development of Black Insurgency, 1930–1970* (Chicago: University of Chicago Press, 1982) and Aldon D. Morris, *The Origins of the Civil Rights Movement: Black Communities Organizing for Change* (New York: Free Press, 1984). This is not to imply that the NAACP and the black churches played no role in Bogalusa, only that they did not dominate the struggle. The pastor of the Mt. Moriah Baptist Church opposed CORE and the Civic and Voters League; on May 23, 1965, while vigilantes struck back at the black movement by attempting to burn the Ebenezer Baptist Church. Similarly, many activists had previously had ties with the NAACP, but the organization did not play a leading role in the Civic and Voters League protests.

18. Telephone interview with Richard Haley, January 30, 1984.

19. Ibid.

20. CORE Report on Bogalusa.

21. The Papers of the Congress of Racial Equality, 1941–1967. "Bogalusa, Louisiana, Incident Summary: January 25–February 21."

22. CORE Report on Bogalusa.

23. "Bogalusa, Louisiana, Incident Summary," Papers of the Congress of Racial Equality.

24. Ibid.

25. Ibid.

26. CORE Report on Bogalusa.

27. Letter from Bogalusa Civic and Voters League to Bogalusa City Council, April 6, 1965, Civil Rights Collection, University of California, Los Angeles, box 2, folder 7B.

28. CORE Report on Bogalusa.

29. "Bogalusa, Louisiana, Incident Summary," Papers of the Congress of Racial Equality.

30. CORE Report on Bogalusa.

31. *Baton Rouge Morning Advocate*, April 16, 1965, p. 1, Bogalusa Clippings File, Troy Middleton Library, Louisiana State University, Baton Rouge. *Gregory Hicks et al.* v. *Claxton Knight et al.* in the U.S. District Court for the Eastern District of Louisiana, Civil Action 15727, Federal Records Center, Fort Worth, Texas, pp. 29, 278.

32. CORE Report on Bogalusa.

33. *Baton Rouge State Times*, May 20, 1965, p. 1. *Hicks* v. *Knight*, pp. 275–78.

34. Interview with Ivory Perry, July 13, 1982, St. Louis.

35. Telephone interview with Jacquelyn Butler Barnes, October 27, 1984.

36. Ibid. Telephone interview with Richard Haley, January 30, 1984.

37. Telephone interview with Ivory Perry, July 3, 1985.

38. *Bogalusa Daily News*, July 9, 1965, p. 1. Parker, *Violence in the U.S.*, 115.

39. Affidavit by Marvin Austin, July 16, 1965, *Hicks* v. *Knight*.

40. Interview with Ivory Perry, September 13, 1983, St. Louis.

41. Affidavits by Victor David Levine, July 17, 1965, and by Carolyn Bryant, July 16, 1965, *Hicks* v. *Knight*.

42. Affidavit by Jacquelyn Butler, July 17, 1965, *Hicks* v. *Knight*. Telephone interview with Jacquelyn Butler Barnes, October 27, 1984.

43. *New York Times*, July 18, 1965, p. 1. Telephone interview with Ivory Perry, July 3, 1985.

44. *New York Times*, July 28, 1965, pp. 1, 40. *New Orleans Times-Picayune*, July 30, 1965, pp. 1, 3.

45. *Hicks* v. *Knight*, pp. 137, 439, 442.

46. *New York Times*, July 31, 1965, p. 1, and July 30, 1965, p. 23. *New Orleans Times-Picayune*, July 30, 1965, pp. 1, 3.

47. Docket and related materials, *Hicks* v. *Knight*.

48. Paul Good, "Klantown, U.S.A.," *Nation*, February 1, 1965, p. 1.

49. *Ebony*, September 1965, p. 28.

50. See the Papers of the Congress of Racial Equality, and August Meier and Elliott Rudwick, *CORE: A Study in the Civil Rights Movement, 1942–1968* (New York: Oxford University Press, 1973), 344–50.

51. Meier and Rudwick, *CORE*, 350. Meier and Rudwick stress the paltry results secured by the Bogalusa campaign, but overlook the gains in community organization and limits on police and vigilante harassment. The Civic and Voters League remained an enduring factor in local politics, playing an especially militant role in the late 1960s. A. Z. Young went on to develop important influence in state politics, and served in Edwin Edwards's gubernatorial administrations.

52. Telephone interview with Ivory Perry, July 3, 1985.

53. Ibid.
54. Interviews with Ivory Perry, July 13, 1982, and April 19, 1987, St. Louis.
55. Morris, *Origins of the Civil Rights Movement*, 158.
56. Telephone interview with Ivory Perry, July 3, 1985.

Chapter 5

1. Harvard Sitkoff, *The Struggle for Black Equality* (New York: Hill and Wang, 1981), 200–202. William O'Neill, *Coming Apart: An Informal History of the 1960s* (New York Times: Quadrangle, 1975), 170–72.
2. Interviews with Ivory Perry, July 13, 1982, and September 13, 1983, St. Louis.
3. *St. Louis Globe-Democrat*, June 14, 1965, p. 9A. *St. Louis Post-Dispatch*, August 8, 1965, p. 1; September 8, 1965, p. 1; September 13, 1965, p. 3; September 14, 1965, p. 1.
4. *St. Louis Post-Dispatch*, September 16, 1965, p. 1.
5. Ibid., September 17, 1965, p. 3.
6. Ibid.
7. Ibid.
8. Metropolitan Police Department of the City of St. Louis, Peace Disturbance and Common Assaults, Complaint Number 315452, September 16, 1965. *St. Louis Post-Dispatch*, September 17, 1965, p. 3.
9. *St. Louis Post-Dispatch*, September 26, 1965, p. 1.
10. Ibid., October 4, 1965, p. 5A.
11. Interview with Ivory Perry, September 16, 1984, St. Louis.
12. Interview with Maurice Williamson, September 17, 1984, St. Louis.
13. Interviews with Anna Cox, December 27, 1983, Sacramento; and with Howard Buchbinder, March 31, 1984, Toronto.
14. Interviews with Ivory Perry, October 3, 1982, St. Louis; and with Howard Buchbinder, March 31, 1984, Toronto.
15. Telephone interview with Pearlie Evans, July 21, 1987.
16. Interviews with Ivory Perry, October 3, 1982, St. Louis, and July 3, 1985 (telephone).
17. Interviews with Ivory Perry, July 3, 1985 (telephone); and with Mickey Rosen, June 17, 1987, St. Louis.
18. Interview with Mickey Rosen, June 17, 1987, St. Louis.
19. Interviews with Judge Theodore McMillian and with Judge Clyde Cahill, September 18, 1984, St. Louis.
20. Interview with Howard Buchbinder, March 31, 1984, Toronto.
21. Ibid.
22. Interview with Ivory Perry, April 9, 1985, St. Louis.
23. Interview with Judge Theodore McMillian, September 18, 1984, St. Louis.

24. Interviews with Ivory Perry, January 20, 1984 (telephone); with Anna Cox, December 27, 1983, Sacramento; and with Kathen Wright, September 16, 1984, St. Louis. *St. Louis Post-Dispatch*, September 18, 1968, p. 49.

25. Interview with Mickey Rosen, June 17, 1987, St. Louis.

26. Harry Edward Berndt, "The Community Development Corporation." (Ph.D. diss., Washington University, 1975).

27. *St. Louis Post-Dispatch*, November 21, 1965, p. 1. *St. Louis Globe-Democrat*, November 22, 1965, p. 13A.

28. The sentence was reduced to a $25 fine and two years' probation, see *St. Louis Post-Dispatch*, February 17, 1966, p. 22D.

29. Interview with Dorie Ladner, June 24, 1987, Washington, D.C.

30. David L. Lewis, *King: A Critical Biography* (New York: Penguin Books, 1970). Robert L. Allen, *Black Awakening in Capitalist America* (New York: Doubleday, 1969), 113. Telephone interview with Ivory Perry, January 20, 1984.

31. Telephone interview with Ivory Perry, January 20, 1984. Stephen B. Oates, *Let the Trumpet Sound* (New York: Harper & Row, 1982), 387–95, 405–19.

32. *St. Louis Post-Dispatch*, September 28, 1966, p. 1.

33. Ibid.

34. Interview with Ivory Perry, September 16, 1984, St. Louis. *St. Louis Globe-Democrat*, September 29, 1966, p. 1.

35. *St. Louis Post-Dispatch*, October 16, 1966, p. 3A; October 18, 1966, p. 3. *St. Louis Globe-Democrat*, October 15, 1966, p. 3. Interview with Ivory Perry, July 13, 1982, St. Louis.

36. Interviews with Ivory Perry, April 19, 1987, and with Mickey Rosen, June 17, 1987, St. Louis.

37. *St. Louis Globe-Democrat*, October 21, 1966, p. 3A.

38. *St. Louis Post-Dispatch*, October 20, 1966, pp. 2B, 4. Interview with Ivory Perry, September 16, 1984, St. Louis.

39. *St. Louis Post-Dispatch*, March 25, 1967, pp. 1C, 3A. Interviews with Ivory Perry, September 16, 1984, St. Louis, and August 26, 1987 (telephone).

40. Ivory Perry testimony, hearings before the National Commission on Urban Problems, St. Louis, Missouri, May 8, 1967, U.S. Government Printing Office, Washington, D.C., vol. 5. William Paul Locke, "A History and Analysis of the Origin and Development of the Human Development Corporation," (Ph.D. diss., St. Louis University, 1974), 177. Missouri House Resolution #778, September 6, 1984.

41. Interview with Ivory Perry, April 17, 1983, St. Louis.

42. Interviews with Anna Cox, December 27, 1983, Sacramento; with Ivory Perry, April 17, 1983, St. Louis.

43. Interview with Ivory Perry, April 17, 1983, St. Louis.

44. Interview with Anna Cox, December 27, 1983, Sacramento.

45. Interview with Ivory Perry, April 17, 1983, St. Louis.

46. Interview with Anna Cox, December 27, 1983, Sacramento.

47. Interviews with Monsignor John Shocklee, March 16, 1984, and with Ivory Perry, October 3, 1982, St. Louis.

48. Telephone interview with Pearlie Evans, July 21, 1987.

49. Lawrence Friedman, "The Social and Political Context of the War on Poverty: An Overview," in Robert Haveman, ed., *A Decade of Federal Anti-Poverty Programs* (New York: Academic Press, 1977), 21.

50. James T. Patterson, *America's Struggle Against Poverty, 1900–1980* (Cambridge: Harvard University Press, 1981), 109–10.

51. Ibid., 109.

52. Ibid., 111.

53. Frances Fox Piven and Richard Cloward, *Poor People's Movements* (New York: Pantheon Books, 1977), 267. John Mollenkopf, *The Contested City* (Princeton: Princeton University Press, 1983). Patterson, *America's Struggle Against Poverty,* 129.

54. Patterson, *America's Struggle Against Poverty,* 151. Allen J. Matusow, *The Unraveling of America* (New York: Harper & Row, 1984), 240.

55. See Patterson, *America's Struggle Against Poverty,* chap. 6.

56. Piven and Cloward, *Poor People's Movements,* 271.

57. Matusow, *The Unraveling of America,* 243–46.

58. Roger Friedland, *Power and Crisis in the City* (London: Shocken Books, 1983), chap. 6, esp. pp. 125–35.

59. Telephone interview with Ivory Perry, January 20, 1984.

60. For the context for this, see Piven and Cloward, *Poor People's Movements,* 271, and Mollenkopf, *The Contested City,* 90–93.

61. Interview with Judge Clyde Cahill, September 18, 1984, St. Louis.

62. Telephone interview with Ivory Perry, January 20, 1984.

63. Interview with Judge Clyde Cahill, September 18, 1984, St. Louis.

64. Ibid.

65. Interview with Ivory Perry, October 3, 1982, St. Louis.

66. *St. Louis Post-Dispatch,* July 23, 1968, p. 3A. Interview with Ivory Perry, October 3, 1982, St. Louis.

Chapter 6

1. For an introduction to the theoretical issues connected with rent strikes see the excellent book edited by Ronald Lawson, with the assistance of Mark Naison, *The Tenant Movement in New York City, 1904–1984* (New Brunswick, N.J.: Rutgers University Press, 1986).

2. Telephone interview with Ivory Perry, July 3, 1985.

3. Charles Kimball Cummings, "Rent Strike in St. Louis" (Ph.D. diss., Washington University, 1975), 128. "Federal Subsidies for Low Income Housing"

(box 2) and "Profile of the Negro Community," Douthit files (box 6), Urban League Collection, Washington University Libraries, St. Louis, Missouri.

4. Raymond Tucker Papers, Washington University Libraries, St. Louis, Missouri, series 3, box 18. *Congressional Record,* June 15, 1964, 13276.

5. Eugene Meehan, *The Quality of Federal Policymaking: Programmed Failure in Public Housing* (Columbia: University of Missouri Press, 1979), 17, 20, 27, 28, 48, 49. Cummings, "Rent Strike in St. Louis," 71.

6. *Federal Role in Urban Affairs,* Senator Joseph Clark testimony, hearings before the U.S. Senate Subcommittee on Government Operations, August 15–16, 1966, U.S. Government Printing Office, Washington, D.C. Kenneth Jackson, "Race, Ethnicity, and Real Estate Appraisal," *Journal of Urban History* 6 (Summer 1980): 419–52. *Home Owners Loan Corporation City Survey Files,* Confidential Survey of St. Louis, 1941, National Archives, Washington, D.C. Letter from Leo Bohannon to Aloys P. Kaufman, March 10, 1953, Raymond Tucker papers. Jackson's article describes the advantages extended to white suburbs by federal loan policies, the HOLC files detail clear discrimination against blacks in securing house loans in St. Louis, and the Bohannon letter explains how urban renewal in the city worked particular hardships on blacks.

7. Report of Housing and Land Clearance Commission to the Board of Aldermen, St. Louis, Missouri, March 18, 1966. A. J. Cervantes Papers, Washington University Libraries, St. Louis, Missouri, series 1, box 32. Meehan, *The Quality of Federal Policymaking,* 17, 20, 27, 28, 105–106.

8. *St. Louis Post-Dispatch,* February 3, 1969, p. 1, and October 29, 1969, p. 1. Interview with the Reverend Buck Jones, March 6, 1982. "Social Protest in St. Louis," Missouri Committee for the Humanities. Meehan, *The Quality of Federal Policymaking,* 83.

9. *St. Louis Post-Dispatch,* April 13, 1969, p. 20A. The phrase "willful use of conflict" comes from Rev. Buck Jones's reminiscences about the rent strike, delivered at a symposium on social protest in St. Louis on March 28, 1982: "Social Protest in St. Louis," Missouri Committee for the Humanities program.

10. Memo of April 27, 1969, A. J. Cervantes Papers, series 1, box 49. Interview with Ivory Perry, October 3, 1982, St. Louis. Meehan, *The Quality of Federal Policymaking,* 93.

11. Telephone interview with Ivory Perry, July 3, 1985.

12. Declaration of support for the rent strike, signed by representatives of CORE, ACTION, the Black Liberators, the Zulu 1000s, and the Black Nationalists. A. J. Cervantes Papers, series 1, box 49.

13. Steven Burghardt, *Tenants and the Housing Crisis* (New York: New Press, 1972), 16. Interview with Ivory Perry, April 17, 1983, St. Louis.

14. Telephone interview with Ivory Perry, July 3, 1985.

15. *St. Louis Post-Dispatch*, April 18, 1969, p. 20.

16. Ibid., April 25, 1969, p. 4A.

17. Ibid., June 18, 1969, p. 3.

18. Speech by Joseph Badaracco, May 1, 1969, and letter from Thomas Elliott Huntley of the Central Baptist Church to Mayor Cervantes, June 6, 1969, A. J. Cervantes Papers, series 1, box 49.

19. Letter from Jean King to A. J. Cervantes, May 19, 1969, A. J. Cervantes Papers, series 1, box 49.

20. Memo to A. J. Cervantes, April 27, 1969, A. J. Cervantes Papers, series 1, box 49.

21. Arnold Schuchter, *Reparations* (Philadelphia and New York: Lippincott, 1970).

22. *St. Louis Post-Dispatch*, July 7, 1969, p. 1.

23. Ibid., p. 5A.

24. Interview with Father John Shocklee, March 16, 1984, St. Louis.

25. A. J. Cervantes Papers, series 1, box 49, July 18, 1969, August 7, 1969. Meehan, *The Quality of Federal Policymaking*, 90.

26. Telephone interview with Ivory Perry, July 3, 1985.

27. Ibid. *St. Louis Post-Dispatch*, September 9, 1969, p. 3.

28. *St. Louis Post-Dispatch*, September 28, 1969, pp. 1, 3. Telephone interview with Ivory Perry, March 12, 1983.

29. *St. Louis Post-Dispatch*, May 11, 1969, p. 3B, and May 12, 1969, p. 3B. George Lipsitz, "Beyond the Fringe Benefits: Rank and File Teamsters in St. Louis," *Liberation* 18 (September–October 1973): 30–53.

30. Leif J. Sverdrup to W. R. Persons, October 23, 1969; Leif J. Sverdrup Papers, Washington University Libraries, St. Louis, Missouri, box 79. For information about Gibbons and Busch and the formation of the CAH, see *St. Louis Post-Dispatch*, October 1969, p. 1., and CAH Minutes, October 1969, Harold Gibbons Papers, Southern Illinois University–Edwardsville Special Collections. Also see Cummings, "Rent Strike in St. Louis," 537. Letter to Civic Progress from Maurice Chambers, December 1, 1969, Leif J. Sverdrup Papers, box 78.

31. *New York Times*, August 14, 1969, p. 14, and September 24, 1969, p. 1.

32. Meehan, *The Quality of Federal Policymaking*, chap. 4. The CAH secured funding from HUD, Congress passed legislation putting a cap on public housing rents of 25 percent of adjusted income, and the Ford Foundation gave money to set up tenant management boards in St. Louis public housing.

33. Interviews with Ivory Perry, October 3, 1982, April 17, 1983, and September 13, 1983, St. Louis. Guida West, *The National Welfare Rights Movement: The Social Protest of Poor Women* (New York: Praeger, 1981), 39. Ronald M. Arundell, "Welfare Rights as Organizing Vehicle," in Paul A. Kurtaman, ed., *The Mississippi Experience* (New York: Association Press, 1971), 84. Frances Fox

Piven and Richard Cloward, *Poor People's Movements* (New York: Pantheon Books, 1977). *On The Line*, St. Louis, Missouri, no. 3, 1971, p. 4.

34. Interview with Ivory Perry, September 13, 1983, St. Louis.

35. Piven and Cloward, *Poor People's Movements*, chap. 5.

36. Ibid., p. 273.

37. James T. Patterson, *America's Struggle Against Poverty, 1900–1980* (Cambridge: Harvard University Press, 1981), 102.

38. For letters contrasting redevelopment spending with urban problems, see A. J. Cervantes Papers, October 23, 1968, and November 8, 1968.

39. Telephone interview with Ivory Perry, July 3, 1985.

40. Ibid.

41. *St. Louis Post-Dispatch*, October 29, 1969, pp. 1, 6A.

42. Telephone interview with Ivory Perry, March 12, 1983. *St. Louis Globe-Democrat*, January 9, 1970, p. 1.

Chapter 7

1. Interview with Ivory Perry, September 16, 1984, St. Louis.

2. Interview with Ivory Perry, October 3, 1982, St. Louis. For damages caused by lead poisoning see Paul P. Craig and Edward Berlin, "The Air of Poverty," *Environment* 13 (June 1971): 2–9.

3. Daniel T. Magidson, "Half Step Forward," *Environment* 13 (June 1971): 11.

4. Interview with Ivory Perry, July 13, 1982, St. Louis.

5. Interview with Ivory Perry, September 16, 1984, St. Louis.

6. *St. Louis Globe-Democrat*, January 1, 1970, section D, p. 10.

7. *St. Louis Post-Dispatch*, April 5, 1970, p. 1. Interview with Ivory Perry, September 16, 1984, St. Louis.

8. Interview with Ivory Perry, October 3, 1982, St. Louis. *St. Louis Post-Dispatch*, July 7, 1970, p. 22A.

9. *St. Louis Post-Dispatch*, August 2, 1970, p. 23A.

10. Magidson "Half Step Forward," 13.

11. Interview with Ivory Perry, October 3, 1982, St. Louis. J. A. Lobbia, "Tough Talk," *Riverfront Times*, April 15–21, 1987, p. 5A.

12. Interviews with Maurice Williamson, September 17, 1984; and with Ivory Perry, September 13, 1983, St. Louis. *St. Louis Sentinel*, August 8, 1970, p. 1.

13. Telephone interview with Pearlie Evans, July 21, 1987.

14. Interview with Judge Theodore McMillian, September 18, 1984, St. Louis. *St. Louis Post-Dispatch*, February 11, 1971, p. 3.

15. Urban League Award, March 17, 1971, personal possession Ivory Perry. See also *St. Louis Post-Dispatch*, March 18, 1971. Letter from Mayor A. J. Cervantes to Ivory Perry, March 21, 1971, personal possession Ivory Perry. *St. Louis Post-Dispatch*, March 21, 1971, p. 18A.

16. *St. Louis Post-Dispatch*, April 22, 1971, p. 10A. *On the Line*, no. 3, August 1971.

17. *St. Louis Post-Dispatch*, April 26, 1971, p. 2V, and May 23, 1971, p. 6A.

18. *St. Louis Post-Dispatch*, September 28, 1971, p. 10A. *Lead Poisoning News* no. 31, October 4, 1972, Lead Poisoning File, A. J. Cervantes Papers, Washington University Libraries, St. Louis, Missouri.

19. *Lead Poisoning News* no. 31, A. J. Cervantes Papers. Daniel T. Magidson, "Half Step Forward," *Environment* 13 (June 1971): 13.

20. *Lead Poisoning News* no. 32, October 25, 1972, p. 1, Lead Poisoning File, A. J. Cervantes Papers. St. Louis Post-Dispatch, June 22, 1972, p. 1, and November 17, 1972, p. 1.

21. Interview with Judge Theodore McMillian, September 18, 1984, St. Louis.

22. *St. Louis Post-Dispatch*, December 10, 1973, p. 5A. Interview with Ivory Perry, July 13, 1982, St. Louis.

23. *St. Louis Post-Dispatch*, December 10, 1973, p. 5A.

24. Ibid., p. 3, and December 21, 1973, p. 2C.

25. Interview with Robert Joiner, June 17, 1987, St. Louis.

26. Interviews with Anna Cox, December 27, 1983, Sacramento; and with Kathen Wright, September 16, 1984, St. Louis.

27. Interview with Anna Cox, December 27, 1983, Sacramento.

28. See Sara Evans, *Personal Politics* (New York: Random House, 1980).

29. The separation between the home and work spheres emerged as part of the transition to industrial capitalism in the nineteenth century. The cult of true womanhood established an ideal of women as domestic, submissive, pious, and pure, while male character traits focused on an ideal of conquest and capital accumulation in the public sphere.

30. Jacqueline Jones, *Labor of Love, Labor of Sorrow* (New York: Basic Books, 1985), 110–12.

31. Interviews with Anna Cox, December 27, 1983, Sacramento; and with Ivory Perry, April 9, 1985, St. Louis.

32. *St. Louis Post-Dispatch*, May 2, 1971, p. 2.

33. Interviews with Ivory Perry, April 9, 1985, and April 18, 1987, St. Louis. *St. Louis Post-Dispatch*, May 2, 1971, p. 2.

34. Interview with Anna Cox, December 27, 1983, Sacramento.

35. Ibid.

36. *St. Louis Post-Dispatch*, September 16, 1970, p. 3A.

37. Federal Bureau of Investigation File on Ivory Perry, File #44-0-25256, June 1, 1973, released to the author by Ivory Perry.

38. *St. Louis Sentinel*, August 2, 1973, p. 1.

39. Ibid. *St. Louis American*, August 2, 1973, p. 1.

40. Interview with Maurice Williamson, September 17, 1984, St. Louis.

41. Nelson Blackstock, *COINTELPRO* (New York: Vintage Books, 1975), 89–90.

"Black Extremist Hate Groups," Federal Bureau of Investigation, *Cointelpro Files,* 100-448006, Section 5, FBI Building, Washington, D.C.

42. "Black Extremist Hate Groups," Federal Bureau of Investigation, *Cointelpro Files.* Telephone interview with Ivory Perry, July 3, 1985.

43. Interview with Ivory Perry, July 13, 1982, St. Louis. *St. Louis Post-Dispatch,* March 11, 1971, p. 3.

44. *St. Louis Argus,* December 13, 1973, p. 1. Interview with Ivory Perry, September 16, 1984, St. Louis.

45. Interview with Ivory Perry, June 10, 1983, Pine Bluff, Arkansas. The figure about lead poisoning among whites is from Magidson, "Half Step Forward."

46. *St. Louis Globe-Democrat,* July 6, 1970, p. 10A.

47. *St. Louis Argus,* December 13, 1983, p. 1. Interview with Ivory Perry, April 9, 1985, St. Louis.

48. *St. Louis Globe-Democrat,* July 6, 1970, p. 10A. Interview with Ivory Perry, July 23, 1982, St. Louis.

49. Telephone interview with Ivory Perry, July 3, 1985.

50. Telephone interviews with Corliss Cruz, February 1, 1986; and with Earline Terry Whitfield, February 2, 1986.

51. Interview with Anna Cox, December 27, 1983, Sacramento.

52. *St. Louis Globe-Democrat,* June 22, 1975, p. 3A, and March 27, 1976, p. 14A. *St. Louis Sentinel,* September 29, 1977, p. 1.

53. Interview with Maurice Williamson, September 17, 1984, St. Louis.

Chapter 8

1. Interview with Maurice Williamson, September 17, 1984, St. Louis.

2. John Mollenkopf, *The Contested City* (Princeton, N.J.: Princeton University Press, 1983), 129.

3. Robert Fisher, *Let the People Decide: Neighborhood Organizing in America* (Boston: Twayne, 1984), 124, 125.

4. Ibid., 124.

5. Quoted ibid., 125.

6. Quoted ibid., 126.

7. James Neal Primm, *Lion of the Valley* (Boulder: Colo.: Pruett, 1981), 448.

8. George Lipsitz, "Promises to Keep," *St. Louis Magazine,* December 1982, pp. 46–48.

9. *St. Louis Post-Dispatch,* March 9, 1978, p. 3A. *Perry v. Laclede Gas Company,* Missouri Commission on Human Rights, case #E5/78-9019; obtained from the commission by request. *St. Louis Post-Dispatch,* May 19, 1978, p. 10C. Letter from Alvin Plummer, Deputy Director, Missouri Commission on Human Rights, to Ivory Perry, November 28, 1978. Interview with Ivory Perry, October 3, 1982, St. Louis.

10. *St. Louis Post-Dispatch,* August 23, 1978, p. 3A.

11. Ibid., October 13, 1978, p. 3A. Interview with Ivory Perry, September 13, 1983, St. Louis.

12. Interview with Anita Reed, September 16, 1984, St. Louis.

13. Ibid.

14. Interview with Ivory Perry, April 19, 1987, St. Louis.

15. Wini Breines and Linda Gordon, "The New Scholarship on Family Violence," *Signs* 8 (Spring 1983): 515.

16. *St. Louis Post-Dispatch,* April 6, 1979, p. 1.

17. Ibid.

18. Interview with Ivory Perry, September 16, 1984, St. Louis.

19. *St. Louis Sentinel,* January 24, 1980, p. 4.

20. *Cleveland Plain-Dealer,* March 16, 1980, p. 25A.

21. *St. Louis Post-Dispatch,* September 17, 1980, p. 1A. Interview with Ivory Perry, July 13, 1982, St. Louis.

22. Mollenkopf, *The Contested City.*

23. Fisher, *Let the People Decide,* 124.

24. *New York Times,* June 22, 1985, p. 26.

25. Fisher, *Let the People Decide,* 125.

26. Interview with Robert Joiner, June 17, 1987, St. Louis.

27. Interview with Ivory Perry, April 9, 1985, St. Louis.

28. Interview with Ivory Perry, April 9, 1985, St. Louis. The Jeff-Vander-Lou Corporation grew out of Macler Shepard's Nineteenth Ward Improvement Association; see Chapter 5.

29. Interview with Ivory Perry, April 9, 1985, St. Louis.

30. Ibid.

31. *St. Louis Globe-Democrat,* March 10, 1983, pp. 1, 5A.

32. *St. Louis Post-Dispatch,* March 10, 1983, p. 18A. Interviews with Ivory Perry, March 12, 1983 (telephone), and April 9, 1985, St. Louis.

33. Interviews with Father John Shocklee, March 16, 1984, and with Ivory Perry, April 9, 1985, St. Louis. *St. Louis Globe-Democrat,* December 3, 1983, p. 8A. *St. Louis Post-Dispatch,* December 2, 1983, p. 3A.

34. David Garrow, *The FBI and Martin Luther King, Jr.* (New York: Norton, 1981), 53. *St. Louis Globe-Democrat,* December 28, 1974, p. 2E.

35. *St. Louis Post-Dispatch,* August 23, 1984, p. 3A. Interviews with Maurice Williamson, September 17, 1984, and with Ivory Perry, September 16, 1984, St. Louis.

36. Interview with Ivory Perry, April 9, 1985, St. Louis.

37. *St. Louis Post-Dispatch,* August 23, 1984, p. 3A. *St. Louis Sentinel,* August 30, 1984, p. 1.

38. Interview with Ivory Perry, April 9, 1985, St. Louis.

39. Ibid.

40. Allen Tullos, "Voting Rights Activists Acquitted," *The Nation*, August 3–10, 1985, p. 78.
41. Interview with Ivory Perry, April 9, 1985, St. Louis.
42. Ibid.
43. *St. Louis American*, July 31–August 6, 1986, p. 1, and August 7–13, 1986, p. 1.
44. Interview with Ivory Perry, April 19, 1987, St. Louis.
45. Interviews with Pearlie Evans, July 21, 1987 (telephone); and with Robert Joiner, June 17, 1987, St. Louis.
46. Interview with Maurice Williamson, September 17, 1984, St. Louis.
47. Andrew H. Malcolm, "New Generation of Poor Youths Emerges in the U.S.," *New York Times*, October 22, 1985, p. 1. Susan Brenna, "Poverty Sneaks Up on U.S. Middle Class," *Dallas Times Herald*, reprinted *Springfield (Massachusetts) Morning Union*, December 9, 1985, p. 7.
48. John Atlas and Peter Dreier, "Mobilize or Compromise? The Tenants' Movement and American Politics," in Chester Hartman, ed., *America's Housing Crisis* (Washington, D.C.: Institute for Policy Studies, 1983), 152, 153, 155.
49. Melvin Oliver and Mark Glick, "An Analysis of the New Orthodoxy on Black Mobility," *Social Problems* 29 (June 1982), esp. pp. 521–22.
50. Chandler Davidson, "Minority Vote Dilution: An Overview," draft supplied to the author by Chandler Davidson.
51. Interview with Ivory Perry, July 13, 1982, St. Louis.
52. Telephone interview with Pearlie Evans, July 21, 1987.
53. Interviews with Jacquelyn Butler Barnes, October 27, 1984 (telephone); and with Anita Reed, September 16, 1984, St. Louis.
54. Interview with Robert Joiner, June 17, 1987, St. Louis.
55. Interview with Dorie Ladner, June 24, 1987, Washington, D.C.

Chapter 9

1. Interview with Ivory Perry, April 18, 1987, St. Louis.
2. Langston Hughes, *The Langston Hughes Reader* (New York: George Braziller, 1958), 88.
3. Interview with Ivory Perry, April 18, 1987, St. Louis.
4. Quoted by John Dos Passos, *The 42nd Parallel* (New York: New American Library, 1969), 52.
5. Sara M. Evans and Harry C. Boyte, *Free Spaces: The Sources of Democratic Change in America* (New York: Harper & Row, 1986).
6. I recognize that Diggins is hardly alone in this judgment of Brown. My own interpretation of Brown relies on the persuasive arguments about him advanced by W. E. B. Du Bois, among others.
7. Aileen Kraditor, *The Radical Persuasion, 1890–1917* (Baton Rouge: Louisiana State University Press, 1981). John Patrick Diggins, *The Lost Soul of American*

Politics (New York: Basic Books, 1984) and "Comrades and Citizens: New Mythologies in American Historiography," *American Historical Review* 90 (June 1985): 614–38. T. J. Jackson Lears, *No Place of Grace* (New York: Pantheon Books, 1981) and "The Concept of Cultural Hegemony," *American Historical Review* 90 (June 1985): 567–93.

8. Albert Murray, *The Omni-Americans* (New York: Vintage Books, 1983), 22.

9. Antonio Gramsci, *Selections from the Prison Notebooks*, ed. Quintin Hoare and Geoffrey Nowell Smith (New York: International Publishers, 1971), 196.

10. William Kornhauser, *The Politics of Mass Society* (New York: Free Press, 1959). Neil Smelser, *Theory of Collective Behavior* (New York: Free Press, 1982). James Geschwender, "Social Structure and the Negro Revolt: An Examination of Some Hypotheses," *Social Forces* 43 (December 1964): 248–55.

11. William Gamson and Emilie Schmeidler, "Organizing the Poor," *Theory and Society*, no. 13 (1984), 567–86. William Gamson, *The Strategy of Social Protest* (Homewood, Ill.: Dorsey Press, 1975). Charles Tilley, "Reflections on the Revolution of Paris: A Recent Review of Historical Writing," *Social Problems*, no. 12 (Summer 1964), 99–121. Michael Lipsky, *Protest in City Politics* (Skokie, Ill.: Rand McNally, 1970). Anthony Oberschall, *Social Conflict and Social Movements* (New York: Prentice-Hall, 1973).

12. Doug McAdam, *Political Process and the Development of Black Insurgency, 1930– 1970* (Chicago and London: University of Chicago Press, 1982), 21.

13. The connection between spontaneous social protest and direct democracy has been skillfully established in Naomi Rosenthal and Michael Schwartz, "Spontaneity and Democracy in Social Protest," paper delivered at American Sociological Association meetings, Chicago, August 1987.

14. Interview with Ivory Perry, September 16, 1984, St. Louis.

15. Interviews with Ivory Perry, April 9, 1985, and October 3, 1982, St. Louis.

16. Frances Fox Piven and Richard Cloward, *The Politics of Turmoil* (New York: Pantheon Books, 1974), 85.

17. Aldon D. Morris, *The Origins of the Civil Rights Movement: Black Communities Organizing for Change* (New York: Free Press, 1984). McAdam, *Political Process and the Development of Black Insurgency.*

18. Theodore Rosengarten, *All God's Dangers* (New York: Random House, 1974). Nell Irvin Painter, *The Narrative of Hosea Hudson* (Cambridge: Harvard University Press, 1979). Clayborne Carson, *In Struggle: SNCC and the Black Awakening of the 1960s* (Cambridge: Harvard University Press, 1981). August Meier and Elliott Rudwick, *CORE: A Study in the Civil Rights Movement, 1942– 1968* (Urbana: University of Illinois Press, 1975). William Chafe, *Civilities and Civil Rights: Greensboro, North Carolina and the Black Struggle for Freedom* (New York: Oxford University Press, 1981). None of these accounts is devoid of historical influences, but their focus necessarily truncates that dimension of their stories.

19. George P. Rawick, *From Sundown to Sunup* (Westport, Conn.: Greenwood, 1972).

20. Jerome Karabel, "Revolutionary Contradictions: Antonio Gramsci and the Problem of Intellectuals," *Politics and Society* (1976): 123–72. E. P. Thompson, *The Making of the English Working Class* (New York: Vintage Books, 1963), 11.

21. Students through volunteer work in screening and testing, tenants through the MTO, black business owners through the testing and screening programs, politicians in the lead control ordinance, social workers in the Yeatman Center's outreach programs and in the People's Coalition Against Lead Poisoning, and pediatricians through the statement at the April convention.

Epilogue

1. Dr. Martin Luther King, Jr., "The Drum Major Instinct," a sermon delivered on February 4, 1968, in Atlanta, Georgia, *Free at Last* (Gordy Records) 929.

2. Interviews with Ivory Perry, July 13, 1982, and April 19, 1987, St. Louis.

3. Interview with Anita Reed, September 16, 1984, St. Louis.

4. Interview with Ivory Perry, April 18, 1987, St. Louis.

5. Interviews with Pearlie Evans, July 21, 1987 (telephone); with Ivory Perry, July 13, 1982, St. Louis; with Maurice Williamson, September 17, 1984, St. Louis; and with Donald Rankins, August 6, 1985 (telephone).

6. Interviews with Judge Clyde Cahill, September 18, 1984; and with Robert Joiner, June 17, 1987, St. Louis.

7. Interview with Percy Green, September 18, 1984, St. Louis.

8. Interview with Anna Cox, December 27, 1983, Sacramento.

9. *St. Louis American*, January 23–29, 1986, p. 1.

Interviews and Archives

Interviews

Jacquelyn Butler Barnes, telephone interview, October 27, 1984.
Leo Branton, January 9, 1984, Los Angeles, California.
Wiley Branton, November 30, 1983, Washington, D.C.
Howard Buchbinder, March 31, 1984, Toronto, Ontario, Canada.
Judge Clyde Cahill, September 18, 1984, St. Louis, Missouri.
Doris Caldwell, June 10, 1983, Pine Bluff, Arkansas.
Anna Cox, December 27, 1983, Sacramento, California.
Corliss Cruz, telephone interview, February 1, 1986.
Pearlie Evans, telephone interview, July 21, 1987.
Leon Gilbert, November 4, 1987, York, Pennsylvania.
Tia Gilbert, November 3, 1987, Philadelphia, Pennsylvania.
Jewel Gonder, June 10, 1983, Pine Bluff, Arkansas.
Percy Green, September 18, 1984, St. Louis, Missouri.
Richard Haley, telephone interview, January 30, 1984.
Katherine Jiner, June 10, 1983, Pine Bluff, Arkansas.
Robert Joiner, June 17, 1987, St. Louis, Missouri.
Myrtle Jones, June 10, 1983, Pine Bluff, Arkansas.
Dorie Ladner, June 24, 1987, Washington, D.C.
Maggie Lewis, June 11, 1983, Little Rock, Arkansas.
Judge Theodore McMillian, September 18, 1984, St. Louis, Missouri.
Charles Oldham, March 16, 1984, St. Louis, Missouri.
Marian Oldham, March 16, 1984, St. Louis, Missouri.
Ivory Perry, July 13, 1982, St. Louis, Missouri. July 23, 1982, St. Louis, Missouri.
  October 3, 1982, St. Louis, Missouri. March 12, 1983, telephone interview.
  April 17, 1983, St. Louis, Missouri. June 10, 1983, Pine Bluff, Arkansas. September 13, 1983, St. Louis, Missouri. January 20, 1984, telephone interview.
  September 16, 1984, St. Louis, Missouri. April 9, 1985, St. Louis, Missouri.
  July 3, 1985, telephone interview. April 18, 1987, St. Louis, Missouri. April 19,
  1987, St. Louis, Missouri. August 26, 1987, telephone interview.
The Reverend Robert Pierce, June 10, 1983, Pine Bluff, Arkansas.

Donald Rankins, telephone interview, August 6, 1985.
Anita Reed, September 16, 1984, St. Louis, Missouri.
Mickey Rosen, June 17, 1987, St. Louis, Missouri.
Monsignor John Shocklee, March 16, 1984, St. Louis, Missouri.
Harold Terrell, June 10, 1983, Pine Bluff, Arkansas.
Gene Tournour, telephone interview, July 28, 1987.
Earline Terry Whitfield, telephone interview, February 2, 1986.
Maurice Williamson, September 17, 1984, St. Louis, Missouri.
Kathen Wright, September 16, 1984, St. Louis, Missouri.

Archival Collections

Bogalusa Clippings File, Louisiana Room, Troy Middleton Library, Louisiana State University, Baton Rouge, Louisiana.
A. J. Cervantes Papers, Washington University Libraries, St. Louis, Missouri.
Civil Rights Collection, University Research Library, University of California at Los Angeles.
COINTELPRO files, Federal Bureau of Investigation Reading Room, Washington, D.C.
Congress of Racial Equality Papers, State Historical Society, Madison, Wisconsin.
Harold Gibbons Papers, Southern Illinois University, Edwardsville Libraries, Edwardsville, Illinois.
Lt. Leon A. Gilbert, Verbatim Record of Trial, Office of the Judge Advocate General, HQAA JAAJ, CC NASSIF Building, Bailey Crossroads, Virginia.
Gregory Hicks et al. v. Claxton Knight et al., U.S. District Court for the Eastern District of Louisiana, Civil Action 15727, Federal Records Center, Fort Worth, Texas.
Home Owners Loan Corporation Files, National Archives, Washington, D.C.
Local History Collection, Public Library, Pine Bluff, Arkansas.
National Association for the Advancement of Colored People Collection, Library of Congress, Washington, D.C.
National Urban League Papers, Library of Congress, Washington, D.C.
Ivory Perry, Verbatim Record of Trial, Office of the Judge Advocate General, HQAA JAAJ, CC NASSIF Building, Bailey Crossroads, Virginia.
Leif J. Sverdrup Papers, Washington University Libraries, St. Louis, Missouri.
Raymond Tucker Papers, Washington University Libraries, St. Louis, Missouri.
Twenty-fifth Infantry Division Records, Washington National Records Center, Archives Branch, NCWN, Suitland, Maryland.
Unit Histories, U.S. Army Military History Institute, Carlisle Barracks, Pennsylvania.
Urban League Collection, Washington University Libraries, St. Louis, Missouri.

Index

Abernathy, Ralph, 114
Action Committee to Improve Opportunities for Negroes, Action Committee to Improve Opportunities Now (ACTION), St. Louis, 84, 89, 128, 149, 150, 154, 158, 161, 190, 194, 216, 231
Agricultural Adjustment Act (AAA), 22
Ahmadiyya Movement in Islam, 194
Aid to Dependent Children (ADC), 166, 167, 222. *See also* National Welfare Rights Organization
Allen, Richard, 235
American Academy of Pediatrics, 179
Amos 'n Andy, 29, 260 n.42
Anheuser Busch, 163
Antipoverty Program, 121. *See also* Human Development Corporation, Office of Economic Opportunity, War on Poverty
Appleman, Roy F., 262 n.32
Arkansas, sharecropping in, 20
Arkansas AM&N, 23, 33, 35
Arthur J. Kennedy Skills Center (St. Louis), 189
Article 75, U.S. Uniform Code of Military Justice, 43, 49
Austin, Marvin, 106

Baker, Josephine, 67
Banks, Samuel L., 50
Banton, William C., 177, 178
Baraka, Amiri, 52
Barry, Don "Red," 30, 260 n.44
Bastrop, Louisiana, 15
Baton Rouge, Louisiana, 101; bus boycott, 72

Benny, Jack, 215
Benson, George, 19
Black Liberators (St. Louis), 149, 191
Black Nationalists (St. Louis), 149, 194–95
Black United Front (Cairo, Illinois), 187
Blumberg, Ralph, 111
Bogalusa Daily News, 111
Bogalusa, Louisiana, 3, 91–92, 231, 269 n.17, 270 n.51; Civic and Voters League, 93, 100, 101, 102, 104, 106, 108, 109, 110, 112, 115, 231; CORE, 93, 94, 95–96, 99, 100, 102–103, 104, 105, 106, 107, 111, 112, 217; counter-demonstrators, 104; Deacons for Defense and Justice, 93, 94–96, 109, 113; economy, 96–98; racial incidents, 99, 101, 102, 106–107
Bogart, Leo, 47, 262 n.32
Bolden, Otis L., 183
Bootlegging, 17
Bosley, Freeman, Sr., 217
Boyte, Harry, 231
Branch Normal College for Negroes, 23. *See also* Arkansas AM&N
Branton, Leo, 31, 32, 33, 34, 35, 229
Branton, Leo, Sr., 32, 34
Branton, Wiley, 31, 32, 34–35
Braxton, Phillip, 59–60
Breines, Wini, 205
Brostron, Curtis, 118–19, 120
Brown, J. N., 19
Brown, John, 233, 280 n.6
Bryant, Carolyn, 107
Buchanan, Fern, 207
Buchbinder, Howard, 121, 124–25
Busch, August A., Jr., 163, 165

INDEX

Walker, John J., 58
Walsh, Timothy, 130
Wamser, Jerry, 214
War on Poverty, 121, 135–43, 200, 236. *See also* Antipoverty Program, Human Development Corporation, Office of Economic Opportunity
Warren, Arkansas, 29; Southern Land Hotel, 29, 39
Washington, Harold, 214
Washington University, 122, 174, 175
Waters, Muddy, 30
Watson, Dr. John Brown, 33
Watts (California) Riot, 117
Webbe-Darst Housing Project, 148, 169
Wheatstraw, Peetie, 67
White, Horton V., 43, 45–46
White, Walter, 49, 52

Wilkins, Roy, 67
Williams, Hosea, 114
Williams, Larry, 215
Williamson, Maurice, 121, 177, 190, 196–97, 199, 216, 222, 253
Willner, Robert, 59
World War II, 25–26
Wright, Kathen Perry, 15, 16, 17, 38, 65, 69, 126, 134, 184

Yates, Bill, 100–101, 103
Yeatman Health Center, 175, 176, 179, 180, 246
Young, A. Z., 93, 95, 108, 270 n.51
Young, Andrew, 114

Zulu 1000s (St. Louis), 149, 191